The Power of Networks

The Power of Networks

Organizing the Global Politics of the Internet

Mikkel Flyverbom

Copenhagen Business School, Denmark

Edward Elgar

Cheltenham, UK • Northampton, MA, USA

Published by
Edward Elgar Publishing Limited
The Lypiatts
15 Lansdown Road
Cheltenham
Glos GL50 2JA
UK

Edward Elgar Publishing, Inc.
William Pratt House
9 Dewey Court
Northampton
Massachusetts 01060
USA

A catalogue record for this book
is available from the British Library

Library of Congress Control Number: 2011925754

MIX
Paper from responsible sources
FSC® C018575

ISBN 978 1 84980 422 6

Typeset by Servis Filmsetting Ltd, Stockport, Cheshire
Printed and bound by MPG Books Group, UK

Contents

Acknowledgements

This book is the result of many encounters, and I could not have written it without the help of the numerous people who have kindly and generously informed, guided and challenged my work along the way. To investigate how and with what effects the global politics of the digital revolution was organized as a multi-stakeholder process, I made a number of visits to the UN headquarters in New York and Geneva, participated in more than a dozen meetings held in diplomatic capitals and exotic locations around the world, and followed two UN World Summit processes closely. In addition to these ethnographic observations, this book builds on extensive interviews and conversations with the members, directors, employees and participants of the different UN-based organizational arrangements involved in the making of the digital revolution as an object of global politics. Finally, the analyses draw on documents and working papers, files from the private archives of UN employees, as well as publications, transcripts of meetings and discussions in online forums. Clearly, I could not have done this work without multiple kinds of support, and while I cannot thank everyone individually, this is my opportunity to acknowledge the most important ones.

First of all, I want to thank my colleagues for their encouragement and guidance. The research project 'Media and Democracy in the Network Society' provided the first home for the project and even covered many of the costs of doing global, multi-sited ethnography. All along, my generous mentor, Hans Krause Hansen, as well as Dorte Salskov-Iversen, Anna Leander and other members of the research group 'Business in Global Governance' at the Copenhagen Business School have nurtured and shaped my work profoundly. More recently, the research group on 'Communication and Organization' led by Dan Kärreman, has been a valuable forum for discussing the final shape of this book. Other people have helped me at crucial stages, in particular Ronald Deibert, Wendy Larner, Jens Hoff, Henrik Bang and Bent Flyvbjerg. I also want to thank Thomas Weiss, who let me come to the Ralph Bunche Centre at CUNY as a visiting scholar, and whose reputation helped open the first doors into the UN system.

Secondly, the project would not have been possible without the trust and generosity of the many people who allowed me to study their daily work. In particular, I am grateful that Markus Kummer, Sergei Kambalov, Wolfgang Kleinwächter, Derrick Cogburn, Rikke Frank Jørgensen, Bill Drake and my interviewees would share their insights and experiences with me. Finally, I am grateful to my wife and dearest friend, Ursula Plesner for the love and the conversations that keep me going, and to Lucca and Theo for making me laugh and marvel every day.

Introduction: hybrid networks and political domains

To most people the global politics of the Internet is simply off the radar. We tend to think of the Internet as yet another medium able to transmit a wide variety of messages, data and cultural products very quickly, a technological innovation allowing stock traders, architects and activists to work in new ways, or as a new social space, where we can connect with old and new friends. But the Internet is not just a medium, a technology and a social space (Cavanagh 2007: 4). It is also a new political domain. For instance, the news regularly reports on the use of filtering in China, Internet users may think about getting caught if they download music and films illegally, and parents wonder if enough is done to keep their kids safe online. But we rarely think of such scattered issues as political, and as long as the Internet works, we have more pressing regulatory, legal and safety concerns to worry about. Nevertheless, what started as a technical experiment connecting a small number of computers in US universities (Abbate 1999) has now become a crucial infrastructure for economic, social and cultural flows, and a site of political contestation. The rapid growth in the number of Internet users into the billions and the importance of networked technologies for most spheres of life has raised questions about how to foster and govern – on a global scale – what has been termed, variously, the 'information society', the 'digital revolution' or the 'information economy'. And these concerns raise questions about power, control and governance. The discovery or creation of new valuable objects – whether we talk about oil and other natural resources, technological infrastructures like the telegraph, or even the New World or outer space – always raises questions about governance and politics. And the Internet is no exception to this rule. When new objects become sites of contestation, questions about governance and power move to the fore: who does this space belong to, what rules and forms of governance should apply, and who should set and enforce them? In the past, the replies to such questions have often revolved around national sovereignty, representative democracy and intergovernmental agreements. But there are also more hybrid forms of governance at work in global politics. Alongside national and intergovernmental forms of steering, we see the emergence of new forms of global governance (Held and McGrew 2002), new multilateralisms (Bull 2010), private authority (Hall and Biersteker 2005), and networks involving both public and private actors (Slaughter 2004). At the margins of conventional politics, we see the emergence of novel organizational arrangements that not only make new objects political, but also open up formal politics to contestation and unsettle the boundaries between the economic, the political and the technical. To make sense of the importance of such forms of steering, we need to think of politics as not only a matter of allocating values through formalized and authoritative political systems (Easton 1971), but also of positioning objects as political, and creating sites where such forms of contestation can take place (Barry 2001).

PURPOSE AND FOCUS

This book examines *how and with what implications the global politics of the Internet has been organized around multi-stakeholder processes, under the auspices of the United Nations*. Multi-stakeholder arrangements, *or what we may term 'hybrid forums'* (Callon, Lascoumes et al. 2009), comprising governments, business, technical associations and civil society groups have emerged as a novel way of addressing emergent socio-political problems and opportunities. This book claims that the current shape of the global politics of the Internet is the result of intense and prolonged interactions in such organizational arrangements operating in and around the United Nations. While not necessarily central to formal politics and decision-making as they are played out in, say, national parliaments and the Security Council of the United Nations, hybrid forums do important work in the making and unsettling of politics and governance. While there is a growing interest in the shifting relationship between government and governance (Rosenau and Czempiel 1992), the emergence and workings of such hybrid forms of organization and steering remain under-studied. In particular, we have only just started to make sense of the myriad of transnational networks comprising governments, business and civil society groups currently shaping emergent socio-political problems and opportunities. While such networks play an increasingly important role in global politics and governance, we know very little about the inner workings, organizational strategies and effects of such hybrid arrangements. This book joins other attempts to fill this gap by providing a rare, in-depth, empirical study of the operations and outcomes of UN-driven experiments with hybrid forms of organization and governance in the area of information and communication technologies (ICTs). Puzzled by the proliferation of such organizational arrangements in global governance, and based on a rich, multi-sited and longitudinal study, this book offers a detailed account of the inner workings of the hybrid forums that have played a pivotal role in the reconfiguration of the global politics of the digital revolution under the auspices of the UN. It shows how hybrid forums become important to the making of politics and governance because they facilitate what I term *collaboration without consensus* and *entangled authority*, and unsettle the boundaries of conventional politics and 'open up new sites and objects of contestation' (Barry 2001: 194).

Reading this book, you will encounter a number of different organizational forms taken by the attempts to address the politics of the digital revolution. But two of these – the UN ICT Task Force and the Working Group on Internet Governance – take centre stage because they laid the foundation for the strong link between hybrid forums and the global politics of the Internet. While also investigating what came before and after these two organizational arrangements, the analyses focus on the practical, yet significant ways in which these early experiments laid the foundations for the entanglement of a techno-political object and an organizational form. Empirically and conceptually, the chapters of the book explore the linkages between an emergent, transnational issue area in global politics, networked forms of organization, and dialogical approaches to governance. The analyses shed light on the practices, actors, controversies, objects of governance, organizational forms, mechanisms and strategies, as well as the technological and regulatory imaginaries, which make up this transnational, socio-political space.[1] The book shows how multi-stakeholder processes facilitate interactions between very different social worlds, but also challenge established UN practices. Finally, the book offers an overview of the emergent shape of the global politics of the Internet and discusses the effects of multi-stakeholder processes in relation to questions about power and authority.

The book speaks to at least three audiences. Those who are interested in the global politics of information and communication will find a wealth of detail about how this issue area has been shaped by a wide range of actors in recent years. Furthermore, the book offers novel insights into the complex relationships between governance, organization, politics and power, and contributes to emergent, 'alternative' approaches to the study of global governance, politics and regulation. For those who are looking for an analytical vocabulary and a research strategy based on insights from ethnography, actor-network theory, governmentality studies and other situated, process-oriented approaches, this book shows where such analyses may start, what they may yield and what their limits may be. For those involved in organizing initiatives that facilitate interactions between different actors, groups, and sectors, this book offers an overview of various techniques and strategies that can be put to work in multi-stakeholder processes and hybrid forums. Similarly, there are those who may have participated in multi-stakeholder processes in national or international settings, in which case this book offers an invitation to reflect on, and maybe shape, such attempts at organizing hybrid forums and engaging stakeholders in new ways.

THE GLOBAL POLITICS OF THE DIGITAL REVOLUTION

The global politics of the Internet resembles other attempts at making new objects governable, but it also differs on a number of counts. Unlike many other spaces, the Internet is transnational in scope, boundless in scale, and subject to distributed forms of control (Mueller 2010). The governance of the Internet involves a wide range of activities, from the technical management of domain names and root servers, through intellectual property rights and the regulation of content to questions about access and development. These forms of steering and coordination involve a multitude of public and private actors at both national and international levels. Furthermore, the Internet is subject to such different types of governance as laws, standards, memoranda of understanding, technical coordination and multi-stakeholder dialogues. Furthermore, many forms of regulation are built into the architecture of the Internet and its applications, such as its codes and protocols (Lessig 1999; Galloway 2004). So rather than the ungovernable space imagined by some Internet pioneers (Barlow 1996) and politicians (Clinton 2000), the Internet is not outside the reach of regulation and control, and has in fact always been subject to various forms of governance.

The relationships between information and communication technologies, governance and development have a long history as intergovernmental concerns and are institutionally anchored in international, multilateral bodies. The acceptance of this linking of technological and societal 'imaginaires' (Flichy 2007), and the focus on making such opportunities available to the poorest parts of the world is not new. In particular at the level of national politics, such hopes for technology-driven social transformation have figured prominently for many years. In international politics, this issue has also been discussed frequently and in a number of institutional settings, such as the G8 and the UN, but has gained new momentum at the global level in recent years, particularly under the heading 'the global digital divide'. As Chadwick points out:

> In recent years, a plethora of global information society initiatives has emerged. Some have developed as part of much broader approaches to financial, trade, social, and development issues. Others are highly specific programs in the area of information and communication technologies. But what unites the vast majority of these is the view that the information society is a positive force that should be encouraged in a global context. (Chadwick, 2006: 211)

In the context of the UN, these different aspects of the global politics of the digital revolution have intersected with long-standing concerns about development and human rights, as well as media-specific issues such as access and infrastructure. Importantly, recent initiatives like the United Nations-sponsored World Summit on the Information Society in 2003–05 and a growing number of more focused initiatives have invigorated discussions about the potentials and problems of the digital revolution in relation to social transformations.

An important starting point for this book is that Internet regulation has become tied to attempts at governing the transformations associated with the use and spread of this technological innovation. Thus, rather than thinking of Internet regulation in narrow terms, this book seeks to contribute to the understanding of the contours of what may be termed the global politics of the digital revolution. But what is the digital revolution and how can this be understood as an object of global governance? At the outset, it suffices to point out that the global politics of the digital revolution implies a linking of digital, networked media technologies (such as computers, mobile phones and the Internet) and their (potential and manifest) consequences for social, economic, political and cultural development. To think of such links between the Internet and social transformations as an object of governance implies a broad understanding of governance as a matter of solving socio-political problems and creating socio-political opportunities (Kooiman 2003).

This book shows how two aspects of the problems and opportunities of the digital revolution have taken centre stage in recent UN processes to address the global politics of the digital revolution, namely the *global governance of the Internet* and the *potential of ICTs for development efforts*. The socio-political opportunities and problems related to the digital revolution have emerged as a heated political issue at the global level. While the emergence of this political controversy is marked by well-known conflicts between developed and developing countries, hopes for international agreements and attempts at unilateral control, it is also addressed and shaped in novel ways. Most importantly, the global politics of the digital revolution are organized around interactions between a wide range of international organizations, governments, civil society groups and business and technical associations. The main contribution of this book is to provide a rich and unique exploration of the multi-stakeholder arrangements that have facilitated the construction of the digital revolution as an object of global governance.

When these UN processes started in the early 2000s, there was very little agreement on key questions about the global politics of the digital revolution. As pointed out by Drake,

> The global debate on Internet governance is in a liminal state. There is a total lack of consensus about how to define Internet governance, and about which issues and institutions are and should be involved in what manner. Similarly, there is a lack of agreement as to whether there are significant problems with existing governance mechanisms, and whether there are any pressing but unresolved issues that need to be tackled through international cooperation. Adding to the complexity of the situation, the technological and market environment is changing rapidly, making this a classic example of 'shooting at a moving target,' and some stakeholders' interests and policy preferences are in flux. Indeed, there is fairly widespread uncertainty about how best to proceed, and perhaps even some frustration and burn out among participants whose full engagement will be needed if the policy debate is to achieve anything significant. (Drake 2004: 122)

This book shows how multi-stakeholder arrangements have emerged as an important way of dealing with this lack of shared definitions, institutional anchorage, responsibilities, mechanisms and clear policy preferences in the global debate on the politics of the digital revolution. While priorities continue to differ and conflicts persist, the acceptance of multi-stakeholder participation as the most appropriate mechanism for the facilitation of dialogue and cooperation in this area constitutes a path-breaking development, particularly in an intergovernmental setting such as the UN where national governments are in control.

AN ETHNOGRAPHY OF ORDERING

In order to examine and conceptualize emergent forms of governance, politics and organization, this book offers an analytical framework that directs attention to everyday practices, associations and processes of ordering. Unlike more conventional approaches, it does not dissect the messy richness of the empirical material – the result of the encounter with a massive international organization such as the UN, years of observations in summits, meetings and working groups, conversations with participants, and piles of documents – into neat variables, theory-driven deductions or structural, social, cultural or other 'outside' explanations. Instead, the book explores the organization of this space of governance at the level of practices and associations.

This research approach may simply be described as ethnographic, but the book is an ethnographic study of a social and political phenomenon, which is not easily delimited. Anthropological research has tended to study discrete communities and bounded 'fields' (Shore and Wright 1997: 14). In contrast, this book sets out to investigate a social and political space that is not bounded by geography, social unity or the walls of an organization. Unlike more traditional, ethnographic 'fields', this space cuts across many institutions, involves such different people as policy and technical specialists, human rights activists, government officials, business leaders and directors of international organizations, moves from one geographical location to the next, and takes the shape of high politics as well as grassroots activism. In order to be approachable as objects of ethnographic inquiry, such political and social spaces require a 'method for analysing connections between levels and forms of social process and action, and exploring how those processes work in different sites – local, national and global' (Shore and Wright 1997: 14).

To guide the analyses of such dispersed and fluid spaces, I propose that we need a *practice-oriented, relational and agnostic research strategy for the study of ordering*. This approach brings together insights from Foucauldian work on power and governmentality (Burchell 1991; Larner and Walters 2004), actor-network theory (ANT) (Callon 1986; Law 1994; Latour 2005a) and science and technology studies (STS) (Clarke and Star 2008; Hackett, Amsterdamska et al. 2008) as well as global ethnography (Cunningham 1999; Burawoy 2000) and process-oriented approaches to organization (Czarniawska 2008; Hernes 2008). These theoretical underpinnings will be fleshed out in Chapter 1. At this stage, it suffices to point out that an analysis of ordering implies that we study the everyday ways in which 'particular agents, practices, objects and subjects are assembled at different locales' (Larner and Walters 2004: 11). By foregrounding processes of entanglement and ordering (Law 1994; Latour 2005a), the analyses break with the view of governance and organization as reified entities (Larner and Walters 2004: 11) and refrain from invoking shorthand explanations, such as society, culture or interests. Instead, the focus on ordering invites us to conceive of objects, actors and interests as articulated and constituted in a situated and relational manner, and not given in advance (Hoff 2003). For instance, as pointed out by Latour (1987: 108–9), '"interests" are what lie in between actors and their goals', and are articulated as actors select what, in their own eyes, helps them reach these goals. The concern with ordering also builds on Foucauldian insights about power, agency and the governance of socio-political spaces. For instance, Foucault's famous work on sexuality and madness set out to expose the normalization of distinctions between the heterosexual and the homosexual, the sane and the insane. By analysing the forms of knowledge, discourses, subjects, institutions and practices, Foucault sought to denaturalize these forms of social regulation and expose their power effects. Along similar lines, this study sets out to map and denaturalize the practices through which the digital revolution was constructed as an object of global governance and multi-stakeholder arrangements connecting different social worlds were posited as the primary mode of organization in this arena.

Such approaches share the assumptions that processes of ordering involve associations and constellations of human and non-human elements; that they must be investigated at the level of practices; and that they must be understood as fragile and contingent articulations and orderings. To make sense of the implications of this research strategy for the empirical, analytical and conceptual steps taken in this book, it is useful to foreground the three analytical principles around which it revolves.

Three Analytical Principles

Most studies of global governance have little interest in situated practices, give ontological priority to entities rather than associations, and tend to start from pre-defined categories and objects. In contrast, this book pursues the study of global politics, governance, and organization at the level of *practices*, focuses on *relations*, and proceeds in an *agnostic* manner. Let us look briefly at the implications of the three analytical principles.

The first analytical principle underpinning this study is that the smallest unit of analysis is that of *practices*, understood as 'organized sayings and doings' (Nicolini 2009: 1401; Orr 1998). Such mundane ways of doing things together (Clarke and Star 2008) may take the shape of discursive and other practices, such as conducting a meeting, interacting in an online forum or building and running an organization. As Nicolini (2009: 1400) points out, 'When it comes to practice, distinguishing material and discursive aspects only has an analytical, not a substantive value, and one should not be given ontological priority over the other.' Starting the analyses from practices allows us to demonstrate how myriads of mundane practices and associations produce what we normally think of as 'society', 'governance', 'an organization' or an 'issue area'. The orientation to practices is central to an ordering perspective because it means '[w]e start from "irreducible, incommensurable, unconnected localities, which then, at great price, sometimes end into provisionally commensurable connections"' (Kendall 2004: 73, quoting Latour 1997).

Practice-oriented studies are rare in the literature on governance and global politics, and sociological and ethnographic approaches still operate at the margins of disciplines like international relations (IR). Still, we have some proponents of what may be termed a 'practice turn', including Laffey and Weldes's (2005) work on the practices of 'policing', Bigo and Walker's (2007) discussion of the 'international' as practices, Sending and Neumann's (2006; Neumann and Sending 2007) writings on governmentality and global governance, and Doty's (1997) discussion of how the attention to practices may move us beyond the agent-structure problematique in IR theory. In political science more broadly, the works of Bevir and Rhodes (2003), Flyvbjerg (2001), Schram and Caterino (2006) and Hajer and Wagenaar (2003) have established practices as an important entry point for studies of politics, power and governance. Finally, the concern with practices has been fuelled by scholars seeking to bring ethnographic approaches into IR theory, such as when Mandaville (2002) stresses the value of anthropological readings of, for instance, the nation-state. Such studies tie in with the call for practices to move centre stage, and shed light on the sites and situations where governance and politics are articulated and carried out.

Second, this book is underpinned by an analytical principle that may be termed *relational*. A relational approach urges us to refrain from thinking in terms of discrete entities, and instead unpack associations. While studies of global governance explore the regulatory and authoritative *relationships* that state and non-state actors develop and institutionalize, most conventional approaches nevertheless consider relationships to be composed of pre-constituted entities. While various forms of (new and old) institutional theory (Gössling, Oerlemans et al. 2007), social network theory (Jones, Hesterley et al. 1997; Wasserman and Faust 1994) and transaction cost economics (Dekker 2004) may study relations, they do so from a substantialist focus on entities, rather than a relational perspective considering the social world to consist of dynamic and unfolding processes (Emirbayer 1997). That is, they reflect the assumption that 'entities precede interaction, or that entities are already entities before they enter into social relations with other entities' (Jackson and Nexon 1999: 293). In contrast, a relational approach implies the view that 'the very terms or units involved in a transaction derive their meaning, significance, and identity from the (changing) functional roles they play within that transaction. The latter, seen as a dynamic, unfolding process, becomes the primary unit of analysis rather than the constituent elements themselves' (Emirbayer 1997: 287). As an analytical principle, a relational approach implies that we give primary attention to the 'constitutive relations' (Barnett and Duvall 2005: 9) where the various elements of governance – objects, procedures, subjects, power and knowledge – are established, negotiated and challenged.

The question of whether we consider the social world to consist of entities or processes, in 'static "things" or in dynamic, unfolding relations' (Emirbayer 1997: 281) is a well-established debate, just like the argument that we need to study power, identities, interests, technology and other phenomena in a relational manner has been made consistently and in multiple disciplines. For instance, such perspectives stress that identities are constituted in interactions and can only be understood in the context of the relations through which they are realized, negotiated and contested (Hylland Eriksen 1999). Or that power is not a resource or a thing simply possessed by some and wanted by others, but the product of relationships in particular sites (Foucault 1977b: 122). Still, such 'postfoundational' (Bevir 2004: 608) and 'radical decentered' (Doty 1997: 376) insights remain under-explored in studies of governance, networks and power.

The third analytical principle is that the analyses have an *agnostic* starting point. As a research strategy, an agnostic approach implies that we do not 'decide in advance what the phenomenon consists of on the basis of prior formal analytic studies' (Garfinkel and Rawls 2002: 171). In line with ethnography, ethnomethodology and actor-network theory, an agnostic approach sets out to 'follow the actors' (Latour 2005a) without being 'conceptually committed to [. . .] prior objects' (Larner and Walters 2004: 5), such as theoretical, managerial, structural, social or other 'outside' explanations (Latour 2005a; Clarke 2005). So to be agnostic 'entails a move of "bracketing" the world of underlying forces and causes, and instead examining the different ways in which the real has been inscribed in thought' (Larner and Walters 2004: 16). By not settling on the shape of, for instance, power and networks in advance it is possible to foreground the making and ordering of actors, issue areas and organizational arrangements, rather than taking them for granted.

In contrast, conventional approaches tend to start from analytical units such as 'structures', 'institutions' or 'ideas', or to define some factors as independent variables and others as dependent ones. But as Bevir (2004: 609) points out: 'Aggregate concepts, such as a class or an institution, cannot be adequate markers for people's beliefs, interests or actions. Such aggregate concepts stand only as abstractions based on the multiple and complex beliefs and actions of the individuals we locate under them.' To be agnostic about the shape and locations of power allows us to explore the operations of power in all (potentially significant) aspects and processes of dialogue about the global politics of the digital revolution. It provides an alternative to the view of institutional arrangements as monolithic structures, and invites us to investigate them more openly – as contingent assemblages under constant (re)construction. Such agnostic approaches explore how interests, authorities and identities are articulated and stabilized through linkages in concrete situations.

These principles have consequences for how we approach the empirical material, engage theoretical insights and conceptualize governance, organization and power. This study sets out to map the assemblages and emergent orderings that make up the organizational forms, governance discussions, and forms of authority involved in the global politics of the Internet. Along the lines of governmentality studies and actor-network theory, we may think of this techno-political space as a complex web of humans, non-humans, discourses, processes, positions and ideas. To approach governance and organization as practical associations among different elements in temporally and spatially demarcated situations has a number of resemblances to what Clarke (2005) terms 'situational analysis' – a poststructuralist rethinking of grounded theory. Following the Straussian line in grounded theory, she shows how social formations can be studied in a situated, relational manner. One important insight is to refrain from thinking about 'context' as something outside our objects of investigation: 'The conditions of the situation are already in the situation. There is no such thing as "context". The conditional elements of the situation need to be specified in the analysis of the situation itself as they are constitutive of it, not merely surrounding it or framing it or contributing to it. They are it' (Clarke 2005: 71–2). By studying entanglements of elements from within situations, Clarke shows how we can study events and their conditions as one, and thus capture the social formations, positions, discourses and other complexities of situations. Although not framed as a form of grounded theory, the present study has many affinities with Clarke's situational analysis and carries out similar analytical operations.

THE BOOK AHEAD

The first chapter advances the concept of ordering and situates the book in relation to the existing literature on governance, organization and power in global politics. Proposing that ordering is best understood in terms of assemblages and translations, the chapter fleshes out these two analytical concepts and shows how they are engaged in this study of hybrid forums and the global politics of the Internet. Paving the way for analyses of the ordering of this emergent space of governance, the chapter goes on to outline four significant effects of ordering, namely the making, shaping and stabilization of subjects, objects of governance, political rationalities and organizational techniques. Finally, the chapter proposes that ordering is ultimately about power, and suggests how theories about power, authority and control may guide the conceptualization of the effects of ordering on subjects, objects, techniques and rationalities. Chapter 2 launches the empirical analysis of the first attempts at ordering the global politics of the digital revolution. It shows how this was driven by a strong belief in the ability of technology to spur social transformation, and captures the ways in which this emergent space of governance has been problematized and shaped through experiments with multi-stakeholder processes in and around the UN system. Chapter 3 shifts the attention to the enrolment of stakeholders as a key part of ordering in hybrid forums. Focusing on processes of inclusion, exclusion and categorization, this chapter provides insights into the power effects of engaging social worlds as stakeholders. Chapter 4 focuses on the organization of hybrid forums in dialogues about the global politics of the Internet. It provides a rich account of the positioning, structuring and steering of multi-stakeholder processes, with particular attention to the multiple organizational techniques used to make members work together and connect with broader groups of stakeholders. Chapter 5 focuses on the ability of hybrid forums to position themselves as platforms for dialogue about the global politics of the digital revolution, and shows how they have ordered this object of governance in new ways. Chapter 6 addresses the ways in which multi-stakeholder processes to address the politics of the Internet continue to take new shapes and directions. Finally, the conclusion conceptualizes the power of hybrid forums and the effects of governing through dialogue for political subjects, objects of governance, organizational techniques and political rationalities.

1. Governance and organization as ordering

Setting out from the three analytical principles outlined in the introduction, this chapter articulates how politics, governance and organization may be understood as processes of ordering. Discussing alternative analytical vocabularies, such as governance, management and control, the chapter seeks to advance the value of ordering as a starting point for practice-oriented, relational and agnostic investigations of politics and organization, provides some analytical concepts to guide such studies, and reflects on ordering processes as central to power and authority.

WHY ORDERING?

As a starting point, we may think of ordering as ways of acting on the world, that is, 'all practices concerned with the control and management of things' (Kendall and Wickham 2001: 28). The concern with ordering can be identified in and across a wide range of disciplines. Such studies take the shape of situated, sociological accounts of the ordering of social life (Clarke 2005), the concern with 'organization as process' (Czarniawska 2008; Hernes 2008) and the 'organization of organizations' (Ahrne, Brunsson et al. 2007) in organization studies, and the making and governance of international spaces, such as in recent work on 'global governmentality' (Larner and Walters, 2004) and networked forms of governance (Barry 2001; Kendall, 2004). The two most important sources of inspiration, however, are the Foucauldian literature on power, governmentality and subjectification (Foucault 1973; Miller and Rose 1990; Rose 1999; Fleming and Spicer 2007) and research based on insights from actor-network theory (ANT) and science and technology studies (STS) (Callon 1986; Callon, Lascoumes et al. 2009; Law 1994; Bowker and Star 1999; Latour 2005a; Hackett, Amsterdamska et al. 2008; Law and Mol 2008; Çalışkan and Callon 2010).

We return to the contributions of these two bodies of literature shortly, but first we need to consider what it means to study ordering, and how this entry point differs from alternative ones, such as governance, management and control. If ordering refers to attempts at managing and controlling things, why not use better-known terms like governance, management, organization or control instead? The most obvious candidate for an umbrella term to frame this book would be the concept of governance. But governance tends to have a more specific meaning than ordering, and to refer to activities that have tangible, regulatory effects. Also, we normally associate concepts such as government and governance with activities undertaken by the state or other formal rule-makers. Clearly, the literature on the shifting relationship between government and governance (Rosenau and Czempiel 1992; Held and McGrew 2002) has directed our attention to the multiple forms of steering below and beyond the nation-state. Also, the literature on governance has captured the emergence of more informal and complex forms of steering, stressing for instance 'recent trends in the weakening of national regulatory systems, the strengthening of multinational corporations, increasing importance of brands, and growing demands from civil society actors for new mechanisms of corporate accountability' (O'Rourke 2006: 899). Finally, some of the international relations literature gives attention to fluid organizational processes, subtle forms of power and the intersection of formal and informal politics (Keck and Sikkink 1998; Rosenau 1999; Weiss and Thakur 2010). Despite these important advances, we tend to think of governance as a 'the rule of a nation state, region or municipal area' (Kendall and Wickham 2001: 32), and focus on formal and bounded organizations and their ability to gain or leverage control in relation to marked-off, well-established policy areas or regimes. To talk of the activities studied in this book as governance would immediately raise the question of what was actually being governed in dialogues about the global politics of the Internet and why the book does not focus on the real governors and hard regulation of cyberspace. In contrast, a focus on ordering in the sense of 'attempts to act on the world' paves the way for a more agnostic inquiry into the possible shape and effects of ordering, and remains more open to the idea that any sort of steering is never simply successful or inefficient, but always contains an element of failure (Kendall and Wickham, 2001).

This investigation could also have been cast in terms of power or control. Although many conceptions of power are open to the multiple shapes taken by control – ranging from direct through bureaucratic to concertive (Barker 1993; Fleming and Spicer 2007) – and the dialectics of domination and resistance (Mumby 2005), they would not invite a focus on the layered and multiple practices of acting on the world (Kendall and Wickham 2001) captured in this book. Thus, ordering casts a wider net than studies of power, control and resistance. Still, it is important to stress that ordering is certainly about power and authority, and this book also ends on that note. But to start from a concern with ordering rather than power allows us to substantiate the important point that power is an effect of practices and associations, not their source (Latour 1986). Thus, power is not only the ability to regulate behaviour, but also to constitute the world in particular ways, define problems to be solved and assemble useful allies (Barnett and Finnemore 2005: 179). Along these lines, the analyses show how the ability to construct and organize spaces for dialogue, to define the identities of different actors as 'stakeholders' and to make them work together constitute important, but often overlooked forms of power.

Finally, this could have been presented as a study of management. However, the concept of management has gained a very specific meaning and is often associated with rational or scientific attempts at optimizing managerial practices and organizational functions (Alvesson and Willmot 1992). But increasingly, the term is also used in ways more similar to ordering, such as in work on the management of meaning (Smircich and Morgan 1982) and in critical management studies (Alvesson and Willmot 1992). Still, to approach the organization of the global politics of the digital revolution through the lens of management would leave important features and discussions in the dark. Clearly, there is management involved, but to focus on these aspects would, for instance, sideline the concern with the shape of this emergent issue area in global politics.

To sum up, the concern of ordering has a number of advantages. It allows us to stay in line with the practice-oriented, relational and agnostic research strategy advocated in the introduction. It broadens the scope of the investigation to include multiple and layered attempts to act on the world, without distinguishing between organization, governance or power at the outset. As a result, the focus on ordering allows us to capture how processes of organizing and governing may be entangled. Also, it demonstrates that power is a result of linkages and practices, and not simply a resource or position, and sheds light on the associations and processes whereby authority emerges and dissolves.

THE ORIGINS OF ORDERING

To fully appreciate the value of the concept of ordering, we need to reflect on the contributions of actor-network theory and governmentality studies. While research based on these two strains of literature has taken rather different directions, they share a focus on ordering as attempts to act on humans, things and the world.

Studies of governmentality focus on the subtle operations of steering, power and discipline. Such approaches employ and develop Foucault's concerns with 'conditions of possibility', 'power/ knowledge' and the practical 'art of government' (Foucault 1973, 1980, 1991b; Hunt and Wickham 1994). The better-known Foucauldian works on the normalization and institutionalization of sexuality and madness hint at the usefulness of this literature for studies of governance and organizations as a matter of ordering. By singling out for analysis the practices, rationalities, relations and governmental techniques on which forms of steering rely, governmentality approaches pave the way for investigations of how particular ways of acting and thinking emerge as taken-for-granted ideas with wide-reaching consequences for the objects and subjects involved. Furthermore, the conception of power as relational, the concern with the ability to 'govern at a distance' and the focus on the effects of such processes for political subjects in this body of literature invites us to explore the circulation and stabilization of particular configurations of practices, rationalities and codifications. In using these insights in a study of the formation of a new issue area in global politics, this book also contributes to the emergent literature on 'global governmentality' (Larner and Walters 2004; Lipschutz and Rowe 2005; Hansen and Salskov-Iversen 2008). Such investigations use the term global governmentality as 'a heading for studies which problematize the constitution and governance of spaces above, beyond, between and across states' (Larner and Walters 2004: 2). While Foucault's own work, and later research drawing on his ideas, has focused mainly on steering within the boundaries of nation-states, such research shows the value of governmentality studies of transnational forms of steering (Lipschutz 2005: 235–6).

Actor-network theory (ANT) challenges taken-for-granted categories and distinctions, such as 'society' and 'organizations', and the 'political' and the 'technical', and calls instead for analyses of the practical ways in which human and non-human elements become linked and stabilized (Latour 2005a). Such analyses show how such phenomena consist of unstable and hybrid associations or 'actor-networks' and momentary stabilizations established through 'translations' (Latour 1986; Law and Hassard 1999; Callon 1986). With ANT, the goal is to capture how particular entities become linked and are made durable. Such accounts refrain from treating, for instance, an organization as an entity with a set of definable characteristics, and focus instead on the process of organizing – that is, how a constellation of elements comes together and apart over time and through constant negotiations (Czarniawska 2008). Studies of ordering start from the basic tenet of actor-network theory – namely to replace a 'sociology of the social' with a 'sociology of associations', because the former 'have simply confused what they should explain with the explanation. They begin with society or other social aggregates, whereas one should end with them' (Latour 2005a: 8). In contrast to such 'sociologies of the social', which consider the world to consist of structures, layers and actors and relies on 'society' or 'culture' as explanations, a 'sociology of associations' stresses that 'modern societies cannot be described without recognizing them as having a fibrous, thread-like, wiry, stringy, ropy, capillary character that is never captured by the notions of levels, layers, territories, spheres, categories, structure, systems' (Latour 1997: 2). Such practice-oriented, relational and agnostic approaches to the study of ordering start from the basic tenet that what we think of as society, power or action are produced by the creation and stabilization of associations. So rather than use 'the social' to explain other phenomena, such as behaviour or control, ANT posits that the social is merely the coming together of networks into a momentary, fragile form of order (Latour 2005a). Furthermore, this implies that what we normally think of as actors with the ability to exercise power is also an effect of associations. A 'sociology of associations' considers actors to be constituted and positioned through associations, and power to result from the ability to link and engage objects and subjects in stabilized configurations. This turns the basic tenet of network theories – that people create networks to order things – upside down. Instead, it proposes that we consider subjects, order or power as possible outcomes of associations. So 'connections create actors, not the other way around' (Czarniawska 2008: 20–21) and power is 'something that has to be obtained by enrolling many actors' (Latour 1986: 271).

Despite their different orientations and underpinnings, actor-network theory and governmentality studies share an interest in practices of acting on subjects and objects, sorting things out and shaping the world. Also, they acknowledge that all action on the world is partial, contingent and must compete with other attempts at ordering (Law 1994; Kendall and Wickham 2001), just as ordering implies multiplicity, has a 'layered importance' and may do 'various things at the same time' (Mol 2002; Law and Mol 2008). Furthermore, both approaches seek to disentangle and denaturalize taken-for-granted phenomena and explanations, such as 'the economy' (Çalışkan and Callon 2010), 'sexuality' (Foucault 1985, 1998) or 'the law' (Latour 2010). Accordingly, rather than thinking of Internet governance as an issue area or regime, or treating organizations as bounded and fixed – that is, as if they were in order – a focus on ordering means that we start by looking at the practices involved in the making of governable objects and organizational arrangements. Rather than following one organization, focusing on one group of stakeholders or defining the issues at stake in advance, the analyses in this book approach processes of organizing and governing as assemblages of multiple, hybrid elements (Latour 2005a; Çalışkan and Callon 2010) and seek to conceptualize the resulting forms of ordering. As we will see, governance and organization, as well as power, are about the ability to connect multiple humans and non-humans in forums where objects can be opened up to contestation and ordering. By conceptualizing the multiple activities involved in the making of hybrid forums and the global politics of the digital revolution as forms of ordering, we are able to focus on their emergence, consolidation and displacement, as well as the mundane workings of power involved.

THE STUDY OF ORDERING

Starting from practices and associations has important methodological implications for studies of governance and global politics: 'When thinking about global government, then, we have to interpret successfully governed space, not as a self-evident object, but as the result of the associations of networks, which are composed of humans and non-humans, and which are painstakingly built from the ground up' (Kendall 2004: 64). One illustration of this kind of analysis is to imagine that you are making a film. As a filmmaker, you cannot simply put 'society' on the screen, but must assemble a number of different elements and invite viewers to connect enough dots to realize that 'this is France', a 'totalitarian society' or something else. Similarly, an analysis of assemblages moves beyond shorthand categories, such as structures, societies and humans, normally at work in social science, and starts by unpacking the different parts and associations from which they are made. To explore hybrid forums and the global politics of the digital revolution in this manner help us capture the fragility and negotiations underpinning what would otherwise come across as faits accomplis – an organizational entity with a mission, a clearly defined issue area or regime, or some actors with conflicting or converging interests.

But how, more concretely, can we then study ordering in a practice-oriented, relational and agnostic manner? To demonstrate what kind of vocabulary is necessary in analyses of ordering, let us look at my first encounters with the phenomenon that this book tries to make sense of. The first occasion was a meeting arranged by the UN in Geneva in the spring of 2003 to prepare the first part of the World Summit on the Information Society (WSIS). After a relatively cumbersome process, my university had obtained a formal status as an accredited civil society entity, which in turn made it possible for me to get the necessary UN badge to enter the premises. The meetings were held in the lower levels of the massive, grey building housing the International Labour Organization (ILO) and the long corridors and many meeting rooms were buzzing with activity. In the large upstairs rooms, with translators and assigned seats, representatives from more than 150 UN member states were working out the procedures and substantive issues around which the formal negotiations would revolve. From time to time they would ask non-state participants to leave the room, and at other times they would invite some or all of us back in. Downstairs, in the smaller rooms in the basement, groups of people were setting up working groups, distributing photocopied statements about human rights, civil society and the global information society, and fuming about the lack of inclusion and the way in which the International Telecommunication Union (ITU) had imposed its technocratic ideas on the process. Some coalitions led to more meetings and new pieces of text, while others fell apart at the first meeting. But all of them seemed to end with announcements about other upcoming meetings.

My second encounter took place two days later, in one of the many buildings in Geneva catering to the needs of missions and international organizations based in the city. That day Conference Centre Varembé housed a meeting of the United Nations Information and Communication Technologies Task Force. This was its first meeting outside the UN headquarters in New York, where the body had been conceived with the support of Kofi Annan, the UN Secretary-General at the time. Aiming to address questions about ICTs and development, the body had members from UN agencies, private companies, international organizations and research institutions. Unlike the WSIS meetings, there was no way of gaining access to the meeting without a formal invitation. My newly acquired badge was of no use, and I only managed to find out where the meeting was held and enter the building by tagging along with someone who was formally invited. Inside the large, wood-panelled room, speakers such as the European Commissioner for Enterprise and Information Society, CEOs from Hewlett-Packard and Oracle, people from the World Economic Forum, and the author of a number of books on the 'network society', Manuel Castells, gave their views on how the Task Force could contribute to development efforts in Sub-Saharan Africa, push for deregulation in the ICT sector and engage in preparations for the World Summit on the Information Society. Coming from the WSIS meetings, I was struck by the organized character of these discussions and the ease with which everyone in the room interacted with others. There was no need to shut doors and nothing to disagree about.

This digression invites us to consider more carefully how we may enter the analysis of the kinds of socio-techno-political spaces that concern this book. What was I witnessing, and how could I make this phenomenon observable in more analytical terms? Deciding what something is a case of (Ragin and Becker 1992) and picking a theoretical entry point is challenging and consequential, so we tend to get it done as quickly as possible.

To simply decide that this was about 'epistemic communities' (Haas 1992), two organizations (March and Simon 1958), or a new regime in the making (Krasner 1983) would settle a lot of uncertainties and questions. But the basic tenet of a practice-oriented, relational and agnostic research strategy is that it may be valuable to postpone these decisions until we have developed a more situated, practical understanding of our empirical material (Flyvbjerg 2001; Clarke 2005). To start from a focus on ordering means that we follow Latour's advice: 'When your informants mix up the organization, hardware, psychology, and politics in one sentence, don't break it down first into neat little pots; try to follow the link they make among those elements that would have looked completely incommensurable if you had followed normal procedures' (Latour 2005a: 141–2). In this way, ordering is about 'following the actors' (Latour 2005a) and implies a focus on practices, associations and stabilization. In line with Foucault's famous studies of sexuality (Foucault 1998a, 1985) and madness (Foucault 1965), or Latour's study of the 'Pasteurization of France' (Latour 1988) or the making of scientific facts (Latour 1987), the study of ordering seeks to capture how different elements or 'networks of forces' are assembled and stabilized.

Let us return to Geneva for a moment. While still in an embryonic form, an assemblage was shaping up. Prior to the meetings I attended in Geneva, important linkages between technologies, people, documents and ideas had already been made. But the assemblage was expanding rapidly, and by the time of my first encounter, it was already a diverse and malleable mixture consisting of technological visions, UN procedures and badges, government representatives, working papers, statements, civil society activists, negotiations, academics, email lists, acronyms, organizational arrangements, technical experts, procedures, industry people and so much more. And the assemblage was certainly at work on something. At the time, I had no idea what it was, and limited knowledge of the inner workings of the UN. Furthermore, it was not an easy object to study. Over the next seven years I would try to keep up with this assemblage and examine its various shapes and tentacles. Following this 'net-set' or 'global information society circus', as some of those involved jokingly called themselves, has involved many trips to exotic locations and diplomatic capitals, hundreds of hours sitting in on meetings, managing a mountain of documents and field notes, and many conversations with those involved. At the many meetings to follow, in emails, books, and discussion groups, a wealth of questions emerged, for example, how to expand the number of top-level domain names, how to spur development, how to protect Internet users from spam, or establish access to communication as a human right. With time, it also became clear that the assemblage – its elements, shape and orientation – was constantly changing. As this book will show, the assemblage has taken multiple forms. Variously, I found myself studying UN conferences, an online community, close-knit expert groups and a very fuzzy social movement. Many of the people involved did not know each other, and very few of them agreed on what the real problems were, or how they should be solved. But many of the activities were organized in very similar ways, even if the settings were markedly different. In the process these different social worlds (Clarke 2005) seemingly came to appreciate the value of getting together, engaging in dialogue and staying clear of direct confrontations, formal negotiations and 'naming and shaming'. Furthermore, some groups and elements in the assemblage were very durable and tightly linked, while others would disappear. But looking back, this messy assemblage had actually produced something fairly tangible, namely an ordering of the global politics of the digital revolution as a multi-stakeholder process.

But how do we capture this assemblage, its ordering and its effects in analytical terms? As the account of my first encounters indicates, and as noted in the discussion of ordering above, we need an analytical vocabulary that is flexible enough to deal with associations among a myriad of heterogeneous elements. Also, it must help us understand and account for the different shapes and configurations taken by assemblages. To this end, I utilize the analytical concepts of 'assemblages' and 'moments of translation' drawn from Callon (1986) and Latour (2005a).

ASSEMBLAGES

To understand how objects, subjects and other elements are constituted and positioned relationally through associations, the concept of assemblages is useful because it implies a focus on the practical ways in which associations are made and start to act (Çalışkan and Callon 2010). The term originates from Deleuze and Guattari (1998), is a key concept in actor-network theory (Kendall 2004; Latour 2005a; Çalışkan and Callon 2010), and has also been taken up in parts of global ethnography (Ong and Collier 2004; Marcus and Saka 2006) and organization studies (Czarniawska and Hernes 2005). The focus on assemblages allows us to connect insights from governmentality studies and actor-network theory to capture hybrid configurations of technologies, actors, discourses and other elements. Studies of governance and organization tend to approach issue areas and institutional arrangements as fixed, separate and bounded entities. In contrast, a focus on ordering implies that we treat issue areas and organizational arrangements in a symmetrical manner (Law 1994) and refrain from separating them in advance. The analytical value of the term 'assemblages' is that it offers a focus on the co-constitution of objects of governance and institutional arrangements and a way to explore how these are continuously constructed, consolidated and contested. Such assemblages are 'composed of various longer or shorter connections [. . .] mixing freely the human and the non-human, the material and the social, the semiotic and the natural' (Kendall 2004: 71).

A number of recent publications have contributed to the operationalization of the term 'assemblages' and related ideas. Clarke's concept of 'situational analysis' is one way of approaching such 'assemblages of sorts: people, things and actions brought together at a particular time and place under particular conditions' (Clarke and Friese 2007: 392, n. 19). Barry uses the term 'technological zones' to describe similar formations. Drawing on a combination of insights from actor-network theory and Foucauldian scholarship, Barry stresses three facets of an analytics of technological zones. Firstly, the study of technological zones must be agnostic: it 'must attend to the complexity of their conditions of emergence and subsequent evolution, rather than assume that the form that technological zones have come to take is inevitable, or simply fills some particular political or economic need'. Secondly, it must take into account human and non-human elements. And thirdly, technological zones should not be perceived as structural phenomena, but rather as landscapes, as in 'the historical construction of particular political and economic spaces, and the specificities of the materials, practices and locations which they transform, connect, exclude and silence' (Barry 2006: 242–3). The conception of a technological zone as 'a structuring of relations, which has a normative force' (ibid.) makes the debt to Foucault clear: the concern with practices, ordering and political rationalities is a key theme in his work and in later discussions of governmentality and power (Kendall and Wickham 2001). Finally, Latham and Sassen's (2005) concept of a 'digital formation' is also useful if we want to capture how visions about information technologies facilitate new complex arrangements of human and non-human elements.

As an analytical starting point, the focus on assemblages allows us to study governance and organizational arrangements in a practice-oriented, relational and agnostic manner. It opens up our analytical gaze to the possibility that what we study may not be captured by shorthand categories, such as 'technology', 'society' or 'organization', and invites us to focus instead on configurations of heterogeneous elements. But ordering is never complete, and to act on the world assemblages need to transform continuously. So to fully understand how assemblages act and are acted upon, we need a way to capture how – in the search for stability and durability

– assemblages have to reconfigure and change. To this end, the analytical concept ‘moments of translation’ (Callon 1986) is useful.

TRANSLATIONS

The concern with translations is central to actor-network theory and is a useful entry point if we want to explore how assemblages become durable by reassembling and reconfiguring (Latour 1986; Nicolini 2009). My use of the term translation and the concern with different moments of translation draws heavily on the work of Callon (1986). In his classic study of the scallops, scientists and fishermen of St Brieuc Bay, Callon used the term to capture how the associations between these human and non-human actors were stabilized, at least momentarily:

> Translation is the mechanism by which the social and natural worlds progressively take form. The result is a situation in which certain entities control others. Understanding what sociologists generally call power relationships means describing the way in which actors are defined, associated and simultaneously obliged to remain faithful to their alliances. The repertoire of translation is not only designed to give a symmetrical and tolerant description of a complex process which constantly mixes together a variety of social and natural entities. It also permits an explanation of how a few obtain the right to express and to represent the many silent actors of the social and natural worlds they have mobilized. (Callon 1986: 224)

Callon discerned four key moments of translation – problematization, ‘interessement’, enrolment and mobilization – and stressed that these ‘constitute the different phases of a general process called translation, during which the identity of actors, the possibility of interaction and the margins of maneuvre are negotiated and delimited’ (Callon 1986: 203). That is, at various moments of translation, the elements and associations of assemblages reconfigure. In the context of this book, ‘moments of translation’ are used to capture the most significant shapes taken by the ordering of the global politics of the digital revolution, and to foreground how, over time, hybrid forums redefine their purposes and procedures in order to connect and mobilize particular subjects and objects.

Focusing on moments of translation invites us to trace and map the operations that make assemblages come to life, achieve a degree of consolidation and eventually become absorbed in new orderings. At the same time, the narrative in this book is structured around crucial moments of ordering, so that each of the five analytical chapters addresses a distinct phase in the invention, construction, stabilization and positioning of the link between hybrid forums and the global politics of the digital revolution.

FORMS AND EFFECTS OF ORDERING

But the purpose of this book is not merely to capture the assemblage and its different configurations. Ultimately my aim has been to bring out how the global politics of the Internet has been ordered as a result of these many associations and configurations, and what this may tell us about power and authority. To address the first of these steps, we need to bring out exactly what is being ordered, that is, what the assemblage and its momentary configurations consist of and seek to shape. As already hinted at, the assemblage contains multiple and constantly changing elements. But four elements stand out as particularly salient. In short, the hybrid forums involved in the global politics of the Internet have ordered organizational techniques, worldviews, subjects and objects. Unpacking these terms, their theoretical backdrop and empirical bearing is a daunting task, and is really what the rest of this book is about. At this point, it suffices to say that the following chapters study the workings and effects of multi-stakeholder processes by foregrounding the techniques used to organize them, the worldviews they are underpinned by, how they engage subjects in their work, and how they construct the objects they seek to shape. Returning briefly to the recollection of my first encounters with the assemblage described above we can exemplify the value of these four analytical themes. Firstly the assemblage was made durable because it developed and refined a suite of techniques to organize activities and interactions. The analyses capture how particular governmental techniques (Miller and Rose 1990; Foucault 1991a) made it possible to construct and organize multi-stakeholder arrangements and mobilize different social worlds. Secondly, the chapters investigate the constellation of worldviews, motivations and desires involved in multi-stakeholder arrangements to address the digital revolution. The concern with 'political rationalities' (Miller and Rose 1990; Rose and Miller 1992) allows us to investigate the reasoning and aspirations that underpin and drive attempts at ordering. Thirdly, the book captures how multi-stakeholder arrangements engage social worlds as stakeholders. These analyses build on the Foucauldian insight that power operates through subjects and must be studied as relational practices, which constrain and enable the conduct of subjects (Foucault 1982). Fourthly, the analyses explore how the digital revolution has emerged as an object of governance at the global level, and how multi-stakeholder processes problematize, construct and shape such objects. This attention to the making of governable objects ties in not only with the call for studies of materiality and the symmetrical treatments of humans and non-humans in ANT (Law 2000), but also the importance of studying how physical and abstract objects become central to the creation and maintenance of social worlds, organizational arrangements and collaborations (Blumer 1969; Clarke and Star 2008).

The ordering of these four facets of the assemblage and their configurations run through the book, and pave the way for the analyses of the operations and effects of multi-stakeholder processes. One way of thinking about these focal points is to consider them as 'sensitizing concepts', which guide and extend the more basic analyses of assemblages and translations, by 'suggest[ing] directions along which to look' (Charmaz 2003; Blumer 1969: 147–8). These four themes are informed by ANT and governmentality studies, but are also extensions of the findings in the empirical data. Without going into any sort of detail on this matter, many of the analytical operations involved in this book tie in with forms of grounded theory that have been pushed around the 'postmodern turn' and away from ideals about formal theory-building, especially through the cross-fertilization with insights from Foucauldian discourse analysis and ANT (Clarke 2005).

Out of these analyses of assemblages, translations and the forms and targets of ordering, the book finally addresses questions of power and authority. As noted above, the effects of ordering may be multiple, unpredictable and layered. In principle, we could find the effects of organizing the global politics of the Internet around hybrid forums to be a shrewd new form taken by neoliberalism, a new type of direct democracy or a corporate takeover of the UN, or a combination of any of these. Admittedly, the findings in this book are less spectacular. Reflecting on the effects and costs of ordering for the subjects, objects, techniques and rationalities involved, the discussions revolve around how the ability to mobilize resources and engage social worlds is about power, how dialogue and participation may be conceived as forms of steering, and how we may conceptualize hybrid forums as entangled forms of authority.

This chapter has developed an analytical vocabulary to rely on when examining the organization of the global politics of the Internet as a multi-stakeholder process. We now have an overall research strategy guiding the study (practice-oriented, relational and agnostic), a unit to study (an assemblage and its translations), an awareness of some particularly salient forms and targets of the ordering involved (techniques, rationalities, objects, subjects) and an ultimate goal with the analysis (power and authority). It is time to return to the making and operations of the socio-techno-political assemblage that this book is about.

2. Problematizing the digital revolution

The Internet entered the UN towards the end of the 1990s. It did so not only as a useful alternative to fax machines and regular mail, or as a way to rethink how files in the massive UN archives could be accessed. This technological innovation linking individual PCs in a quickly expanding global network brought on a wave of experiments with ways of organizing UN processes, suggested new directions for media regulation and development strategies to explore, and paved the way for unprecedented interaction and dialogue between business and other non-state actors. The emergence of these UN processes to flesh out the global politics of the digital revolution was made possible by a number of associations between multiple, heterogeneous elements. To understand how this happened, we need to address how these associations were made and stabilized, and particularly how they were driven by ideas about the relationship between technology and social transformation.

As we will see, these associations cast the digital revolution as a project in need of attention, that is, they turned it into a 'matter of concern' (Latour 2004, 2005b). When matters of fact emerge as matters of concern, they 'begin to look different, to render a different sound, they start to move in all directions, they overflow their boundaries, they include a complete set of new actors, they reveal the fragile envelopes in which they are housed' (Latour 2005b: 39). This chapter captures the moment where this transformation started, and shows how we may think of it as an important moment of ordering. Callon uses the term 'problematization' to refer to moments of translation where particular (human and non-human) actors position themselves as indispensable to others by defining the nature of a problem and offering a possible solution (Callon 1986: 203). The problematization of the digital revolution unsettled a number of concerns and practices, and in the process a particular ordering came about.

The UN interest in the socio-political problems and opportunities created by the rapidly growing importance of the Internet constitutes an important foundation for the bigger project of organizing the global politics of the digital revolution. To appreciate the significance of these activities we need to bring out the ways in which a technological innovation can give new direction to politics and transform organizational arrangements, and how multi-stakeholder processes help scramble and reorder the boundaries between the technical, the political, the organizational and the social. This is where the attention to processes of ordering becomes central. As pointed out in Chapter 1, the dual concern with assemblages and translations helps us capture how such different elements as networked ICTs, societal transformations, regulation and organizational reforms become not only linked, but also ordered. To understand the emergence of the global politics of the Internet and the reliance on multi-stakeholder processes, we need to explore the associations and translations of technology, politics and organization that made these activities possible. This involves an investigation of how such different elements as the Internet and the IT boom, a growing interest in corporate social responsibility, an increased focus on partnerships and entrepreneurship in development efforts, demands for UN reforms and a mounting discomfort with US-mandated private control with the technical infrastructure of the Internet became assembled in and around the UN. This linking of controversies about regulation, visions about the potentials of networked technologies and innovative ways of doing governance paved the way for the organization of the global politics of the Internet. By engaging a number of different social worlds and nurturing relations with corporations, technical experts, civil society groups and other international organizations, the activities to address these issues also paved the way for one of the most significant UN attempts at developing inclusive and participatory forms of engagement with non-state actors.

ASSEMBLING THE OPPORTUNITIES AND CHALLENGES OF THE DIGITAL REVOLUTION

In California, enthusiastic and savvy young computer wizards and entrepreneurs were constructing the pillars of the 'new economy'. Working out of university dorms and small start-ups in the San Francisco Bay area now known as Silicon Valley, engineers, techies and programmers developed the software, devices and business models that would make the dot.com boom possible. The mid-1990s were marked by a wild optimism about the potential of new media technologies for social transformation (Barney 2000; Mosco 2004; Flichy 2007). In the burgeoning literature on new media, observations about such economic growth in the computer industries were combined with theories about the 'knowledge society'

(Mansell and Wehn 1998), the 'information society' (Beniger 1986) and the 'network society' (Castells 1996). These visions of technology-induced social transformation, in turn, caught the attention of national governments, international organizations and corporations. While the dot.com bust in 2000 certainly put out some of these hopes, the belief in the transformative potential of ICTs continued to propel considerable investment in computers, cables and education to spread the digital revolution – in the shape of e-strategies, e-commerce, e-governance, e-health, e-education and e-literacy – in the US and Western Europe.

Picking up on these ideas, UN-based discussions about the global politics of the Internet revolved around four core themes related to the role of ICTs in societal transformations. The first of these brought together the elements developed in the literature cited above – observations about economic growth in the computer industries and theories about the 'knowledge society', the 'information society' and the 'network society' – into visions of technology-induced social transformation that many states, international organizations and corporations found attractive.

The second element of the global politics of the Internet involved considerations about the potential of ICTs for poverty reduction and economic growth in the poorest parts of the world. Building on long-standing concerns about the 'global digital divide' – an expression coined in the mid-1990s, which has since figured prominently in campaigns and initiatives to make ICTs available to developing countries and constitutes an important pillar of the global politics of the digital revolution – the problematization involved visions of how this 'digital divide' could be bridged. For instance, would it be possible for the poorest parts of Africa to 'leapfrog' stages of development if Internet access was made affordable and widely available? If so, maybe development efforts ought to shift the focus away from traditional development efforts such as food and water supplies and more towards computers and cables.

Third, these UN processes were driven by concerns about global Internet governance. The growing realization that the Internet certainly can be – and already is – regulated in a number of ways played an important role in the problematization. Especially for the UN, the governance of the Internet only emerged as a key concern quite late, namely when the UN World Summit on the Information Society (WSIS) turned into a fierce conflict over this matter. As we will see, even such contestations strengthen associations among multiple social worlds.

Fourth, the potential of ICTs vis-à-vis institutional reform, particularly within the UN system, constituted a less visible, but nonetheless important component in the UN discussions of the Internet and the global information society. In this respect the Internet offered a new solution to the long-standing problem of modernization and reform in the UN. The issue of ICT-driven UN reforms was not just taken up by member states already calling for institutional reforms, but also by civil society groups and computer companies willing to share their experiences and visions regarding networked forms of organization.

These visions became entangled with other UN projects in very concrete ways. For instance, the Economic and Social Council (ECOSOC), which coordinates the many specialized UN agencies and commissions, invited CEOs from some of the most successful ICT companies to reflect on how the UN might latch onto the digital revolution. The rapid spread of the Internet also spurred a wealth of regulatory initiatives in specialized agencies such as the International Telecommunications Union (ITU) and the World Bank. Excitement about the Internet also coincided with the decision to re-orient UN development strategies towards more targeted initiatives, such as those spelled out in the Millennium Development Goals. One of these targets was to cooperate with the private sector in developing global partnerships to 'make available benefits of new technologies, especially information and communications' (UN 2000). This linking of business, partnerships, ICTs and development was central to the emergence of ICT-for-development (ICT4D) as a key component of the global politics of the digital revolution. As pointed out by Heeks (2008: 27) 'The digital technologies of the 1990s, then, supplied a new tool in search of a purpose; development goals were new targets in search of a delivery mechanism. These two domains intersected and gave rise to ICT4D in a flurry of publications, bodies, events, programs, and project funding.' Furthermore, hopes about the transformative potential of the Internet were brought to bear in efforts to reform and revitalize the UN. These visions took the shape of calls for digital partnerships (Dossal 2002) and networked forms of organization to replace the traditional 'bureaucratic hierarchy' (Holohan 2003). Finally, the growing awareness about the significance of the Internet shaped UN activities and strategies in the area of global media regulation. In particular, the ITU became closely involved with attempts at constructing the Internet as yet another form of telecommunication in need of international agreements and UN-based forms of steering. These many concerns and activities spurred by the spread of the Internet emerged as the most significant components of the assemblage that made it possible for the global politics of the Internet to become a key concern in the UN. As we will see in this chapter, these broad concerns were soon consolidated into more tangible projects. In other words, they were ordered through a process of assembling and translating. It is this process that we now turn to.

DEVELOPMENT AND THE DIGITAL DIVIDE

Discussions about the global digital divide – the inequality of access to ICTs and the resulting socio-economic disadvantages for excluded parts of the world – spurred the ongoing UN attempt at engaging with the global politics of media and communications. Calls for the need to bridge the digital divide were propelled by the widespread excitement about the potential of digital technologies for social transformation and economic development, and took the shape of roll-outs of cables and infrastructure as well as capacity-building and education. The idea that technological innovations, such as the Internet, can contribute to development efforts in the poorest parts of the world ties in with long-standing concerns about the importance of technology, information and knowledge within the development sector. In the 1950s radio was perceived as an important tool for development and was integrated into development efforts (Schech 2002) alongside many other activities, such as nation-state formation, political and economic reforms and other core components of the developed world (Escobar 1995). As a number of scholars have pointed out (May 2002; Wade 2002; Flyverbom and Hansen 2006), the emergence of ICTs as a priority in development efforts builds on a highly optimistic view of the ability of technology to transform societies, economies and politics. Such forms of technological determinism underpin not only digital divide campaigns, but also broader visions of the 'global information society', the 'new economy' and 'ICT-for-development'. Currently the concern with technology transfer goes hand in hand with ideas about the need for knowledge as a key component of development (King and McGrath 2004; Flyverbom and Hansen 2006), and intersects with initiatives such as micro-financing, corporate citizenship and philanthropy.

Concerns about the global digital divide have emerged alongside the growth of the Internet, but leading up to the UN processes under scrutiny here, these discussions were particularly visible within the major development agencies such as the World Bank and the United Nations Development Programme (UNDP), for instance as documented in UNDP's Human Development Report from 2001 entitled *Making New Technologies Work for Development*. But the World Economic Forum (GDDI 2002) and the Group of Eight (G8) also played parts in the construction of the global digital divide as a relevant issue for states, business and a number of civil society groups to take up. During the G8 summit in Okinawa, Japan in 2000, a 'Charter on the Global Information Society' was adopted and subsequently a body called the G8 Digital Opportunity Task Force (DOT Force) was created to develop a plan of action (DOT Force 2000). In contrast to previous discussions about the digital divide this body offered a pro-active and entrepreneurial approach to ICT-driven development – indicated by the focus on the opportunities of the digital revolution. Bringing together groups from government, business, civil society and international organizations, from developed as well as developing countries (DOT Force 2001) this body also gave momentum to the focus on cross-sectoral collaboration as a fruitful way of addressing the digital divide. As we will see, the DOT Force was a key source of inspiration for later UN-driven activities seeking to continue the discussions about digital opportunities and challenges. The linking of a strong belief in the potential of ICTs for development and the call for broad and inclusive collaboration between private and public actors constituted an attractive formula that the UN bought more or less wholesale. The focus on multistakeholder processes resonated not only with other UN concerns, but also with a growing interest in partnerships in the development community. The field of development has been marked by an increased focus on partnerships, alliances and networks bringing together the efforts of different sectors and types of actors (Brinkerhoff 2002), and as noted above, the Millennium Development Goals reproduced this formula by dedicating its eighth goal to a focus on ICT efforts through partnerships (Unwin 2009: 134). At the time, such discussions figured prominently in US politics and in the development sector, and, as we will see, came to shape UN activities in the area of media, communication and development in significant and consequential ways.

GLOBAL MEDIA REGULATION

UN concerns with the Internet also involved the question of global media regulation. Discussions about the politics and regulation of media and communications have a long history and telecommunications policy and governance is a well-established issue area at national and international levels. As Drake points out:

> Long before governments recognized a need to establish international mechanisms to manage global problems like trade, human rights or the environment, they saw that nation-states could only benefit from the possibilities of international telecommunications if there were shared rules of the game governing how national networks would interconnect and messages would be passed from one to the next. (Drake 2000: 124)

In many ways media and communications have been treated like other culturally, socially, politically and economically important resources. States have invoked the principle of national sovereignty, crafted policies and set up regulatory agencies. Collectively, states have delegated authority to intergovernmental agencies and fleshed out the rules, procedures and principles of media regulation (Braithwaite and Drahos 2000; Napoli 2001; Siochrú and Girard 2002). But clearly, there are important differences between various forms of media regulation. Radio and television are not regulated in the same way as the telephone, and the control of cables and other technical infrastructures is separated from the control of content and ownership. Some elements of media regulation are under national and multilateral control, while others are regulated by industry or not regulated at all. The international regulation of telecommunications has primarily been the responsibility of the oldest intergovernmental organization in the world, the UN-based International Telecommunication Union (ITU). But with the emergence of the Internet and broader changes in global politics, such as increasing liberalization (Drake 2000) and the emergence of private authorities (Cutler, Haufler et al. 1999; Hall and Biersteker 2002; Graz and Nölke 2007; Hansen and Salskov-Iversen 2008), global media regulation, and particularly Internet governance, is increasingly diversified and dispersed (Eriksson and Giacomello 2008).

While global media have always been subject to various forms of governance, the Internet has – for many years – been portrayed as outside the reach of regulation, often with reference to its decentralized, global nature (Barlow 1996; Lessig 1999). In technical terms the Internet is different from other media technologies: it is a highly distributed, ever-expanding combination of innovations sharing a versatile technical platform. These technical features – in combination with persistent US pressure for technical and corporate self-regulation – mean that the Internet has not been integrated into ITU and other traditional forms of global media governance. Still, there is nothing inherently ungovernable about the Internet, and in hindsight, the arguments that it cannot be regulated must be seen as political decisions made by governments or wishful thinking on the part of its developers and early users. The growing realization that the Internet certainly can be – and already is – regulated in a number of ways (Goldsmith and Wu 2006; Lessig 1999) has contributed to UN processes to address the global politics of the digital revolution.

Controversies about the global politics of media and communications hail back at least to the mid-1970s when the United Nations Education, Scientific and Cultural Organization (UNESCO) initiated what was known as the New World Information and Communication Order (NWICO). This process was driven by developing countries dissatisfied with the economic and cultural consequences of increasing Western control over global media and contents, and put media and communications on the global agenda for the first time (Siochrú and Girard 2002: 75).

But this UN attempt to link media and communication to concerns about cultural imperialism, unfair trade agreements, lack of national control and developing countries' lack of influence in decisions such as those made in the World Bank and the World Trade Organization (WTO) was far from successful in terms of tangible outcomes. In fact, the most concrete result of the process was that the US and later the UK withdrew from UNESCO, which had taken the lead in this decade-long initiative (Thussu 2000; Kamalipour 2002; Siochrú and Girard 2002). Still, the attention to the politics of media and communication created by NWICO is important in relation to contemporary discussions about the global politics of the digital revolution and the reliance on multi-stakeholder processes. For instance, one major reason for the emergence of multi-stakeholder participation as a key principle in ongoing UN activities in this area may be the realization that a process driven by (developing country) governments with very little interest in the views of other actors may be considered one of the causes of NWICO's failure (Kleinwächter, personal communication).

The emergence of the Internet as a matter of concern in global media regulation revolved around questions such as whether, how and with what consequences a new governance framework could be established in this area. In the context of the UN, one key question was whether Internet governance should be considered a part of the broader regulation of telecommunications or an entirely different thing in need of a unique regulatory approach. While other media could be separated or grouped for purposes of regulation, the emergence of digitalization, technological convergence and shared infrastructures have unsettled this stability (Napoli 2001; Siochrú and Girard 2002). UN activities in this area have contributed to the tension between traditional regulation of telecommunications and emergent forms of Internet governance. In particular, attempts to position Internet regulation as part of the broader telecommunications regime have been met with strong resistance, and the attempt to construct the Internet as unique and in need of a novel approach to governance played a pivotal role in the UN-based activities and processes under scrutiny in this book. As we will see, the emergence of the global governance of the Internet as a visible matter of concern raised and revitalized questions about the power and authority to govern techno-political spaces.

The attempt to address these questions without resorting to traditional UN decision-making processes or fuelling existing conflicts involved a number of experiments with multi-stakeholder forms of organization. The sources of these attempts at engaging various social worlds were not only the DOT Force, but also the broader, technical community involved in the construction and maintenance of the Internet. Bodies such as the Internet Corporation for Assigned Names and Numbers (ICANN), the Internet

Engineering Task Force (IETF) and the Internet Society (ISOC) all seek to bring together different groupings, and to position themselves as inclusive and transparent forums. For instance, ICANN, which manages central parts of the technical infrastructure of the Internet, was conceived as a private, non-profit organization operating under a 'memorandum of understanding' with the US Department of Commerce. While ICANN's mandate is primarily technical, the decision to create this organization was a clear signal that the US wanted to keep the principle of industry self-regulation in place (Siochrú and Girard 2002). Still, an awareness of the importance of even technical aspects of Internet governance and the need for transparency and inclusion when it comes to the decisions and operations of ICANN has made this body the site of a number of ambitious experiments with novel and inclusive forms of global governance. To the dismay of many national governments, ICANN does not operate on the basis of intergovernmental agreements, although states and other actors are consulted. In other words, ICANN and other Internet governance arrangements challenge national, representative forms of democracy and seek to develop novel forms of global governance foregrounding users as the primary constituency. Such experiments also became central to UN activities to address the global politics of the digital revolution. They not only tied in with the technological visions and challenges discussed in this chapter, but also helped the UN find ways of engaging industry, technical and civil society groups in the many consultations, dialogues and forums for discussion to follow.

NETWORKING THE UN

As early as his acceptance speech as Secretary-General, Kofi Annan expressed the need for a leaner, more efficient and responsive UN (http://www.un.org/reform). Such attempts at reforming the UN took a number of shapes in the following decade, but one important track was to explore whether networks, partnerships and virtual forms of organization could be used to these ends. For instance the report on the Millennium Development Goals stressed the need for 'digital connections' and suggested that: 'We can use the new information technology to make the UN more efficient, and to improve its interaction with the rest of the world. But to do so we must overcome a change-resistant culture. The Secretary-General is asking the information technology industry to help us do it' (Annan 2000: para VI).

What drove these strategies was a hope that if the Internet could transform societies and economies, maybe it would also help the UN renew itself, do away with the image of a rusty bureaucracy and instead enable the organization to re-emerge as a responsive, modern network (Holohan 2003). The potential of ICTs for institutional reform, particularly within the UN system itself, constitutes a less visible, but nonetheless important component of the organization of the global politics of the digital revolution as a multi-stakeholder process. These visions of technology-driven reforms gained momentum because they catered to a growing interest in engaging non-state actors in UN processes. As an intergovernmental institution serving its member states, the UN obviously does not allow non-state actors to make decisions and develop policies. While non-state actors, in particular NGOs, may be consulted, as spelled out in Article 71 of the UN Declaration (UN Charter, chapter 10), they are rarely part of agenda-setting and decision-making processes. But many parts of the UN have sought to develop novel forms of interaction with relevant non-state groups and organizations, and these proposals and activities helped pave the way for the emergence of multi-stakeholder participation as a key feature of UN work on the digital revolution. Looking back, the Acting Executive Director of the UN ICT Task Force put it this way,

> I have seen the UN evolve in the last 30 years or so, and in ECOSOC, NGOs consulting with states was always there, but it was a very formalistic kind of relationship, it is not a real relationship, and okay, they are allowed to make statements and submit a document, and they can lobby delegations behind the scenes, but there is no real participation. I mean, at least until, it has changed in the last 5–7 years, but until then there was nothing [. . .] Similarly, private sector was practically non-existent. [Business could] come and speak, but there was no real engagement, you wouldn't actually find a senior vice president of a company coming here and participating in a discussion. That was non-existent, in the UN, it didn't exist, until 1995–6. It didn't happen. (Interview, UNICTTF Acting Executive Coordinator 2004)

Although NGOs have always played an important role in the UN system – through consultations and in relation to implementation on the ground – and business associations have been present in the background of UN processes, this was one of the first times they were recognized as equal partners in advisory bodies, decision-making processes and in meetings. This distinction between 'consultation' and 'real participation' is central to the emergence of hybrid forums to address the global politics of the digital revolution.

The origins of multi-stakeholder processes in the UN are numerous. UN summits in particular have emerged as important test beds for attempts at engaging a wide range of social worlds in efforts to address issues such as the environment, gender inequality and development. In activities to follow up on the 1992 UN Conference on Environment and

Development in Rio de Janeiro, participation and inclusion evolved as priorities (Ferenz 2002), and by the 2002 Johannesburg Summit, multi-stakeholder processes were a key concern (www.johannesburgsummit.org). These and other UN experiments with participation were part and parcel of an increasing focus on participation in global governance. As pointed out above, many UN organizations involved in development have made partnerships with the business community a key priority. In particular, the emergence of corporate citizenship and the massive growth of the ICT sector fuelled such attempts at doing development in ways that combine 'doing well' with 'doing good', to quote one of the business gurus in this area, C.K. Prahalad (Prahalad 2010: 159), who is also mentioned as influential by UN staff members (Interview, UNICTTF Acting Executive Coordinator 2004). But discussions about the politics of ICTs also involved concerns about how to develop new forms of global governance that could engage – and improve the cooperation between – different sectors and stakeholders. This drive for new modes of political coordination and decision-making beyond national orientations and intergovernmental systems of rule entered the UN system fairly recently. Probably the most concrete instance of such attempts to challenge the view of the UN as an intergovernmental organization, where governments alone agree on internationally binding rules, guidelines and principles, is the report by the Commission on Global Governance, *Our Global Neighborhood*, published in 1995. This report stated that 'the world needs a new vision that can galvanize people everywhere to achieve higher levels of cooperation in areas of common concern and shared destiny' (Commission on Global Governance 1995:1) and used this as backcloth for a lengthy investigation of how the UN could position itself as a key player, bringing together governments, intergovernmental institutions, NGOs, transnational corporations, academia and the mass media. Following up on these recommendations, and in another attempt to update and develop Article 71 and more inclusive forms of global governance, the 'Cardoso Report' in 2004 called for UN reforms to strengthen formal collaboration with civil society and other non-state actors, particularly through so-called 'multi-constituency processes' ('Cardoso Report' 2004: 9).

Summing up, it is clear that collaborations with non-state actors have a long history in the UN, but that the scale and importance of these have increased in recent years. More institutionalized, collaborative arrangements go back to the tripartite structure of the International Labour Organization, in place since 1919, the access to conferences and summits, and the consultative status that ECOSOC has given to NGOs from the 1950s onwards. More recently, collaborative arrangements have been used extensively in the preparations for world summits, in the Global Compact, and in a number of working groups, task forces and other more informal contexts. Such strategies to strengthen participation and partnerships and to establish networked arrangements have been presented as effective, legitimate and salient ways of responding to complex issues and problems. Clearly, these experiments tie in with discussions about the transformation of 'government' into 'governance' and a growing excitement about networked forms of organization. In the UN, many of these arrangements – both in the shape of policy discussions and concrete projects – were pursued with direct reference to the potential and strengths of digital media, for instance when it is argued that 'improved access to and use of ICT is needed to forge such win-win partnerships worldwide' (Dossal 2002: n.p.)

Taken together, these discussions about the potential of networks, partnerships and other forms of engagement with non-state actors comprised an important component of the emergent assemblage. These concerns about inclusion and partnerships, and the hopes about the potential of ICTs for institutional reform contribute to the emergence of the global politics of the digital revolution in important ways: they indicate an acceptance of a new distribution of roles and responsibilities among public and private sectors, such as business getting involved in development activities that were previously carried out by (inter)governmental donor organizations and business stressing the same values as the development community in their corporate social responsibility activities. At the same time, the idea of ICTs as a source of social and political transformation paved the way for the global politics of the digital revolution – not only as a new issue area, but also as a novel way of organizing interactions with non-state actors.

ORDERING THE ASSEMBLAGE

Turning these relatively scattered hopes and concerns about the digital revolution into a more ordered project involved a number of activities in ECOSOC and ITU. To make sense of these ordering activities, the concept 'problematization' (Callon 1986; Foucault 1991d; Bratich, Packer et al. 2003) is useful. Problematizations are moments when the question of 'how to govern' becomes central (Dean 1999) and particular actors are able to position themselves as indispensable to others by not only identifying a problem to be addressed but also a way to resolve it (Callon 1986: 203). Problematizations involve the movement or reduction of macrocosms into microcosms (Callon, Lascoumes et al. 2009: 48) – in this case ordering highly dispersed discussions about media regulation, the technology-society nexus, the use of ICTs in development efforts, and networked forms of organizing into some more organized UN processes.

Two particular UN-driven initiatives laid the foundation for the multi-stakeholder processes to address the global politics of the digital revolution: a series of ICT-for-development activities undertaken by the Department of Economic and Social Affairs (DESA) and ECOSOC, tackling questions about development, globalization and new ICTs, and ITU's decision to arrange a world summit on the 'global information society'. Shifting the attention to these organizational activities is a way to capture how the assemblage was ordered through processes of translation, that is, how these matters of concern (Latour 2004) were turned into matters of intervention.

ACTING ON THE GLOBAL DIGITAL DIVIDE

From 1999 onwards, ECOSOC devoted a number of General Assembly sessions to discussions about the digital revolution. Couched in traditional terms such as 'technology transfer' and tied very closely to the broader prospects of globalization processes, these discussions considered how the UN may help 'enable [developing countries] to benefit from globalization through full and effective integration into the emerging global information network' (General-Assembly 1999). As a result of these discussions the General Assembly suggested that the Secretary-General should prepare a report

> containing action-oriented recommendations on promoting further the role of the United Nations system in the transfer of information and communication technology to the developing countries and also on its role in promoting policy coherence, complementarity and coordination on economic, financial, trade, technology and development issues at the global level in order to optimize the benefits of globalization. (General-Assembly 1999: 4)

As one of the components of the problematization of the global politics of the digital revolution, these discussions helped construct ICT-driven development as a relevant project on which to embark, and proposed the transfer of technology as an important starting point. But they also invigorated the idea that this matter of concern should be addressed by engaging actors other than UN agencies and member states. In the General Assembly resolutions and reports to follow, it was suggested that the project should be undertaken in close collaboration with the Bretton Woods institutions, the International Monetary Fund (IMF), the International Bank for Reconstruction and Development (IBRD) and the World Trade Organization (WTO) and the Group of 8 (G8). Along with experts such as Vincent Cerf – one of the many founding fathers of the Internet – business leaders from the world's major ICT companies, such as Nokia, WorldCom and Sun Microsystems were invited to meetings. While the majority of UN discussions about the question of ICTs took the shape of more traditional intergovernmental negotiations, these meetings with non-state actors played an important role in General Assembly attempts to give momentum to the project (Interview, UNICTTF Acting Executive Coordinator 2004). One proposal was that the Secretary-General should ask a 'high-level panel of experts on information and communication technology' to prepare a set of recommendations for further action (General-Assembly 1999: 4). As we will see, the decision to set up this panel paved the way for one of the first organizational forms taken by the assemblage at this moment of translation: a small hybrid forum. This group came to play a pivotal role in the activities to follow, and constitutes an important pillar of the problematization phase, particularly because their report translated the scattered discussions described above into a proposal for action.

Arranged by the DESA and UNDP, the 'High-Level Panel on Information and Communication Technology' held its first meeting in New York in April 2000. The panel was chaired by a former president of Costa Rica, Jose Maria Figueres, and consisted of 17 experts: ministers, directors of companies, ICT specialists and members of national boards and various organizations from all five official UN regions, Africa, Asia, Eastern Europe, Latin America and the Caribbean, and Western Europe. According to one member, who participated in her capacity as a telecommunications policy and gender specialist from Latin America, the panel 'included people with a variety of responsibilities, many of whom were actually managing ICT strategies in their countries' (Interview, TfDev Member of UNICTTF 2004). And what came out of this attempt at cross-regional, cross-sectoral dialogue was 'a very rich set of discussions, not only about the challenges, but also the opportunities and mechanisms for actually promoting and accelerating the rates at which developing countries were using ICTs for development' (Interview, TfDev Member of UNICTTF 2004). The work of the panel resulted in a small blue book, which presented 'the challenge' of the digital divide, 'the opportunity' for developing countries if they got access to ICTs, and 'the mission' through which this goal may be reached. The report – a material proof that some kind of ordering was in place – stressed that the UN could play an important role in efforts at using ICTs for development purposes and called for an 'international ICT action plan'. Amidst a number of policy-oriented proposals and general recommendations for the orientation of this action plan, such as the need to overcome gender barriers, to strengthen capacity-building, to initiate ICT sector reforms and to make access to information and communication services a human right, there was also a very concrete proposal to set up a task force to address the issue of ICT and development. The report suggested that the

> United Nations should create, under the leadership of the Secretary-General but outside United Nations organizational structures, an ICT Task Force. This task force should bring together multilateral development institutions, private industry, foundations and trusts and would facilitate, including by investment, the expansion of the market for ICT in developing countries, thereby helping to bridge the digital divide [. . .] This task force would provide overall leadership and strategy for ICT development. A fund should be created that the task force would administer and for which up to $500 million would be solicited from sources such as the United Nations Fund for International Partnerships. This amount would be matched by funds raised from the private sector and foundations. (Panel 2000: 3–4)

This hybrid forum – the United Nations ICT Task Force (UNICTTF) – was intended to facilitate partnerships between private and public ICT-for-development initiatives and administer a trust fund supporting such projects (UNICTTF 2000c). The vision was that it would mobilize and manage financial resources from UN budgets and private sources – ideally $500 million the first year and twice the amount in the year to follow – and use these to fund projects seeking to bridge the digital divide. These suggestions were quickly picked up and developed by DESA. In the words of the executive director of the UNICTTF, the blue book constituted the primary source of inspiration for the task force, in fact, 'that's how it was founded' (Interview, UNICTTF Deputy Executive Coordinator 2004). According to a UNDP employee, who helped DESA create the UNICTTF (Interview, TfDev Member of UNICTTF 2004), the UN should undertake and lead these efforts, not only because 'the UN has the trust of the developing countries', but also because 'ICT is the future and by effectively seizing the initiative, the UN can immensely benefit from the exposure that will result from demonstrating that it is at the "cutting edge" and facilitating the use of ICT in development' (UNDP employee 2000a: 1). He also stressed that

> my own reading of the present situation is that there is a growing shift away from the discussion about whether there should be a new global ICT initiative for the developing countries to a discussion of how this can be accomplished. Decisive and prompt leadership by one body is now necessary to avoid a far more costly, protracted and difficult task of reconciling the follow-ups that one or more donors/institutions are beginning to consider. (UNDP employee 2000a: 2)

Thus, the question was no longer whether or not these initiatives should be undertaken, but how to move ahead. With this ordering of the project and its translation into organizational arrangements and forms of intervention, it also became the object of muted, but significant struggles and turf wars between the DESA, the World Bank and UNDP – all of which were rushing to appropriate and act on these ideas. The DESA activities helped order the organization of the global politics of the digital revolution in important ways: first by defining the identities of a wide range of actors as partners and stakeholders in relation to the matter of ICT-for-development and, second, by striving for the proposed ICT Task Force to be positioned as the main organizational arrangement for UN efforts in this area.

MAKING THE DIGITAL REVOLUTION GOVERNABLE

Meanwhile, in another part of the UN, discussions about the problems and opportunities related to ICTs were also gaining momentum. Historically, the International Telecommunication Union has played an important role in global media regulation through the development of technical standards in communications equipment, the allocation of radio frequency spectrum and satellite slots, and the negotiation of agreements between international telecommunications operators (Siochrú and Girard 2002: 36). Attempts by ITU and others to integrate the Internet into such existing, multilateral forms of media governance have been relatively unsuccessful. Nonetheless, the global regulation of the Internet played a part in the decision to create a forum for discussion about the global politics of the digital revolution. At a meeting in Minneapolis in 1998, the International Telecommunication Union decided to arrange a UN summit on the 'information society'. The resolution stated that the purpose of the world summit (WSIS) should be

> establishing an overall framework identifying, with the contribution of all partners, a joint and harmonized understanding of the information society; drawing up a strategic plan of action for concerted development of the information society by defining an agenda covering the objectives to be achieved and the resources to be mobilized; identifying the roles of the various partners to ensure smooth coordination of the establishment in practice of the information society in all Member States. (ITU 1998)

The decision to hold a World Summit on the Information Society has been interpreted by some as an attempt to take over the functions of

ICANN (Klein 2006). But according to others, WSIS was rather an attempt to follow up on parts of the failed NWICO process, and establish a new UN platform for discussions about the global information society (Kleinwächter, personal communication). At any rate, the resolution adopted in Minneapolis, and the later resolution endorsed by the UN General Assembly addressed the broader information society issues rather than just ICANN. As this chapter shows, WSIS and the broader problematization of the global politics of the digital revolution came about as an attempt to create a place where intergovernmental discussions about the Internet and new ICTs could take place. Whereas other communication technologies have forums for discussion or institutional homes, the global politics of the digital revolution was homeless, and it was 'almost taboo' to speak about the Internet at the ITU (Shope-Mafole, intervention at WGIG's first consultation 2004). The appeal of WSIS and related processes was not simply that the ITU sought to strengthen its role in Internet governance, but also that developing countries found the lack of coordination and centralized regulation to be a major obstacle to their ability to participate. The number of organizations involved in Internet governance is astonishing – for instance, a report by the International Chamber of Commerce has identified 41 separate entities (ICC 2004). If Internet governance could be addressed within ITU, the missions located in Geneva would be able to take part, be familiar with the procedures, and not have to follow the many Internet governance meetings taking place around the world, where technical jargon and tightly-knit groupings makes participation a major challenge, even if it is formally possible and encouraged, for instance by ICANN (Interview, WGIG Executive Coordinator 2005). WSIS provided an opportunity to address these challenges, as well as the many other questions raised by the emergence of the Internet. Also, it catered to the many international organizations and national governments challenging the existence of private, regulatory bodies, such as ICANN, which do not follow the rules and practices that have been established in the regulation of other ICTs.

Conferences and world summits have always been a central part of the work of the UN. They have been used to address a huge variety of issues – from trade, energy and disarmament, through crime, poverty and drug trafficking to development, human rights, gender inequality, education and climate change (Schechter 2001). While building on this tradition, WSIS differed from other UN summits in two ways: unlike previous summits, WSIS sought to bring attention to an emergent issue, rather than a well-known and long-standing problem. Also, unlike other summits, WSIS consisted of two meetings – one in 2003 and one in 2005 – with a number of preparatory and follow-up events in between. Building on the experiments with multi-stakeholder participation described above, WSIS allowed for broad-based participation by non-state actors. With 175 states, and hundreds of international organizations, NGOs and private sector groups, WSIS brought together more than 11,000 people in 2003 and more than 19,000 in 2005 (www.itu.int/wsis/participation/index.html (accessed 3 March 2011)).

The Geneva phase of WSIS addressed a wide range of issues related to the digital revolution, but Internet governance and development funding in particular created deadlocks. As a result, the Secretary-General was asked to set up two working groups to address these questions and prepare the grounds for negotiations to resume during the Tunis phase of WSIS in 2005. One of these was the Working Group on Internet Governance (WGIG), which was set up to deal with the conflict over the global governance of the Internet. WSIS provided an opportunity to discuss this controversial question – and the disagreements turned out to be deep-rooted. Some governments, particularly that of the US, demanded that the established practice of self-regulation should continue, while a number of developing countries, particularly Syria, Iran, China, Pakistan and India argued for intergovernmental oversight, preferably carried out by ITU. The decision to create WGIG was driven by the realization that this deadlock could not be solved in the final hours of negotiation. Instead, it was agreed that the UN Secretary-General should create a forum where further discussions could take place. In preparation for the Tunis phase of the summit, this body was asked to produce a report, which would 'develop a working definition of Internet governance', 'identify the public policy issues that are relevant to Internet governance' and 'develop a common understanding of the respective roles and responsibilities of governments, existing intergovernmental and international organisations and other forums as well as the private sector and civil society from both developing and developed countries' (WSIS 2003b, para 13b). In the process, this hybrid forum became a test bed for multi-stakeholder participation with significant implications for the objects, subjects, techniques and rationalities involved.

PROBLEMATIZATION AS ORDERING

Returning to this book's overall concern with processes of ordering raises the question of what was ordered in the problematization phase. This moment of ordering linked a number of different activities, concerns, visions, actors and organizations in and around the UN and sought to position the Internet and socio-political transformation as a matter in need of intervention. WSIS is particularly important to the problematization of the global politics of the digital revolution because the world summit provided the 'institutionally legitimated claims to truth, or one or another type of sanctioned seriousness' (Rabinow 2005: 44) that turned the scattered concerns about the digital revolution discussed in this chapter into a more solid and ordered project. The problematization of the global politics of the digital revolution sheds light on the ways in which governance and organization are entangled. The problematization locked objects, subjects, rationalities and techniques in a particular configuration, and capturing the shape of this configuration brings us closer to understanding the operations and effects of multi-stakeholder processes. Using insights from ANT and governmentality studies we can conceptualize the making and workings of these first UN activities in more abstract terms.

This first moment of translation involved the first steps towards positioning a number of 'social worlds' (Clarke and Star 2008) as potential allies, exploring the organizational techniques to be used, and settling on what was to be governed. The following section looks at these in turn, and then moves on to consider in some more detail how the problematization revolved around a particular set of political rationalities that constitute important tools and targets of ordering. The first moment of ordering positioned particular social worlds as central to the project under construction. The activities involved not only considerations about who to ally with, but also about who to target. For instance, major donor agencies and large IT companies were considered as central to the project of creating a well-funded UN task force to pursue the ICT-for-development project. Similarly, WSIS encouraged not only UN member states but also civil society groups and industry to participate, and other attempts to address the global governance of the Internet considered carefully how to engage the different technical and regulatory bodies already carrying out these governance activities. This moment of ordering took the first step towards the categorization of particular social worlds as stakeholders, and as we will see in the chapters below, such attempts at classification and codification are central to the workings and effects of hybrid forums.

When it comes to the organizational techniques at work in these first attempts to address the global politics of the digital revolution, it is clear that most of them were traditional UN procedures. ICT-for-development was approached as a matter to be dealt with by the ECOSOC General Assembly, and the result was a UN resolution to pursue the matter further. Similarly, the focus on the information society and Internet regulation took the shape of a decision to arrange a UN world summit. And when this organizational arrangement ended in deadlock, a working group was set up to find ways of addressing the matter. So at this stage of ordering, most of the techniques were well-developed, traditional UN instruments. However, they were put to uses that challenged established practices in the UN system. In particular, the growing engagement with non-state actors tested the limits of such procedures and arrangements. In the search for organizational arrangements and mechanisms, actors within the UN looked not only in their own toolbox, but also picked up on developments in other places, such as ICANN and the G8.

Another important outcome was that the problematization posited a number of scattered questions and aspirations as a matter of concern and intervention. The first moment of ordering in the organization of the global politics of the Internet particularly focused on the construction and delimitation of the digital revolution as a governable object. Making this object governable involved multiple observations, delimitations and mappings of phenomena such as the IT boom, the digital divide, media regulations, partnerships and networked organizations, and new approaches to development. These linked-up activities not only examined how development was carried out and the Internet was controlled, but also questioned institutional arrangements and procedural practices and the division of labour between public and private actors, and reflected on the political subjects involved.

RATIONALITIES AT WORK

But most importantly, the first moment of ordering revolved around a distinct set of worldviews, or 'political rationalities' (Miller and Rose 1990; Rose and Miller 1992). To fully appreciate the importance of rationalities as tools and targets of ordering, we need to reflect briefly on the meaning and origins of this term. Political rationalities can be understood as the ideas, ambitions and values that underpin practices of ordering. In the words of Foucault '"practices" don't exist without a certain regime of rationality' (Foucault 1991c: 79). More recent work on governmentality has spelled out the analytical value of this term and proposed that we think of political rationalities as 'the changing discursive fields within which the exercise of power is conceptualised, the moral justifications for particular ways of exercising power by diverse authorities, notions of the appropriate forms, objects and limits of politics, and conceptions of the proper distribution of such tasks among secular, spiritual, military and familial sectors' (Rose and Miller 1992: 175).

In Rose and Miller's rendition, political rationalities have three key characteristics: they are discursive in character, they have a moral nature, and they contain assumptions about what, how and who should be governed (Miller and Rose 1990; Rose and Miller 1992). To study political rationalities therefore implies a focus on the forms of knowledge and reasoning that are invoked when particular objects of governance are constructed and action upon them is sought.

Clearly, the concern with values, ideas and reasoning is also central to other approaches to social and political science. In international relations, the literature on ideas points to the ways in which values and forms of knowledge affect policy choices and governance activities. Here ideas are often described as cognitive – inner forces that determine action (Jacobsen 1995). This stands in stark contrast to the Foucauldian idea of political rationalities as socially and historically assembled and negotiated. From such perspectives, beliefs and forms of reasoning cannot simply be determined (Haas 1992: 34–5), but must be studied as they become articulated, linked and stabilized. As Garland points out, 'Since particular techniques and devices are often compatible with a variety of different political rationalities, the contingent historical processes whereby one becomes linked up to another are obviously of great importance to analysis' (Garland 1997).

Furthermore, the conception of political rationalities in the governmentality literature can be distinguished from the Weberian view that capitalist societies are marked by a process of rationalization (Weber 2002). For instance, Foucault suggested that

> It may be wise not to take as a whole the rationalization of society or of culture, but to analyze such a process in several fields, each with reference to a fundamental experience: madness, illness, death, crime, sexuality, and so forth. I think that the word *rationalization* is dangerous. What we have to do is analyze specific rationalities rather than always invoking the progress of rationalization in general. (Foucault 1982: 329)

In contrast to the idea that one monolithic rationality takes up a dominant position as *the* spirit of society, Foucault referred to rationalities in the plural, and investigated how particular forms of rationality become inscribed in practices (Foucault 1991c: 79). These insights invite us to not think of rationalities as quasi-structures setting very strict limits on what can be said and done, but rather to understand them as fragile constellations of ideas that are continuously established, contested and reordered, but may also become relatively stable. Still, and somewhat surprisingly, particularly the British and Australian governmentality literature has tended to overemphasize one rationality and produced a surge of publications investigating the saturation of neoliberal rationalities in just about all spheres. In contrast, this book explores the multiple rationalities at work in multi-stakeholder processes.

Finally, it is important to stress that while governmental rationalities operate through political subjects, they do not determine or control these. An actor is not 'objectified' but 'subjectified' by a given governmental regime of techniques and rationalities, which 'constructs individuals who are capable of choice and action, shapes them as active subjects, and seeks to align their choices with the objectives of governing authorities' (Garland 1997: 175). Thus, to understand the entanglement of agency, subjectification and steering we must look at political rationalities, subjects and other elements in the practice-oriented, relational and agnostic manner advocated throughout this book.

These insights are useful when we reflect on the political rationalities at work in UN activities to address the global politics of the digital revolution. During the problematization phase, three particular political rationalities that we may term *technological determinism, empowerment* and *networking* stand out. The UN problematization of the digital revolution was made possible by a strong belief in the ability of ICTs to transform societies, economies and politics. While many aspects of the global politics of the Internet were still very fuzzy, there was widespread agreement that the Internet should be seen as an important resource and driver for a wide range of social, political and other transformations. We may describe this political rationality as a form of technological determinism – the belief that history is driven by technological developments. This technological vision was one of the worldviews underpinning the emergence of the global politics of the digital revolution. Secondly, the problematization revolved around 'discourses, programs and other tactics aimed at making individuals politically active and capable of self-government' (Cruikshank 1999: 1), that is, different social worlds were invited to take up positions as entrepreneurs and stakeholders, rather than as aid recipients or critics. While such forms of empowerment were not the only or primary purpose of UN activities, the moral nature and implied assumptions about participation and collaboration mean that this political rationality helped set the course for and give meaning to the construction of the digital revolution as an important object of governance to a wide range of actors. The argument is not that this political rationality saturates all of the UN or a given moment in history, or can be explained as the interest of particular actors, but rather that it was one product of the assembling and translation of concrete practices, governmental techniques and forms of subjectification. Thirdly, the problematization revolved around a growing fascination with networking, partnering and other types of collaborative interactions. This conception of networking as the solution to organizational, management, financial and operational problems can be seen as a third political rationality at work in the first moment of ordering. The value of bringing together different stakeholders, building connections and seeking common ground constitutes an important component in these early UN activities, and one which came to shape subsequent multi-stakeholder processes in important ways. Taken together, these three political rationalities laid the foundation for the organization of the global politics of the digital revolution, and also gave direction to the practical ways of going about this project. The articulation of different rationalities – and their negotiation – is a central concern in the chapters below, and as we will see, down the road these three rationalities encountered other, better-known UN rationalities, such as human rights, democracy and intergovernmentalism.

To sum up: at this stage, the organization of multi-stakeholder processes to address the global politics of the digital revolution had barely taken shape. When it comes to organizational arrangements, the matter was primarily addressed through existing forums and mechanisms. The decision to hold the World Summit on the Information Society created a new forum for discussions, and also showed a strong commitment to the issue on the part of the UN. While such world conferences are a common UN practice, it is important to note that engaging stakeholders was not only seen as important and desirable, but also as central to the success of the project. Without engaging the creators and managers of the Internet, the UN would never become a platform for significant discussions of the global politics of the Internet. But so far, there was little agreement on the meaning, nature and target of these efforts, and in many ways this fluidity was necessary for the project to be possible. As we will see in Chapter 5, the construction of objects with multiple meanings are central to multi-stakeholder processes because such boundary objects facilitate interactions (Star and Griesemer 1989), and because hybrid forums thrive on the lack of discursive closures (Deetz 1992).

In relation to the question of power and authority, the moment of problematization involved an important step in the direction of positioning the UN as a platform for multi-stakeholder processes addressing the politics of the Internet. If we take on the assertion that an important aspect of power is the ability to 'constitute the problems that need to be solved [. . .] through a process of social construction' (Barnett and Finnemore 2005: 179), we start to see how the very emergence of these discussions can have important effects. In the process of organizing the politics of the digital revolution, the first translation of the assemblage had significant consequences for the shape and direction of subsequent discussions and activities. For instance, it established multi-stakeholder participation as a key component, led to the first experiments with networked forms of organization and began to test the limits of what the UN would be able to achieve in this area. This moment of translation resulted in two hybrid forums – a task force addressing ICT-for-development and a working group focusing on Internet governance. As the following chapters will show, these two organizational arrangements allowed for a number of substantive and organizational orderings to fall into place: a myriad of questions about the digital revolution were turned into two more delimited matters of concern, selected social worlds were positioned as stakeholders, and ideas about how to proceed were stabilized.

3. Engaging social worlds as stakeholders

The classification of relevant social worlds as stakeholders is central to hybrid forums (Hallström and Boström 2010), and categories such as 'government', 'business' and 'civil society' are constantly at work in the organization of the global politics of the Internet. Such categories are so well established that we tend to forget that they are the results of acts of classification (Bowker and Star 1999), and not given. The focus on associations, translations and enrolment helps us capture how such diverse 'social worlds' (Clarke and Star 2008) are enacted (Bowker and Star 1999; Czarniawska and Hernes 2005) in the process of being categorized as stakeholders. That is, stakeholders do not exist in advance, but emerge through categorizations (Hallström and Boström 2010) that posit dispersed social worlds as allies in a given project. Conventional approaches to governance tend to take actors and their positions for granted (Bevir 2003) and reproduce such categories as states, business and civil society without reflecting on how these enact particular positions and relations (Law and Urry 2004). The focus on ordering helps us unsettle and question the view of actors as fixed and natural entities that simply carry out activities, shape politics, or set up organizations. In other words, it helps us to capture how categories such as 'stakeholders' are the results of assemblages and translations. To unpack the ways in which stakeholders are codified in hybrid forums, this chapter foregrounds a number of techniques used to engage and categorize social worlds. Because the problematization of the global politics of the Internet was constructed as a set of opportunities and challenges for a wide range of actors, there was a need to engage others than UN member states or international organizations with more narrow mandates. Many governments were concerned about the questions raised by the growth of the Internet, and sought to use the UN to address these in relatively conventional ways. But the emergence of organizational arrangements involving governments, business, technical groups and civil society as the primary way of addressing the challenges and opportunities of the digital revolution differed from established UN practice in significant ways. This created a demand for ways of attracting and engaging particular social worlds, and the techniques used to do this – what Callon (1986) calls 'interessement' – are central if we want to understand the categorization of particular social worlds into stakeholders as central to the making of hybrid forums.

ORDERING THROUGH INTERESSEMENT

Organizational techniques and devices are central to the emergence and ordering of assemblages. Such governmental techniques are used to strengthen links and facilitate mobilizations, and focusing on these offers insights into the mundane practices involved in the creation and consolidation of hybrid forums. The attention to such techniques is a key contribution of governmentality studies. To Foucault,

> the target of analysis wasn't 'institutions', 'theories' or 'ideology', but *practices* – with the aim of grasping the conditions which make these acceptable at a given moment; the hypothesis being that these types of practice are not just governed by institutions, prescribed by ideologies, guided by pragmatic circumstances – whatever role these elements may actually play – but possess up to a point their own specific regularities, logic, strategy, self-evidence and 'reason'. It is a question of analysing a 'regime of practices' – practices being understood here as places where what is said and what is done, rules imposed and reasons given, the planned and the taken for granted meet and interconnect. (Foucault 1991c: 75)

Continuing this theme, this chapter gives primary attention to 'the invention and assemblage of particular apparatuses and devices for exercising power and intervening upon particular problems' (Rose 1999: 19), and shows the importance of such 'humble and mundane mechanisms which appear to make it possible to govern' (Miller and Rose 1990: 8). In this moment of ordering, the most important challenge was to interest and engage relevant allies in the projects to address the global politics of the Internet. Understood as ordering techniques, the practices used to engage and mobilize such social worlds constitute a relevant starting point for the analysis of hybrid forums, in particular because they allow us to capture how ordering is practical and always in-the-making. Furthermore, this is where insights from governmentality studies, actor-network theory and process perspectives on organizing can be used to shed light on the concrete ways in which human, non-human, technical and ideational elements become entangled in governance and organization.

The analyses in this chapter revolve around two governmental techniques which were central to the making of the UN ICT Task Force (UNICTTF) and the Working Group on Internet Governance (WGIG) and had important effects in terms of power. Both hybrid forums found ways of interacting with different social worlds, and sought to mobilize some of these as allies in their projects. Consultations are commonplace in the UN system, and article 71 in the Charter of the UN states that 'The Economic and Social Council may make suitable arrangements for consultation with non-governmental organizations which are concerned with matters within its competence' (UN Charter, chapter 10). But the results of consultations with NGOs and civil society groups are rarely explicitly included in final UN decisions or policy documents. Furthermore, consultations and other forms of participation often take the form of allowing non-state actors to respond to very ambiguous and open questions or to comment on matters that have already been decided (Cooke and Kothari 2001). In contrast, the success or failure of hybrid forums rests on their ability to engage and mobilize a critical mass of relevant groups in a long-term project – not just in allowing their voices to be heard. Thus, in order to turn ideas about stakeholder engagement in UN processes into a more stable organizational arrangement, these consultations were an important first step. As we will see, consultations were used at crucial moments in the ordering of these two UN-anchored hybrid forums, but most extensively in the UNICTTF. While WGIG also relied on consultations in the early phase of interacting with different social worlds, the selection of members and the mobilization of particular groups as stakeholders took the shape of self-nominations. Focusing on these techniques used to attract and engage social worlds, the chapter fleshes out how this moment of translation ordered objects, subjects, techniques and rationalities in new ways, and gives particular attention to the power effects of categorizations.

THE SEARCH FOR ALLIES

As outlined in the previous chapter, as a result of the ECOSOC meetings, the Department of Economic and Social Affairs (DESA) was given a mandate to establish the UN ICT Task Force, and the first step was to arrange a series of worldwide consultations during the fall of 2000. The immediate purpose of these consultations was to investigate who the future members could be and how interested they were in contributing to a trust fund. But the consultations were also used as a way to solicit responses regarding the administration, focus, activities and outcomes of the UNICTTF (UNICTTF 2000d: 2). Finally, the consultations played an important role in terms of legitimizing the creation of the forum and forestalling future opposition. For instance, the person initiating the consultations stressed that the objectives with the consultations should be to

> broaden the basis of support for the S-G's [Secretary General's] Task Force and ensure approval by ECOSOC in January [and] to promote a spirit of inclusion in the process, with the understanding that some of the entities may have little to contribute in terms of fresh ideas, policies, contacts or financial support but that excluding these entities from the process could have a negative impact at some future point in time. (UNDP employee 2000b: 1)

At the outset, the DESA team carrying out the consultations planned to consult globally and with all relevant stakeholders. But as the process got started, new strategies and targets had to be developed. In particular, the meaning of the term stakeholder changed many times. As proposed in the report from the High-Level Panel on Information and Communication Technology, the role of the UNICTTF should be to 'ensure complementarity and synergy' (UNDP employee 2000a: 2) between multilateral development institutions, such as the World Bank, UNDP, the World International Property Organization (WIPO) and ITU, and other bodies involved in ICT-for-development, such as the G8 DOT Force. But 'complementarity and synergy' turned out to be very difficult to establish as particularly the World Bank and UNDP had very little interest in a new competitor funding agency in the area of development. Their unwillingness to cooperate and the struggle over the ICT-for-development project never took the shape of direct confrontation, at least not in the written exchanges. Rather, both organizations – as well as the DOT Force – partnered with the UNICTTF, but simultaneously sought to marginalize and hamper the efforts to create this forum. As the following will show, they managed to narrow the scope and mandate of the UNICTTF to the point where most of the original ideas were given up – in effect transforming it from a financially strong coordination mechanism to a forum for discussion with no resources, thus posing little threat for the other agencies and their projects.

A 'CAREFUL, BUREAUCRATIC DANCE'

Memos written by the UNDP employee involved in the creation of the UNICTTF give important insights into what the coordinator of the UNICTTF refers to as both 'turf battles' and a 'careful, bureaucratic dance' (Interview, UNICTTF Deputy Executive Coordinator 2004) involving different UN entities. For instance, in a note the UNDP employee wrote that it had been difficult for him to get information about 'the state of play' once the High-Level Panel's report and recommendations had been presented to ECOSOC. It had been particularly difficult for him to get information about the visions – both short and long-term

– that UNDP and the World Bank had for their involvement in advancing the ICT-for-development agenda. He had, however, 'detected an attitude within the [World] Bank and UNDP that DESA's continuing ECOSOC initiatives should not be taken too seriously' (UNDP employee 2000c: 1). While ECOSOC's accomplishments in 'awareness raising' were recognized by the other UN agencies, it was not seen as a 'substantive partner' because it lacked 'operational experience, fund-raising, [and] private sector experience'; rather it was perceived as a 'necessary political partner' (ibid.) He stressed that UNDP was seeking to position itself as a major player in ICT-for-development, and saw UNICTTF as a competitor rather than as a collaborator:

> bluntly speaking, it is my impression that the tactic is to leave you with a good feeling of partnership, but in fact to proceed in a manner that pre-empts DESA's initiatives to consult and build broad consensus on the functions of the Task Force and Trust Fund. Thus, contacts proceed apace with some of the same individuals/entities that you have on DESA's list of Advisers. Specific projects and program ideas are being discussed and energetically prepared [. . .] UNDP is building its own trust fund, and already has $11 million (in hand or pledged) and aims at reaching $100 million within the next 12 months. (UNDP employee 2000c: 4)

He suggested that DESA should 'keep some other "critical" players informed including the DOT Force, UNDP and perhaps the Bank, but [do] not seek their formal blessings' (UNDP employee 2000b: 1). Because of this recommendation, the consultation team decided not to consult UNDP and the World Bank formally. In late 2001, UNDP launched its own trust fund (UNDP 2001), which focused on exactly the same issues that the UNICTTF had proposed. Still, DESA held onto the idea of a coordination body administering a trust fund based on contributions from private companies and multilateral institutions, and continued the worldwide consultations. Such struggles for resources and recognition between the different UN agencies constitute one stumbling block for multi-stakeholder processes. So rather than pursuing the project of addressing the digital revolution in close collaboration with UNDP and the World Bank, the team decided to find other parties to consult and from whom to solicit support. The idea that came up was to focus on 'the "new" players, i.e. industry, foundations, and trusts', that is, to pursue the project in collaboration with partners from outside the UN system. The UNDP employee suggested that if, for ' "political" reasons consultations are needed with recipients, then focus initially on Africa and/or one other region where we have data and contacts and the need is greatest' (UNDP employee 2000c: 3).

In this process of planning the consultations, the changing definition of a stakeholder gives insight into the considerations and strategies of the consultation team. At the outset, the World Bank, UNDP and other UN-based development agencies were considered stakeholders. As the project and the strategies changed, new social worlds emerged as possible stakeholders, such as US-based computer companies, philanthropic bodies and foundations, and UN member states and other international organizations. Others, such as 'recipients' (UNDP employee 2000a) and civil society groups were first included and later excluded from the definition of what a UNICTTF stakeholder was. Rather than thinking of stakeholders as given in advance, these processes indicate that we need to focus on the ways in which different social worlds are categorized as stakeholders, and how such negotiations are entangled with searches for organizational and substantive ordering.

SETTING UP NEW TARGETS

Because of the conflicts with UNDP and the World Bank, the original project took on a new shape. Instead of trying to mediate between the major international donor institutions and business, the UNICTTF would work to involve business as its main donor and stakeholder. With this decision to attract other social worlds the substantive direction and political rationalities of the project were also reconfigured.

Having decided to target information technology companies and business foundations instead of development agencies, DESA hired a private consultant from the Seattle-based ICT-for-development initiative Digital Partners. In one of his first contributions to the consultation process, he reflected on what the roles of the different stakeholders should be. He saw the most likely private donors to be corporations, particularly executives in advanced countries, but also considered independent philanthropists with 'new money' and ICT entrepreneurs. They would support the project because 'private sector leaders are aware that the UN and the S-G himself has legitimacy in the countries where they operate and a partnership with him will be welcomed' (Digital Partners Consultant 2000c: 2). The strategy he proposed was the following:

> To use the language of Silicon Valley, the logical course of action for the ICT Task Force is to 'leverage the UN brand' by focusing squarely on how the new digital economy can enhance the UN's core constituency and core concerns – basic health, literacy, grassroots economic enterprise, debt relief, etc. Certainly, no prior high-level initiative has addressed this theme in a comprehensive way – though there is much evidence that all aspects of poverty alleviation can be enhanced in light of the global spread of networked communications, and

> due to the new distribution of power, money and information which digital technologies have unleashed. (Digital Partners Consultant 2000b: 1)

The worldwide consultations were carried out by a team of consultants, experts, DESA and UNDP employees, who had also been involved in the creation of the UNICTTF. More than 40 meetings were held in Europe, Africa and the US between October and December 2000 (UNICTTF 2000b; 2000d). The consultant from Digital Partners approached a number of US-based companies including Hewlett-Packard, Motorola, Microsoft, Real Networks, eBay, WorldCom, Cisco, 3COM and McKinsey, as well as foundations created by these companies and other corporate actors from the ICT sector. These worldwide consultations revolved around issues such as why different actors wished to be part of the UNICTTF, what they expected from their membership, what they believed the body should focus on and what its activities could lead to. At this stage, the object of governance was still very much under construction and these consultations with different social worlds constitute a defining moment.

DEVELOPMENT OR DEREGULATION?

The consultations with business groups were meant as a way to solicit financial support for the initiative. At the time, many information technology companies were growing rapidly and at least some of them seemed willing to channel their surplus into charitable causes. However, the consultations made it clear that hardly any of these companies were looking for new causes to support or a UN body to administer their existing development and aid projects. Instead, the consulted business groups showed an overwhelming interest in using the UNICTTF as a spearhead for policy reforms in the area of ICTs. From their point of view, the first steps towards bridging the digital divide should be to spur deregulation, foster competition and encourage new market development in this area. National governments handle the majority of public policy issues in the area of ICT regulation, so the idea was not for the UNICTTF to have a regulatory role. But the consulted companies wanted it to push for deregulation, increased competition and other initiatives that could encourage the development of new markets. Furthermore, they were interested in using the body as a way to promote their existing activities, such as market development and corporate citizenship projects, and to improve their relations with governments, the media and the public.

The consulted business representatives in Western Europe had a strong interest in government reforms, market liberalization and an 'enabling policy environment' in the area of ICTs. From their point of view, policy reforms were a prerequisite if corporations were to get involved in laying down cables, building new markets and other development activities such as those proposed by UNICTTF. For instance, Andersen Consulting, whom the team met in London, indicated that they would like to join the UNICTTF if the body would take on the task of spreading the 'consensus on deregulation [that] exists'. In particular, the UN could provide the 'legitimacy and the neutral forum to push this issue without being seen as entirely driven by the US' and create 'trust in the deregulation phase and process' (UNICTTF 2000b: 10–12). The US government had a very similar vision of the UNICTTF as a way to create 'pro-competitive, market-led policy and regulatory regimes that will attract private long-term investment and foster the development and deployment of ICT [. . .] As a practical matter, we believe that fostering pro-competitive market-led policy and regulatory regimes is fundamental to bridging the international digital divide and creating global digital opportunity' (USA 2000–2001).

Similarly, the Swedish ICT company Ericsson called for the UNICTTF to take on the task of solving the 'bureaucratic difficulties' that companies run into when creating local projects. They also felt that the UNICTTF could help to identify bottlenecks in the overall policy arena, such as 'ITU which seemed to be only interested in maintaining the status quo' (UNICTTF 2000b:18). In Norwegian consultations, the companies called for a 'better regulatory environment' and the need for removing monopolies in developing countries, which function as 'cash cows for governments'. In the consultations with companies in South Africa, it was argued that 'the private sector will drive connectivity if the public sector provides a conducive environment' (ibid.)

Across the board, ICT companies posited market development as *the* solution to poverty in developing countries, and stressed that deregulation was the incentive that business was waiting for before getting involved in such development activities. Furthermore, only a small number of the consulted parties wished to contribute financially to the trust fund.

Some of those who were consulted questioned the idea of the UNICTTF as an advocate of deregulation and market development. Norwegian civil society groups saw the proposed approach as 'largely driven by interests emanating from the North', and described the focus on the regulatory environment as a 'supply side issue' (UNICTTF 2000b: 18). They proposed that the process should instead be demand- and recipient-driven. The Russian government expressed scepticism towards the very idea of the digital divide, and proposed that 'perhaps the so-called problem of the digital divide is a "trick" of the private companies similar to the

"Millennium Bug"' (UNICTTF 2000b: 1). Agreeing with an earlier statement by Ted Turner, the Bill and Melinda Gates Foundation did not support the idea of ICTs as an important factor in poverty alleviation,[2] and the UK government questioned the link between ICTs and poverty reduction upon which the belief in ICT-for-development rests. They proposed that the focus should be on more traditional forms of poverty reduction, particularly in Africa where even the most basic 'analogue forms of communication' are still beyond the reach of most people (Digital Partners Consultant 2000a: 9).

Although there were some critical voices, the consultations showed a broad-based interest in deregulation and liberalization in ICT policies. To the majority of corporations and a number of Western governments, the UNICTTF could play an important advocacy role in this endeavour. But the ordering of the UNICTTF as a channel for public relations activities and market development initiatives clearly departed from the original idea. All along DESA sought to appeal to the private sector in the hope that business would contribute financially to the trust fund. In return they would benefit from a close affiliation with the UN and opportunities to show policymakers what the benefits of novel approaches to development could be. Although deregulation was not part of DESA's original vision for the UNICTTF, this focus was taken on board and came to play a central role in later activities. Thus, the consultations with business contributed to the ordering of the object of governance in a very significant and direct way, because DESA's vision had to be aligned with those of important allies.

CORPORATE SOCIAL RESPONSIBILITY AND PUBLIC RELATIONS

Apart from a way to push for deregulation, business representatives were also interested in the UNICTTF as a way to increase their visibility and promote their existing corporate citizenship activities, such as supporting education in developing countries. In particular, companies in Europe and the US were interested in a direct and visible affiliation with the UN Secretary-General, Kofi Annan. Many European companies were just as interested in increasing their visibility as they were in profits (UNICTTF 2000b), and large ICT companies in the US would 'enthusiastically seek an alliance with the Secretary-General to add value to their government relations strategies in the developing world' (Digital Partners Consultant 2000a: 8). For instance, Motorola was interested in a direct relationship with the Secretary-General, because 'only the Secretary-General has legitimacy as an honest broker' (Digital Partners Consultant 2000a: 12). Furthermore, by taking part in UNICTTF's work the company saw an opportunity to develop a 'communications strategy that may respond effectively to antiglobalization critics', and help it achieve 'sophisticated media coverage' that 'raises the bar on corporate efforts to reduce the Digital Divide' (Digital Partners Consultant 2000a: 13).

Some of the large ICT companies also offered to lead UN reform efforts, as such initiatives would 'provide leadership roles for their CEOs' (Digital Partners Consultant 2000a: 7). At the time, Hewlett-Packard was involved in a number of ICT-for-development initiatives and stated that 'we are at a moment in time when the interests of Hewlett-Packard are aligned with the interests of the Secretary-General', particularly because the UNICTTF could be 'an opportunity to make a high-profile identification with the Secretary-General's effort' (Digital Partners Consultant 2000a: 10–11). One such project was the $1 billion initiative 'Global e-Inclusion', which the company announced in 2000, but later scaled down considerably. UNICTTF could be one way of spreading the message about such corporate citizenship initiatives. At the same time, the company also expressed hope that the UNICTTF could be used to identify new potential partners and donors. Hewlett-Packard stressed that it had chosen to channel resources to corporate citizenship efforts and development projects because its corporate culture was more expansive than that of 'lean-and-mean new economy companies in Silicon Valley' and because it had 'depth of character and breadth of vision' (Digital Partners Consultant 2000a: 11). But the final goal with its activities was not mere philanthropy: the long-term focus was 'wealth creation' and thereby the creation of 'business opportunities among the very poor' (Digital Partners Consultant 2000a: 10). Hewlett-Packard mentioned the ideas of the business guru C.K. Prahalad – that business can 'do good and do well' at the same time – as a key source of inspiration. From this perspective, with the emergence and proliferation of the Internet, developing countries constitute an undiscovered market opportunity.

In contrast, the sales revenues of Cisco had risen by 50 per cent per year for many years and the company did not expect market saturation in high-end markets, so the representatives showed little interest in market development in developing countries. According to the company itself, its reasons for engaging in the digital divide and ICT and development initiatives were primarily 'human resources considerations – especially increasing the level of trained engineers in the developing world' (Digital Partners Consultant 2000a: 8). Since its inception in 1997, the so-called Cisco Networking Academies project has spread to more than 150 countries, and taught 1.6 million students at more than 10,000 academies in high schools, colleges, universities, and community-based organizations how to develop and maintain computer networks.

What emerged out of these consultations was that large ICT companies mainly saw the UNICTTF as an opportunity to integrate their market-development activities, stakeholder relations and CSR initiatives. But none of the consulted companies wanted to support actual projects financially, particularly as many already had similar activities and therefore preferred to use these channels, rather than a UN body. These consultations reconfigured important facets of the object of governance: rather than coordinating ICT-for-development activities and funding development projects, the UNICTTF was recast as a platform for policy dialogue and the profiling of social responsibility in the corporate sector.

TRUST FUND OR TALKING SHOP?

The consultations also made it clear that while some wanted a financially strong body initiating ICT and development activities, others preferred a non-operational body providing policy recommendations. The consultations with Western European governments made it clear that most of them were against the idea of a trust fund, either because they did not want the UN to rely on voluntary contributions (France) or because they were not convinced about the need for such a fund (United Kingdom). Sweden offered to contribute, but stressed that it could be difficult for the UN to attract 'private capital for its initiatives' and suggested that the UNICTTF should seek to function as a 'co-ordinating group instead of a competing group' vis-à-vis the World Bank, UNDP and other initiatives (UNICTTF 2000b: 3). As we have seen, business too expressed strong reservations about the very idea of the trust fund, stressing particularly the 'institutional constraints' that could result from a transfer of their ICT and development activities to the UN (Digital Partners Consultant 2000a) and fears that the slowness, bureaucracy and inefficiency of the UN system could hamper ICT-for-development efforts. In a similar vein, private foundations pointed to a considerable gap between the slowness of the UN system and the fast pace of the ICT sector (Consultation Team 2000). As we will see, the need to distance the UNICTTF from the image of the UN system as a cumbersome bureaucracy played an important role in the decision to place the body at the margins of the UN.

Other voices had also to be taken into account. The consultations with European governments showed that very few of them were interested in a new donor agency. For instance, the Dutch government argued that the UNICTTF should focus on policy, advocacy and promotion of the ICT4D agenda and not its execution, which could be handled by the World Bank (UNICTTF 2000b: 12). Other European governments wanted the body to coordinate existing and future activities in this area. These visions challenged the original idea of a body with financial resources, and posited the UNICTTF as a coordination mechanism that could oversee existing projects, identify overlaps and make sure that no duplication of efforts occurred. However, a number of those consulted, such as the main donor countries, the World Bank and UNDP, even challenged the idea of coordination. For instance, the European Commissioner for Enterprise and Information Society described the European Commission's reaction to the idea of the UNICTTF as a coordination mechanism in the following way:

> Our interlocutors in Western Europe suggested focusing on synergies rather than on co-ordination. Co-ordination is desirable, but could not be imposed on those organizations, which are not part of the UN system. ICTs provide the opportunity for a decentralised and open way of working together, and I would suggest that full advantage would be taken of that. (Liikanen 2001: 2)

While this comment reproduces the idea of ICTs as a driver of novel forms of organization and collaboration, it also serves to challenge the more modest attempt to position the Task Force as coordinator of existing ICT4D initiatives. The search for a purpose and a position was not over.

Meanwhile, consultations in Africa produced very different results. In stark contrast to the reactions from business, African and other developing countries argued that the UNICTTF would only be able to eradicate the global digital divide if the body had financial resources. African governments welcomed the idea of the trust fund because these resources would allow UNICTTF actually to work for development and finance concrete projects, and not just talk about it, that is, it could add to the 'proliferation of financing windows', the only problem with which 'is getting money from them' (Consultation Team 2000). From the perspective of African governments, the significance of a financially strong, operational body was captured in the distinction between a 'trust fund' and a 'talking shop'. It was also stressed in the West African consultations that technology would not be enough – institutional, political, regulatory, market and human capacity issues should also be addressed. While those on the receiving end were considered stakeholders at this stage of the process, their positions and arguments did not have much effect on the direction of the UNICTTF. And as time went by, developing countries were categorized as the targets of efforts, not as partners in the process.

The transformation of the UNICTTF from a funding mechanism to a forum for dialogue was the outcome of a range of negotiations and considerations. In particular, the lack of support from the consulted businesses,

Western governments, and private foundations as well as the hidden, but strong pressure exerted by the UNDP and the World Bank, led DESA to give up the idea of the trust fund:

> originally the proposal was there should be a global trust fund [. . .] But that was shot down by the donor governments, also by the multilateral institutions, UNDP and World Bank, they were not in favor of that because that would have had implications for their own work. So they did not want to have someone else raising funding [. . .] So the ICT Task Force is now more of a policy body and a platform where partnerships are built and actions gets taken through various partnerships, rather than UNICTTF itself undertaking things. (Interview, UNICCTF Acting Executive Coordinator 2004)

As pointed out by Callon, Lascoumes et al. (2009), moments of translation often involve multiple, smaller translations. In the case of UNICTTF, the transformation of the original idea had taken its third shape: it was no longer a trust fund, nor a coordination body, but a forum for dialogue. From the point of view of DESA, this was not only an attack on the initial vision behind the Task Force – it also impaired its position in the ICT4D domain where it had originally aimed to become *the* main powerhouse. According to the director, the realization that the trust fund had to be given up created 'a certain feeling of let-down, when nothing happened, I have to admit that. And a lot of people lost interest because of the fact that it was not going to flourish in the way it was expected to' (Interview, UNICTTF Acting Executive Coordinator 2004). A non-operational, advocacy body and a forum for dialogue was not what DESA had hoped for, and according to the Coordinator, this role is one of the reasons why 'in terms of its achievements [the UNICTTF] has been modest' (ibid.)

From an ordering perspective, the most important question is not whose visions for the Task Force won out, but rather how this translation locked governmental techniques, political rationalities, objects and political subjects in a particular configuration. The transformation into a forum for dialogue meant that the UNICTTF could not rely on centralized, hierarchical approaches to steering and organization as planned, but had to resort to a more decentralized networking strategy. We may think of it as a transformation from a 'web of reward and coercion' with considerable financial resources and the ability to assert its influence through funding, to a 'web of dialogue and persuasion' relying on facilitation, the identification of best practices and other soft governance techniques (Braithwaite and Drahos 2000; Slaughter 2004; Hansen and Salskov-Iversen 2005). However, as we will see later, this ordering of UNICTTF turned out to be one of its strengths, both in terms of the kind of support that businesses would provide, and in the form of authority that the body was able to establish for itself in attempts to address the global politics of the Internet.

Consultations played a central role in the formation of the UNICTTF and had very important consequences for its substantive focus, modes of governance and constitution. The process of creating the Working Group on Internet Governance also relied on consultations, although these took a different shape. In the following, we turn attention to the governance techniques used in the formation of WGIG. Where the initiators of UNICTTF used consultations as a way to solicit support for the initiative, in WGIG the primary concern was to establish a broadly acceptable group that could bring negotiations about Internet governance out of deadlock. This is one explanation for the consultations taking different shape in the two cases. But there were also other reasons, such as a decision to let some social worlds play a more direct role in the selection of members and a more conscious effort to experiment with multi-stakeholder processes. This part of the chapter analyses the formation of the Working Group on Internet Governance and focuses particularly on the role and significance of stakeholder consultations.

MOBILIZING SOCIAL WORLDS

As noted in the previous chapter, the Working Group on Internet Governance was set up to solve the deadlock over the question of Internet governance during the first phase of the World Summit on the Information Society. WGIG was originally envisioned as operating according to the rules of procedure governing UN summits, but as these would allow only governments 'full and active participation', an important body like the Internet Corporation for Assigned Names and Numbers (ICANN) could only participate as an observer. In the attempt to make room for such bodies, which play a central role in the development and coordination of the Internet's core resources, WGIG had to be established as a consultative body to the Secretary-General. By establishing WGIG outside the formal WSIS structure, it gained greater autonomy and flexibility, both in terms of procedures and membership. This also meant that the mobilization of social worlds as stakeholders was an important starting point.

A number of principles for the operations of WGIG were defined in the Geneva Summit documents, namely that it should be created in an 'open and transparent manner' and allow for 'full and active participation' of all stakeholders (WSIS 2003, para 50). Still, these principles had to be fleshed out and operationalized. ICANN, ITU and UNICTTF, as well as a number of national and regional bodies arranged meetings to discuss the concerns and issues to be dealt with. But the actual job of setting up WGIG was left in the hands of a Swiss diplomat, Markus Kummer, and the Secretary-General's main WSIS adviser, Nitin Desai. Because of his work in the final negotiations, Kummer was asked to initiate WGIG and was later appointed Executive Coordinator of the working group. In setting up WGIG, his first step was to discuss the constitution and composition of the group with potential stakeholders and members. These interactions took two different forms: initially a number of informal, individual consultations with a variety of state and non-state actors were carried out at meetings and events around the world, and later a formal, open consultation was held in Geneva. Here, most participants were government delegations – from 85 different countries – but 44 different non-governmental entities were also represented, among them ICANN, NGOs and academics, some companies, the International Chamber of Commerce (ICC), and international organizations and UN departments (WGIG 2004–05). At these formal consultations, the first attempts at defining the agenda, procedures and composition of WGIG were made.

WGIG relied on consultations as one important technique in this formative phase. But in order to flesh out how WGIG came into existence, we need to grasp another important governmental technique involved, namely the invitation to let various groups nominate candidates for WGIG. Members of WGIG were chosen through a self-nomination process in which two social worlds – business and civil society groups – were asked to suggest candidates. Stakeholder self-nominations constitute a significant feature of this hybrid forum, and the analysis of this governmental technique sheds light on how particular social worlds were cast and mobilized as stakeholders.

STAKEHOLDER SELF-NOMINATIONS

After the formal consultations, the Executive Coordinator of WGIG invited two groups of non-state actors to come up with lists of possible candidates for the group.[3] In the search for a spokesperson for business, he contacted the International Chamber of Commerce (ICC), which also coordinated the business entities involved in WSIS. The Senior Policy Manager of Electronic Business, Telecommunications and IT at ICC then contacted more than one hundred ICC members and asked them to suggest candidates for WGIG. Based on these she created a list of candidates, most of whom later became members of WGIG. According to her, the process of selecting the business sector candidates was unproblematic, although it was more complicated resolving a list that respected all the criteria, such as that WGIG should be balanced along regional, sectoral and gender lines, and that members should be drawn from both developed and developing countries (Interview, ICC Member of UNICCTF 2005). Evidently, the ICC had the experience and procedures for such a nomination process in place.

In contrast, when the Executive Coordinator asked for nominations for representatives of civil society, the result was a prolonged and conflict-ridden debate. The WSIS process had given rise to multiple groups focusing on different thematic and regional aspects of the politics of the digital revolution (www.wsis-cs.org/caucuses.html). One of these – the Internet Governance Caucus (IG Caucus) – focused specifically on the global governance of the Internet, and the Executive Director decided to use this group as a spokesperson for the wider WSIS civil society groups. But the IG Caucus had no procedures in place, and very little experience with such processes. Soon, the question of how some candidates could 'represent' civil society interests in the context of WGIG came up. The nomination process became very contested and time-consuming for the IG Caucus, and gives important insights into the negotiations between the different social worlds that took place in the interessement phase of the WGIG project.

HOW TO SELF-NOMINATE?

The Executive Coordinator's request for a list of possible civil society candidates for WGIG led to an intense debate between subscribers on the IG Caucus mailing list[4] over the summer and fall of 2004. In particular, these discussions revolved around the question of how to select candidates in a transparent and legitimate manner. One concern was how a short list of people could possibly represent the diversity of civil society. Another issue was whether the selection process should be carried out by the IG Caucus – whose members had a targeted and long-standing interest in the issue of Internet governance – or by the civil society bodies developed during WSIS, that is, the Civil Society Plenary or the Bureau.[5]

Before starting the nomination process, members of the IG Caucus discussed a number of possible approaches. As summed up by one member, they had four different options. First, the IG Caucus could choose a 'clean hands approach', that is, not select from among the proposed candidates, but simply forward a list to the WGIG Coordinator. Or they could choose a 'top down approach' where a small group would select from among the proposed candidates – an approach used in Internet governance bodies like IETF and ICANN. A third route could be via a 'voting approach', which would imply an online voting process, either in the IG Caucus or among all civil society groups in WSIS. Finally, an option would be to take an ‘informal approach’, that is, to hold discussions about candidates on a mailing list, and hope that a rough consensus would emerge (IG-Caucus 2004–05). But many members were concerned about the balance between efficiency and legitimacy, and the problems involved in all these different approaches were debated at length on the mailing list. In the process, new approaches were suggested. One idea was to delegate the decision-making process, so that each WSIS caucus could select a number of candidates, as long as they had a relevant background in ICT policy, international experience and conformed to other criteria stressed by the WGIG Coordinator. But a number of objections were made, such as that the group would not be able to work together if its members did not know each other, or that nominees might not have the necessary expertise in the field of Internet governance. Some argued that the IG Caucus consisted of people ‘committed to IG issues’ and therefore, they were the most qualified candidates for WGIG (IG-Caucus 2004–05), while others pointed out that while expertise was important, the very definition of WGIG’s tasks would be the result of discussions in the group, and therefore diversity was important. But there was widespread support for the idea of keeping the selection process open to the other WSIS caucuses and working groups (IG-Caucus 2004–05), and the IG Caucus decided to contact the WSIS Bureau and the Plenary in order to get help and input on how to carry out the selection process. They never received a response.

MOBILIZING WSIS CIVIL SOCIETY GROUPS

Suddenly, the IG Caucus realized that the deadline for nominations was coming up. This meant that they had to make a decision, even if there was still little or no consensus about how to go about condensing a potentially large group of nominees into a more manageable list without getting into conflict with the other groups (IG-Caucus 2004–05). Then one of the Caucus coordinators posted a draft of a call for nominations, and encouraged Caucus members to accept it, even if they did not agree fully. Soon after, the final call was sent out to all WSIS caucuses and groups, inviting each of them to come up with between one and three names for the list of proposed candidates. The call listed the importance of diversity, balance and experience, and stressed the need for candidates to be willing to spend a considerable amount of time on WGIG meetings and activities.

In the following days, the IG Caucus tried to settle on its own candidates. With the WGIG consultations approaching rapidly, different members sought to jumpstart the Caucus's own nomination process. For instance, the member who had previously outlined the four different approaches first asked members to agree on a voting procedure. In another email, sent just 25 minutes later, he proposed another model, namely to set up a 'quick nomcom [nomination committee] approach' where between three and five 'trusted people' would decide who should be chosen for the list of candidates (IG-Caucus 2004–05). Another member cited a lunch conversation he had just had with the WGIG Executive Coordinator, who had told him that the list of nominees would not be needed until a week after the formal consultations, and the member suggested that it might be a good idea for the IG Caucus to postpone the final selection until they had a clearer idea about the exact issues that WGIG would deal with.

Meanwhile, nominations poured in from other WSIS caucuses, some of them containing many more than the three candidates asked for. The IG Caucus itself had built up a list of 15 nominees and had not yet started condensing it. Then at a lunch meeting, held in conjunction with the formal WGIG consultations in Geneva, ten members of the IG Caucus decided to condense the list by excluding all candidates who were not active on the mailing list. This cut the list down to five people. The notes from the meeting explain that the decision was made on the grounds that 'those who feel committed to the caucus and are known for being accessible' would be best suited as members of WGIG (IG-Caucus 2004). In subsequent discussions on the mailing list, it was argued that the Caucus should nominate all five, rather than cutting the list down to three. This idea gained more support when one of the coordinators mentioned that the WGIG Coordinator encouraged them to nominate five rather than three candidates. However, the IG Caucus coordinator also wrote: 'there is one aspect that makes me feel uncomfortable. Proposing 5 names implies that we change on the fly the rules we created and suggested to all other caucuses. Is this an acceptable procedure?' (IG-Caucus 2004–05). One member did not think so, and asked what would happen to all those people who were taken off the list early on – 'Do they get a second chance too?' (IG-Caucus 2004–05). Others, however, argued that the Caucus should listen to what the Executive Coordinator suggested, and that it was no problem to let other caucuses and working groups know that the IG Caucus has simply responded to the 'UN's reasonable request for a larger pool of IG experts to select from' (IG-Caucus 2004–05). When the deadline for nominations expired, the IG Caucus still had not decided which and how many of its five candidates to nominate. In the event, one of the coordinators called for immediate action as the Executive Coordinator had just communicated to her that the slate of civil society nominees should be sent to him as soon a possible, as he would hold the first meeting about the composition of WGIG just four days later. She had the 'impression' that there was more support for the nomination of five rather than three candidates, and suggested that the IG Caucus should act accordingly.

CHOOSING BETWEEN THE CANDIDATES

The list of 35 nominees, including five from the IG Caucus, was then uploaded to the IG Caucus website. From this pool of nominees, 10–12 candidates were to be picked to represent civil society in WGIG. One of the IG Caucus coordinators suggested that the selection of nominees for WGIG should be carried out by a nomination committee, and mentioned that she had already found three IG Caucus members who were willing to be on this committee. She thought that 'the nomcom should make the ultimate decision and announce the decision to the plenary and the IG caucus list. I don't think it makes sense to ask the plenary list for endorsement of the final slate as someone suggested.' Finally, she noted that, 'Of course, there are plenty of reasons again to wave the transparency, accountability and legitimacy flag. I'd hope though that the list members are pragmatic enough to take into account the tight time frame, thus endorse my suggestions and, if possible, help to improve them' (IG-Caucus 2004–05).

Soon afterwards, one of the members of the nomination committee sent out an email announcing the result of their work. From the 35 names suggested by all WSIS caucuses and working groups, they had chosen nine candidates. Five of these were the nominees that the IG Caucus itself had come up with. To understand how this happened, the explanation offered by the WGIG Coordinator is valuable:

> Well, first of all they [civil society] came up with a sort of process where I think each caucus was represented by two people. It was brought to my attention, [but my reaction was] 'are these really the people we want'? There were several names I knew from various events who had something to say on these particular issues, but they were not on the lists. There were other people who certainly may have had worthy experiences within these areas, but not necessarily of Internet governance – and I said, 'I think it would make more sense to have more people from the Internet Governance Caucus and also, please, give us more people to choose from'. (Interview, WGIG Executive Coordinator 2005)

So this was one reason why the IG Caucus did not forward the more inclusive list, choosing instead to nominate the people most directly involved in Internet governance, namely the members of the IG Caucus. But the nomination committee had also created a new category, namely a list of what they called 'connectors', in which most of the candidates nominated by the other WSIS groups were placed, and whom the nomination committee envisaged as able to 'facilitate interaction with various thematic constituencies as the process expands to a broader range of issues' (IG-Caucus 2004–05). It was a Caucus member – often referred to jokingly as 'Mr Procedure' by his colleagues (IG-Caucus 2004–05) – who came up with the idea of a group of 'connectors'.

But a number of the WSIS caucuses and working groups involved in the process reacted negatively to this invention of a new category of WGIG membership that had neither been mentioned previously nor asked for by the UN. Many found it an unacceptable change in procedure, because there was little clarity as to what role and importance these connectors could have in relation to WGIG. Furthermore, they argued, most of the applied criteria could easily have been met by others who were not IG Caucus members (WSIS Caucuses 2004–05). The decision to create two lists – one with the required nominees and one with connectors intended as mediators between the group and others – must be seen in light of the proposal made by the IG Caucus at the consultations that there should be ways for WGIG to connect to and communicate with a broader group of people outside the process. But the decision to create a list of connectors was also based on the assumption that WGIG would address Internet governance in a narrow sense, that is, it would primarily focus on issues such as the technical infrastructure and other matters handled by ICANN. In an email explaining why they had created two lists, one of the committee members explained that 'Accordingly, the natural first step is to designate candidates for the Working Group that are more connected with this restrictive dimension – that everybody agrees should be addressed' (IG-Caucus 2004–05). But as the discussions about and the interest in the work of WGIG had already grown to include a large and diverse group of actors and organizations, the committee anticipated that the scope of WGIG would widen accordingly, so that the group's work would include a very wide range of issues. Thus, the connectors provided a way of responding to this anticipated broadening of the scope of the WGIG agenda, as well as a way of ensuring that WSIS caucuses and working groups would be kept updated and remain ready to intervene in the process when an issue of interest to them came up.

Shortly after this, on 11 November 2004, an official UN press release announced that the Secretary-General had formally established WGIG. The group consisted of 39 people, with roughly equal numbers drawn from members from government, business and civil society. Of the 11 civil society members, eight were taken from the list of nine civil society nominees, pooled from the WSIS groups and cut down by the IG Caucus nomination committee. But two of the names on the list of connectors were also chosen as members of WGIG, although the idea of connectors was not taken on board (Interview, WGIG Executive Coordinator 2005). As a result most of the nominees from the other WSIS groups found themselves placed in a category that evaporated soon after it left the hands of the nomination committee.

AN OBLIGATORY PASSAGE POINT

As a result of the self-nomination process, actors representing civil society got close to one-third of the seats in WGIG. This was considered a major breakthrough among those involved (Interview, APC Member of WGIG 2005; Drake 2005). Rather than a scattered, uncoordinated group of individuals operating on the margins of formal UN discussions and negotiations over Internet governance, civil society had now been recognized as a formal participant, with the same rights and responsibilities as business and governments. The IG Caucus emerged as a particularly successful interlocutor, as this group managed to get just about all of its candidates accepted by the UN. But the process was not seen as legitimate by a number of WSIS groups, some of which complained vehemently – for months to come – about the way the nomination process was handled. In particular, the WSIS group focusing on patents, copyright and trademarks, and pushing for free, open software, was outraged to be excluded from the WGIG process. From their perspective, issues such as intellectual property rights (IPR) and proprietary versus open source software were central to Internet governance, and therefore should be addressed by those with expertise in the area. One member of the Patent, Copyright and Trademark Caucus, who was included as a connector, but not chosen for WGIG, later commented on the process in the following way, 'I have come to the conclusion that "connector" is essentially a fancy word for "legitimacy donor". It seems obvious that the people in the WGIG are trying to keep me silent with vague offers of sympathy and no real influence on the process' (WSIS Caucuses 2004–05). In response to the repeated attacks on the process, one of the most active IG Caucus members – later chosen for WGIG – explained that free software people were not included because they were seen as 'advocates', not 'facilitators'. He promised that he would try to push the issue himself, along with like-minded governments. To this, the member of the Patent, Copyrights and Trademark Caucus pointed out that they were a group of facilitators, with 20 years of experience. They feared that without any experts able to make the case against the one-sided focus on copyright owners, these issues would not be dealt with properly in the context of WGIG, especially because other members were experts from pro-owners' rights groups. Therefore, the Patent, Copyright and Trademark Caucus would prefer that the IPR issue was taken off the agenda all together. But as we will see, these issues were not taken off the WGIG agenda, but came to play a key role as one of the most contentious and least resolved issues dealt with in WGIG (Flyverbom 2011).

Well aware of the problems involved, it seems that the IG Caucus gave more weight to having their members accepted – using the Executive Coordinator as a highly influential 'silent partner' and an important source of UN wishes and interests – than to carrying out the process in full accordance with the procedures established and communicated to the other WSIS groups. The establishment of the WGIG presented an opportunity for one of the most active WSIS groupings to position itself as an obligatory passage point (Callon 1986). By identifying and positioning itself as the representative of 'civil society' in this hybrid forum, the IG Caucus made itself 'indispensable in the network of relationships they were building' (Callon 1986: 207–8). Such direct interventions are rare in the formation of hybrid forums, and made other social worlds react critically. But it also constitutes a rich moment if we want to capture the power dynamics of hybrid forums.

INTERESSEMENT AS ORDERING

The focus on ordering helps us understand the making of hybrid forums, and particularly the reconfiguration of the governmental techniques, political rationalities, objects and subjects involved. These insights pave the way for the conceptualization of the shape and effects of this moment of translation, and help us to address the ways in which hybrid forums relate to more general questions of power, authority and organization in the global politics of the digital revolution. This conceptualization starts from the assertion that the study of ordering implies that we cannot separate political subjects – such as stakeholders – from the governmental techniques and political rationalities through which they are constituted. The formation of the organizational arrangements sheds light not only on the political subjects involved, but also on governmental techniques, political rationalities and objects, and the assemblage they came to make up.

The previous chapter showed how the problematization of the ICT domain led ECOSOC to devote a number of General Assembly discussions to the issue of the relationship between ICTs, globalization and development, and the ITU to initiate the World Summit on the Information Society. Where the problematization phase revolved around establishing that the politics of the Internet constituted an issue in need of intervention, the interessement phase involved attempts 'to impose and stabilize the identity of the other actors' (Callon 1989: 8). Most importantly, this moment of translation revolved around positioning a number of social worlds as allies. The focus on the practices involved in this search for and categorization of a number of social worlds as stakeholders helps us understand the inner workings of hybrid forums. In particular, the analyses of consultations and self-nominations used in the formation of the two forums discussed here bring out the practical and strategic ways in which the UNICTTF and WGIG engaged and mobilized different social worlds as stakeholders.

In both cases, the formative phase revolved around making particular social worlds interested and engaged in the projects. The attraction and mobilization of these allies relied on two governmental techniques in particular. First, consultations were central to the making of stakeholders through categorizations and negotiations over the goal and shape of the two hybrid forums. The formation of UNICTTF worked around the assumption that companies operating in the ICT sector would be willing to play a role in development activities in the poorest parts of the world with little or no immediate market potential. While none of the consulted companies blindly accepted the subject position on offer, some of the most important ones still chose to take part in the initiative. As the analyses have shown, the representation of business as a socially responsible actor – operating hand in hand with the UN – was the primary appeal. At the same time, the companies wanted an opportunity to advocate a political shift towards market deregulation in the sector and saw the UNICTTF as a possible avenue for such efforts. In various ways, the UNICTTF allowed business to emerge as a politically and socially engaged actor. The formation of UNICTTF shows how the attributes of a stakeholder were developed and stabilized through processes of categorizing and mobilizing social worlds, rather than being given in advance. For instance, two consequences of the process were that business leaders were constructed as philanthropists willing to channel assistance to UN-driven development efforts and that Africa came to be positioned as the target of these UN-based ICT-for-development activities, rather than as a partner. Also the position of the World Bank and UNDP as the most important stakeholders in the project changed drastically when it became clear that they were not allies after all. Second, stakeholder self-nominations were important in the process of categorizing and engaging social worlds. In WGIG, the categorization of social worlds as members and stakeholders shaped the goals and strategies of the working group, and served as a way to mobilize some groups and exclude others. This governmental technique brought together multiple elements: the idea of a nomination committee was inspired by the way such decision-making processes are carried out in bodies such as ICANN and IETF, and the process was cast in terms that we normally associate with democracy, such as representation, legitimacy and constituencies. WGIG's formation also had consequences for the role and identity of non-state actors, who had previously operated at the margins of the WSIS process and now suddenly had a seat at the table alongside government delegates. The process led to discussions about the very definition or identity of a civil society actor in general and a WGIG member in particular. For instance, discussions between the IG Caucus and the IPR and Patents Caucus about the character of WGIG members show how the process involved the ordering of identities, for example, whether civil society actors should function as advocates, experts or facilitators. In comparison with the professional nomination process that the business sector carried out, it is obvious that the self-nominations made the issue of representation visible to the involved civil society groups. The UN reliance on self-nomination as a governmental technique had far-reaching consequences for the civil society groups that accepted the invitation to participate, implying that these groups had to self-organize, professionalize their work and develop a number of procedures. It also meant that they had to tackle the ensuing conflicts and concerns about legitimacy vis-à-vis other civil society groups. The self-nominations clearly constituted a form of discipline in the sense that they made actors do things they would not have done otherwise – such as choosing representatives and getting into conflicts with other WSIS civil society groups. At the same time, the process paved the way for an unprecedented degree of access and participation in UN processes, and created a sense of ownership of the projects among its members.

The formation of the two hybrid forums demonstrates how the making of the global politics of the Internet revolved around a particular set of worldviews. The attempt to position the digital revolution as an object of governance in the context of the UN was driven by a political rationality that positions development not simply as aid, but also as the creation of growth and entrepreneurship. Thus, ICT-for-development casts development as a shared responsibility and interest of business, development agencies and other actors, and positions poor people as potential entrepreneurs and consumers, and developing countries as markets rather than aid recipients. This political rationality ties in with a broader development approach seeking a balance between aid and economic growth. In the formation of the UNICTTF this search for a balance between traditional donor approaches to development and business interests in developing new markets was made visible not only in the ordering of the object of governance, but also in the governmental techniques, political subjects and organizational forms developed for the purpose.

In contrast to the UNICTTF, the formation of WGIG was not about the pursuit of financial and symbolic support for an idea. Rather, the main concern was to mobilize actors with broad backing, acceptance and valuable connections in the social worlds relevant to, and engaged in, Internet governance as this issue played out in the context of WSIS. In short, the WGIG consultations focused on stakeholder representation and the creation of a micro-cosmos reflective of WSIS positions on Internet governance and were based on a view of deliberation as a way to reach a higher level of discussion, consensus and mutual learning.

The ordering activities explored in this chapter also had consequences for the objects of governance. In the case of UNICTTF, the interessement and making of stakeholders had far-reaching consequences for the scope and direction of its work. The many translations of the project – from funding through coordination to dialogue – cannot be understood in isolation from the attempts to construct and engage social worlds as stakeholders. Although less evident in the case of WGIG, we still saw how the interessement of stakeholders reconfigured the scope of the substantive focus of the body, for instance when it came to the question of whether or not IPR should be a central theme on the agenda. These shifting configurations of objects and subjects give substance to the claim that ordering must be understood in a practice-oriented, agnostic and relational manner. For instance, treating stakeholders as a pre-defined entity, or casting ICT-for-development or Internet governance as fixed policy issues would not make us able to capture how ordering involves the co-constitutive making of both objects and subjects.

INTERESSEMENT AND POWER

The ordering through processes of interessement also sheds light on the ways in which power and authority operate in hybrid forums. The ability to invent and engage particular subjects, objects, techniques and rationalities can be understood as a form of power and an attempt to gain authority. As we have seen, the two hybrid forums, UNICTTF and WGIG, were fragile and contested. But this should not make us think that this moment of translation was simply the result of the demands of some powerful actor or authority. Often, as the analyses have sought to show, power operates in much more subtle ways. So rather than something held by a single actor – an individual, an organization or a sector – power must be seen as the ability to stabilize particular rationalities, techniques, objects and ways of distributing roles and responsibilities. As noted by Clegg (1998: 30), 'Power [is] a more or less stable or shifting network of alliances extended over a shifting terrain of practice and discursively constructed interests. Points of resistance will open up at many points in the network.' As the analyses in this chapter show, the formation of the two hybrid forums took place in the midst of distinctly unstable alliances and various points of resistance. To capture how power operates in hybrid forums, we need to pay attention to the different forms it takes. Sometimes power is about the ability to exclude and include particular social worlds in the making of hybrid forums. Clearly, questions of inclusion and exclusion are central to networks of all sorts (Cammaerts 2008) and, as we have seen above, gaining and controlling access is one form taken by power in multi-stakeholder arrangements. But power also takes the shape of attempts to categorize and codify subjects in processes of ordering. To make sense of the categorization of social worlds as stakeholders we need to consider how governance and organizing involve forms of 'subjectification'. That is, how do social worlds emerge as political subjects, how are they codified as part of a governmental field through political rationalities and steering techniques, and what does this entail in terms of agency and power? To understand how multi-stakeholder processes codify and position individuals and collectivities as stakeholders, Foucault's conception of subjects as constituted and disciplined through discursive formations, regimes of practices and other forms of ordering is central (Foucault 1982). These arguments about steering, power and agency were most fully developed in Foucault's late work on governmentality (Foucault 1982, 1991b). In his early work, Foucault understood subjects as the more or less passive products of discourses and regimes of practices (Foucault 1977a, 1998a). But in his later work on power and governmentality he offered a more sophisticated conception of the subject (Foucault 1982). Here, he argued that the subject is not 'objectified' but 'subjectified' by a given governmental regime and that this 'constructs individuals who are capable of choice and action, shapes them as active subjects, and seeks to align their choices with the objectives of governing authorities' (Garland 1997: 175). Discourses and practices do not determine what actors do – rather they shape and manage the 'conditions of possibility' of their agency (Foucault 1982: 341): 'When we are governed, when our behaviour is managed, directed or conducted by others, we do not become the passive objects of a physical determination. To govern individuals is to get them to act and to align their particular wills with ends imposed on them through constraining and facilitating models of possible actions' (Burchell 1991: 119).

In such conceptions, steering and power are not unidirectional, but shape the 'conduct of conduct' of all those involved (Foucault 1982). As we saw in the case of the UNICTTF above, the attempt to codify subjects in particular ways also shaped the conduct of those seeking to govern. Thus, anyone who wants to shape the conduct of others must be able to connect to, engage and work through the governed – that is, 'make it their own affair' (Gordon 1991: 48) – in order to be successful. This reminds us that if government is always relational, it cannot constitute a direct form of control. Still, some research drawing on Foucault's work on power and governmentality focuses primarily on how governmental schemes are imagined, launched and managed. To the degree that such investigations give attention to subjects and their experiences of and roles within such regimes of practices, they focus on the ways in which subjects and identities are codified by governmental regimes, rather than the relations and negotiations needed for these to be possible.

So, while seeking to 'shape, guide or affect the conduct of some person or persons' (Gordon 1991: 2), power does not simply control and restrain, but also produces new opportunities and forms of agency (Foucault 1982). For instance, during the first phase of WSIS, no non-state actors had yet been allowed to take part in UN working groups. The nomination process can be seen as a striking example of the ability of an organization such as the UN to mobilize and encourage civil society members to coordinate themselves, respond to new opportunities and take up subject positions on offer. Still, it is important to note how subtle this ordering of social worlds was: the decision to ask civil society groups to nominate their own candidates meant that contentious decisions about inclusion and exclusion were left in the hands of the IG Caucus. At the same time, this delegation of decision-making authority still involved the Executive Coordinator in managing the process at a distance by releasing bits of information about UN preferences that were otherwise difficult to obtain. But the productive effects of power also take the shape of skills and resources. That is, hybrid forums make it necessary for social worlds to develop particular skills and engage particular resources. A good example in this chapter of the productive effects of power on the conduct of social worlds was the need for the IG Caucus to develop new procedures, deal with the question of representation, and appear united. At the same time, the inability of UNICTTF to shape the conduct of the private sector in the desired direction shows how fragile the operations of power can be.

Another way of thinking about power in relation to hybrid forums is the question of authority. In line with the view of authority as 'institutionalized cooperation' (Cutler, Haufler et al. 1999: 334), hybrid forums seek to facilitate and organize constellations of different human and non-human entities. If we conceive of ordering as a practical and relational process, power and authority must also be understood as the products of assemblages – dispersed, relational and without a centre or source. According to Bang, such an approach to power

> breaks with the modern view of political authority as a hierarchical and uniform sovereign entity. Political authority is considered a distinct type of communicative relationship for articulating binding decisions and actions for a given field, terrain or group of people. Such communication can be hierarchical or bureaucratic in form, but it can also be negotiated and dialogical. (Bang 2003: 9)

Conceptions of authority as a 'matter of connecting' (Bang 2003: 15) rest on the Foucauldian view of power, but an important addition to such relational conceptions of authority is Latour's concept of power as enrolment (Latour 1986). From this perspective, authority turns on the ability to enrol others, because like power, it is not simply held, but 'something that has to be obtained by enrolling many actors' (Latour 1986: 271). Questions about authority shed light on the negotiated and practical ways in which hybrid forums seek to establish themselves as recognized and legitimate – in more or less institutionalized collaborative arrangements.

Thinking about authority as the effect of activities that connect 'locales where action occurs' to 'loci of calculation where knowledge can be accumulated' (Braithwaite and Drahos 2000: 482), reminds us to focus our attention on the concrete activities whereby authority is established. As we will see, these hybrid forums emerged as important platforms for two key themes in the global politics of the digital revolution. Such attempts to facilitate steering are an important aspect of the authority of hybrid forums. At the same time, the formative phase – the moment of interessement – played an important role in terms of constituting and stabilizing the subject positions of the key actors and the objects making up the global politics of the digital revolution. Still, the two arrangements were only just coming together and more ordering was about to happen. We now turn to the moment of ordering where not only social worlds but also objects of governance were locked in place, at least momentarily.

4. Organizing hybrid forums

Ordering involves the stabilization of relations, practices and goals, and one shorthand expression for such forms of ordering is to call them organizations. But in line with the research strategy underpinning this book, the question is what we may learn by investigating the *making* of such orderings. Conventional approaches to organization (March and Simon 1958; Blau and Scott 1962; Pugh 1997; Scott 2004) set out to study 'the structure, functioning and performance of organizations and the behaviour of groups and individuals within them' (Pugh 1997: xii) and tend to start from a number of assertions. Organizations are structures containing people. They have stable relations and predictable and regulated ways of doing things, often in the shape of manuals, rules and values governing behaviour. And organizations have a purpose, often in the shape of a business strategy or a defined set of goals. But hybrid forums seem to lack many of these features of formal organizations. They are fluid arrangements, often organized on the fly and constantly in the process of developing procedures and work modalities. At the same time they are often aiming at a moving target, searching for a project, or being established to construct a new issue area as a matter of concern. That is, they are constantly in the process of ordering. These features offer some empirical arguments for an alternative conception of organization, one which is more attuned to fluidity and becoming.

ORGANIZATION AS PROCESS

As this book seeks to demonstrate, the global politics of the Internet has been organized through a number of different and very fluid arrangements, which cannot simply be described as organizations. This chapter captures the ways in which multi-stakeholder processes are conceived, constructed and consolidated in different, more or less stabilized organizational arrangements. At various moments in time, the organization of the global politics of the digital revolution takes the shape of well-defined working groups, a relatively stable organization with different departments, or a much more loosely coupled network or even a fluid, social movement. The point is that these orderings are never fixed or stable, and must be understood as entangled with attempts at giving substance and direction to the global politics of the Internet. This book stresses that organization and governance can be understood as entangled, and this calls for a distinction between organizations and organizing. To capture shifting organizational forms and their ties to other processes, we need the kind of flexible analytical starting point offered by theories about organizing and disorganization. The received view of organizations as bounded and fixed entities holds on to what I termed a substantialist position in the discussion of analytical principles in Chapter 1. In line with the relationalist research strategy advocated in this book, to shift the attention to organizing as a process of ordering implies that nothing is organized forever and that seemingly fixed entities may soon change (Czarniawska 2008: 16). By foregrounding processes of organizing, we are able to see how organization always involves disorganization (Cooper 1986; Hassard, Kelemen et al. 2008) and constant maintenance and ordering. The focus on processes rather than structures has a long history (for an overview, see Hernes 2008) and multiple proponents in contemporary organizational theory (Czarniawska 2008; Hassard, Kelemen et al. 2008; Hernes 2008), but is still far from mainstream.

The burgeoning literature on networks has paved the way for analyses of more ephemeral and fluid institutional arrangements, but still tends to reify networks by defining their limits and shape in advance (Hassard, Kelemen et al. 2008). Such snapshots of seemingly stable and delimited organizations often fail to grasp which human or non-human elements make a difference in a given network and lack a conception of organizations as always under construction. In contrast, this book starts from an agnostic point of departure when it comes to the components and shapes of organizational forms and tries not to separate these from the other objects with which they are entangled.

While many parts of organizational theory seek to challenge structuralist and substantialist conceptions of organization (Scott 2004), international relations remains less attuned to the idea that organizing may be a useful starting point if we want to account for governance, organization and change. Most IR theories in this area seek to classify different types of organizations and networks and account for their ability to impact on politics and policies. The best-known work on networks has evolved around the concepts of 'epistemic communities' (Haas 1992) and 'transnational advocacy networks' (Keck and Sikkink 1998). In such accounts, networks are seen as important organizational arrangements which operate at the margins of governmental and intergovernmental institutions and carry out strategic knowledge- and information-based forms of political intervention. Haas shows how, in moments of uncertainty and complexity, epistemic communities play a key role in interpreting and presenting policy problems and their solutions to decision-makers. They do so by 'articulating the cause and effect relationships of complex problems, helping states identify their interest, framing the issues for collective debate, proposing specific policies, and identifying salient points for negotiation' (Haas 1992: 2). While this approach draws on Foucauldian ideas about power/knowledge, it is more firmly grounded in cognitive psychology and its focus on 'the conditioning role that prior beliefs and established operating procedures play in determining how individuals will respond to new situations or events and choose a course of action when confronted with uncertainty' (Haas 1992: 28). Transnational advocacy networks consist of activists, NGOs and other civil society groups, which must be seen as important because they ' "frame" issues to make them comprehensible to target audiences, to attract attention and encourage action, and to "fit" with favorable institutional venues. Network actors bring new ideas, norms, and discourses into policy debates, and serve as sources of information and testimony' (Keck and Sikkink 1998: 2–3). Both epistemic community and transnational advocacy approaches combine a rationalist focus on institutions, material constraints and incentives with constructivist ideas, which 'take actors and interests to be constituted in interaction' (Keck and Sikkink 1998: 3, footnote). But because they hold onto a substantialist conception of organizations, actors and issue areas, they have little to say about how these come into existence. By shifting our attention to ordering, we are able to give substance to, for instance, Czarniawska's claim that 'connections create actors, not the other way around' (2008: 20).

ENROLMENT AS ORDERING

This chapter describes the moment when the process of building momentum for the idea of UN-driven multi-stakeholder processes to address the global politics of the Internet took the shape of two hybrid forums. As we saw in the previous chapter, categorizing and engaging social worlds was an important step, but the success of these experiments depended on the ability of different social worlds to collaborate, find common ground and develop a sense of membership. While all members subscribed to some broad principles, such as the link between ICTs and development in the case of the UNICTTF, and the importance of not hampering the growth of the Internet in the case of WGIG, they did not agree on how to reach these goals. According to members of the two bodies, they had 'irreconcilable positions' (Drake 2005a), 'their own agendas' (Interview,

SIDA Member of UNICTTF 2005) and did 'not agree' (Interview, WGIG Executive Coordinator 2005). Accordingly, this moment of ordering revolved around a number of practices and governmental techniques that aimed to make it possible and desirable for people with divergent – often conflicting – goals to work together. Governmental techniques are central to hybrid forums because they provide the organizational infrastructure for collaborations between social worlds, and in order to stabilize the relationships between the social worlds engaged as members, a complex array of techniques had to be developed. Clearly, the process of creating these alliances and relationships began in the interessement phase, and building on the discussions in the previous chapter, organizational techniques also play an important role in the analyses here. Drawing on Callon's concept of translation, we may think of the moment we turn our attention to now as a matter of 'enrolment' (Callon 1986), and the governmental techniques that move to the fore in this phase are 'device[s] by which a set of interrelated roles [are] defined and attributed to actors who accept them' (Callon 1986: 211).

Studying the moment of enrolment and the practices involved in strengthening and stabilizing these relations helps us to understand how hybrid forums are made and start to act. The strategies and procedures developed to facilitate and manage interactions between members, staff and external stakeholders in the enrolment phase of the hybrid forums under discussion here revolve around a particular constellation of techniques, rationalities, subjects and objects. This chapter discusses *positioning*, *structuring*, *acting* and *connecting* as four important facets of the ordering of the UN ICT Task Force and the Working Group on Internet Governance. By foregrounding these steps in the consolidation of multistakeholder processes, the chapter contributes to the understanding of the organization and power of hybrid forums.

POSITIONING: NETWORKS WITHIN A HIERARCHY

From the outset, the two forums were conceived as institutional innovations in the context of the UN system. Like their better-known cousin, the UN Global Compact, they brought together stakeholders in attempts to develop new guidelines, practices and policy proposals through cross-sectoral learning and dialogue (Ruggie 2001, 2002; Rasche and Kell 2010). Such inclusive, learning-based, transnational networks constitute supplements – and more rarely alternatives – to multilateral negotiations, by allowing stakeholders, and not just government delegations, to develop new options, models and policy proposals.

As we have seen, the ordering of the global politics of the Internet was shaped by a growing interest in novel approaches to governance and policymaking that would allow for broad-based participation and position the UN as an important platform for such experiments. In particular, the idea of multi-stakeholder processes figured prominently: these would make it possible to combine the resources of public and private entities, and allow all stakeholders to respond to common concerns in a collective and non-confrontational manner. In the interessement phase, these visions and norms were translated into organizational forms and regularized practices. And in the following phases, this focus on multi-stakeholder participation played a very important role in the attempts to position the two hybrid forums as platforms for discussions about the politics of the digital revolution. Seeking to develop horizontal relationships and the identification and dissemination of best practices, the two networks positioned themselves as solutions to many of the concerns pertaining to development, Internet governance and UN reforms. Although there is a growing interest in multi-stakeholder processes, the nature of the UN as an intergovernmental institution means that such activities have to be launched very carefully. Paving the way for such new norms and forms of organization and governance involved a myriad of critical choices, strategies and careful negotiations.

As many of these considerations, practices and interactions were similar in the UNICTTF and WGIG, this chapter explores the two hybrid forums in a comparative manner. The analyses foreground a number of common features and questions that are central to multi-stakeholder arrangements in the UN, such as institutional proximity and independence, members' identities, skills and expectations, and the balance between action and consensus.

The UN is an intergovernmental institution, and non-state actors still operate at the margins of the system. Hybrid forums therefore need to be positioned very carefully, both in financial and institutional terms. Like other new organizational forms and approaches to governance in the UN, such as the Global Compact, the two forums needed to find a way to benefit from the UN without being dragged down by rigid rules and procedures. Hybrid networks seem to flourish when they are able to keep some distance from the UN agencies, to rely on financial resources from outside and operate at the margins of the system, but are still able to maintain direct and visible ties to the Secretary-General.

The UN ICT Task Force was highly integrated into the UN system and the secretariat handling its daily operations resembled those of many other UN entities. The secretariat was part of the Department of Economic and Social Affairs (DESA) and located in one of the smaller UN buildings in New York, across the street from the majestic UN headquarters. It consisted of the Acting Executive Coordinator, the Deputy Executive Coordinator, and eight lower-level staff members. The two coordinators were involved in the UNICTTF from the very beginning. At the outset, they had the UNICTTF as what they term 'a kind of hobby', before the Deputy Executive Coordinator left his former job as Chief Executive of Policy Coordination at ECOSOC in 2003, to run the secretariat on a full-time basis. The Acting Executive Coordinator of UNICTTF remained Director of the Division for ECOSOC Support and Coordination, and had the UNICTTF as his 'second or third job' and one of 'his many, many hats' (Interview, UNICTTF Deputy Executive Coordinator 2004; Interview, UNICTTF Programme Officer 2004).

While the Task Force was conceived and managed from within the UN, its constitution and level of autonomy was radically different from other bodies within the system. It was described as 'the first body created by an intergovernmental decision of the United Nations in which members, representing governments, civil society (including the private sector, not-for-profit foundations, NGOs and academia) and organizations of the United Nations system have equal decision-making power' (ECOSOC 2001).

Another feature that made the UNICTTF different from other UN bodies was that all members – whether from government, business, civil society organizations or international organizations – had 'full membership, on an equal footing' (Interview, UNICTTF Acting Executive Coordinator 2004). As we have seen, discussions about non-state involvement in UN processes were central in the early phases of the formation of UNICTTF. But in order for this level of non-state participation to be possible within the framework of the UN, the UNICTTF needed a special status. As a result, the UNICTTF was set up by the Secretary-General – a strategy that according to the Acting Executive Coordinator made it possible for the UNICTTF to operate more freely vis-à-vis the UN rules of procedure. When asked what makes the UNICTTF different from other UN bodies, such as the Commission on Sustainable Development and other task forces and committees, the Acting Executive Coordinator responded that the difference lies in 'the way it operates. Because normal UN bodies, they operate under certain rules of procedure, so since it was set up outside the normal UN framework, it can operate completely separately and independently. [The UNICTTF is] very different, very different' (Interview, UNICTTF Acting Executive Coordinator 2004). Unlike other bodies set up on the margins of the UN system, the UNICTTF was not a short-term advisory panel, which 'comes together for six months or one year, and produces a report and submits it to the Secretary-General, and then it is over' (Interview, UNICTTF Acting Executive Coordinator

2004). In contrast to the UN Global Compact, which has a number of similar traits, such as a learning approach to regulation, and a non-binding, partnership approach to collaboration between business, civil society and the UN (Ruggie 2001, 2002), the UNICTTF was less about principles and more about policy (Interview, UNICTTF Acting Executive Coordinator 2004). To those involved, the UNICTTF was different from previous initiatives because it was 'given a mandate to carry out something, although with very little resources' (Interview, UNICTTF Acting Executive Coordinator 2004).

All along, the UNICTTF has drawn on the support of the Secretary-General and used such signs of high-level UN engagement to strengthen its legitimacy and position. But at the same time, it was important for the identity and positioning of the UNICTTF that it worked 'without any involvement of the traditional bureaucratic approach of the UN' (Interview, UNICTTF Acting Executive Coordinator 2004). These concerns about the relationship between the UNICTTF and the UN system responded very directly to the results of the worldwide consultations. Business in particular stressed the importance of drawing on the legitimacy of the UN and its Secretary-General, and at the same time distancing the body from the perceived bureaucracy and inertia of the UN system. While the close ties to the Secretary-General made it possible to have state and non-state members working on equal footing, its close ties to DESA positioned it inside the UN system in administrative terms.

Positioning hybrid forums as legitimate, inclusive and significant is an important part of enrolment, and seems to be a more general feature of multi-stakeholder arrangements in the UN system. In many ways, the careful positioning of the UNICTTF was similar to that of WGIG, which also existed at the margins of the UN system and had to position itself carefully in order to strike a balance between the legitimacy offered by strong UN ties and the need for independence and room to manoeuvre. WGIG was based at the Palais des Nations, the UN headquarters in Geneva, and run by a small secretariat, consisting of the Executive Coordinator, Markus Kummer, a Senior Adviser seconded by the ITU, a consultant and a number of administrative assistants and interns. As pointed out in the previous chapter, it was first proposed that WGIG should be constructed as a WSIS working group, but as the rules of procedure applied in WSIS would not allow for equal participation by all stakeholders, it was decided to establish it as an advisory body to the Secretary-General (Interview, WGIG Executive Coordinator 2005). The position as an advisory body allowed for a high level of autonomy vis-à-vis UN rules of procedure, as well as the full participation of non-state actors. This position also gave the Executive Coordinator a high degree of freedom and responsibility in relation to how the body should operate and whom it should include. As the previous chapter has shown, important inspiration was provided by the civil society people involved in the issue of Internet governance in the WSIS context, most of whom had many years of experience in ICANN and other Internet governance bodies. According to the Executive Coordinator of WGIG and members of the IG Caucus, their discussions about the modalities and composition set out a number of principles that were accepted by all stakeholders in the formation phase of WGIG. At the core of these lay the attempt to translate the principles about participation on equal footing, openness and transparency into practice. But the UNICTTF also played an important role in relation to WGIG. According to the Executive Coordinator,

> the UN ICT Task Force [was important] up to a point, because they already had a precedent, and I'm sure it made it easier also, when you asked 'are there any obstacles in the UN?', [there was] none at all, because in the UN that precedent had been taken. Nobody asked why or said 'we cannot have government and others together', so that certainly helped, I think, ease the process. But we did not really have a particular role model from my point of view – we developed our own model. (Interview, WGIG Executive Coordinator 2005)

However, this description of the relationship between the two stands in stark contrast to the view held by the Deputy Executive Coordinator of UNICTTF, who found that WGIG more or less copied its approach and organizational model from the UNICTTF. From his perspective 'this Working Group [on Internet Governance] is absolutely mimicking everything that the Task Force secretariat [. . .] how it's organized, what it's going to be doing, the modalities of work, the consultation processes' (Interview, UNICTTF Deputy Executive Coordinator 2004). The Deputy Executive Coordinator had the following to say about the creation of WGIG and the role that UNICTTF was allowed to play in the process,

> personally I believe that this is an unnecessary duplication of efforts and work, and an unnecessary burden in terms of funding [. . .] We were not asked to do that. It's a political process, so if you don't give it to ITU, you don't give it to the Task Force either. So none of us are going to [do it]. We were telling them from the very beginning that we exist. We have been existing for two years now; we're a multi-stakeholder platform with participation from developing countries, the private sector, civil society, and academia – everything that WSIS enumerated as the characteristics of this new working group. We are it – and we exist. And we have been doing this for two-and-a-half years now. So we are ready to do this if you want us to do it. And we are going to do it even if you don't ask us to do it, because it's in our mandate, and has been long before WSIS happened. So we are going to do all this. And still the decision was made to create something else. (Interview, UNICTTF Deputy Executive Coordinator 2004)

From this perspective, the creation of WGIG undermined the position of the UNICTTF as the UN multi-stakeholder arrangement concerned with Internet governance, and laid the foundation for a new turf war. These concerns about novelty and uniqueness point to the constant struggles over ownership of ideas and organizational formats in the UN system. At the same time, there was some recognition within both secretariats that their efforts were congruent and part of the same process of innovation – towards new types of bodies, serving externally defined purposes rather than internal, bureaucratic ones.

To stress that the two bodies constituted organizational innovations within the UN system was important because it tied in with the wish among many stakeholders for UN reform (see Chapter 2) and signalled the admission of new forms of global governance and types of authority to the UN system. Like many other governmental techniques employed by the UNICTTF and WGIG, the constitution as multi-stakeholder forums for dialogue – positioned strategically at the margins of the UN system – must be understood as an amalgamation of techniques taken from different contexts. The constellation of these are, simultaneously, the product of very pragmatic attempts at turning principles into action, and the outcome of problems and resistance encountered along the way. Even if they primarily differed from other UN bodies in the combination of elements they drew upon, and did not develop new rules of procedures and new formal positions in relation to the UN system, their innovative nature was stressed and employed strategically. To sum up, positioning – in relation to other agencies and established practice in the UN system – constitutes an important pillar in the creation and ordering of hybrid forums.

STRUCTURING: NETWORKS OF NETWORKS

As we have seen, the inclusion of non-state actors in UN-affiliated hybrid forums is a sensitive issue. This implies careful positioning, but also novel ways of structuring interactions and processes. One of the most important features of the two forums was the inclusion of stakeholders as full and equal members. This constitution as a network involving different types of authorities – scientific, moral, private and public (Porter 2008) – was central to the identity of the two forums and functioned as an important point of identification for their members. The distribution of seats and the involvement of stakeholders were therefore key concerns, and these efforts played a central role in the process of enrolling social worlds in the two projects.

The UNICTTF was driven by ideas about the potential of networked forms of organization for novel approaches to development and the creation of synergies and sustainability. After the consultations with potential allies and the careful positioning at the margins of the UN system, the project of addressing the link between development and the digital revolution was ready to take a more stable form. In setting up this novel organizational arrangement, it was important to engage members who would add momentum as well as legitimacy to the project. In the words of the Deputy Coordinator, they were building

> a networking mechanism basically. And this is what is needed to give ICT for development a truly global dimension, because we are talking about hundreds, if not thousands of individual initiatives, some of them undertaken in heroic circumstances. The problem with that is that they are isolated: most of them have a character of a pilot project and they don't have sustainability. So once a donor or a sponsor withdraws, these things normally fizzle out, leaving frustration. So what the Task Force is trying to do is to sort of link all of these things in a global network of networks. So that individual initiatives, organizations, activities, and even individuals have an idea of what the other guy is doing across the river, or across an ocean, and how this can be used for addressing local needs, and what best practices exist, and how governments can use experience of other governments in developing their own e-strategies and how to integrate these e-strategies in their more general development programs and strategies. This is what we're trying to do: capacity-building, awareness-raising, linking networks and, you know, this kind of stuff. (Interview, UNICTTF Deputy Executive Coordinator 2004)

This organizational arrangement consisted of a core group, a small steering group, a panel of advisers, local and regional groupings and a number of loosely affiliated partners. The core group had 50 members, from both developed and developing countries. Out of these, 20 members were categorized as 'government', 17 members as 'international organizations and multilateral institutions', ten members as 'private sector', and three members as 'civil society groups'. Most members were high-level representatives, such as CEOs of companies, ministers and chairpersons of large organizations. While members had an interest and some expertise in the issue of ICTs and development, very few of them were technical experts. Because the UNICTTF had such a strong focus on stakeholder representation and legitimacy, it was impossible to have as many business members as wanted by the initiators. As a solution, it was decided that Cisco and Hewlett-Packard would share a seat. Had this been an organizational setting where voting and other forms of number-based procedures were used, this would imply that these two companies would only count as one. But in UNICTTF, representation played another role, and no votes were ever cast. So if used well, half a seat was just as good as a full one. As we will see, both Cisco and Hewlett-Packard made the most of their membership. The member from Cisco functioned as vice-chairman, and Hewlett-Packard chaired the Working Group on Entrepreneurship throughout the lifespan of the UNICTTF. In this sense, the strong focus on representation as a matter of numbers stands in stark contrast to the actual abilities and strategies employed in order to gain influence in hybrid forums.

Cooperating closely with the Chairman and the secretariat, the UNICTTF Bureau took care of decision-making and future planning. The Bureau was led by the Chairman, and its other members were chosen from the core group and elected for one-year terms. The tasks of the Bureau were to coordinate the work of the body, maintain its focus, and mobilize resources for initiatives and activities. Members of the Bureau used video-conferencing for regular meetings, and often met face-to-face during UNICTTF meetings. As with the rest of the UNICTTF, work in the Bureau was voluntary and unpaid.

The core group met every six months for one-and-a-half day meetings, often in conjunction with the so-called Global Forums organized by the UNICTTF in major cities, among them Berlin, New York and Dublin. In addition to the core group of members, the body consisted of a panel of advisers. These were 30 ICT experts, including academics like Manuel Castells and Nicholas Negroponte, business leaders like John Gage of SUN Microsystems, the Secretary-General of the International Chamber of Commerce and national leaders. The panel of advisers was used regularly during the formation of the UNICTTF, but less so later on, although some advisers were invited to speak at meetings and Global Forums.

Finally, the UNICTTF consisted of a number of thematically divided working groups and regional nodes. The four open-ended working groups[6] focused on 'ICT Policy and Governance', 'Enabling Environment', 'Human Resource Development and Capacity Building' and 'ICT Indicators and MDG Mapping'. The five regional networks covered Africa, Latin America and the Caribbean, Asia, Arab States, Europe and Central Asia. Both working groups and regional networks were supposed to be 'the ears and eyes of the UNICTTF on the ground' (Abu-Ghazaleh 2002) and allow for the creation of networks and partnerships on multiple levels, ranging from the global to the local and across the issue areas relevant to ICT4D. The working groups and regional networks were intended to 'facilitate a decentralized approach to cooperation on the basis of the identification of problems and gaps in existing activities related to ICT for development' (UNICTTF 2004b). They were open-ended, cooperated with regional, national and local ICT4D initiatives in an attempt to 'facilitate synergy' and imagined as a way for input on 'best practices', initiatives and priorities to reach the UNICTTF from wider groups of stakeholders. In addition to the core UNICTTF members, the working groups and regional networks had a number of members (ranging from 20 to more than 230), who had been invited or had applied to become part of this network of networks. These members included academics, leaders of private companies and representatives from civil society organizations and a number of associations. Neither working groups nor regional networks had resources available – and chairing them meant that only direct expenses, not work hours, could be covered by UNICTTF. This meant that – in practice – little work was done in these parts of the UNICTTF (Interview, APC Member of UNICTTF 2003), unless the group was chaired by someone with resources and enthusiasm (Interview, UNICTTF Deputy Executive Coordinator 2004). Finally, the UNICTTF maintained an extensive set of connections to relevant organizations, projects and initiatives which carry out similar activities at regional, national and local levels. These so-called partners included the G8 DOT Force, the World Economic Forum, Global Business Dialogue on Electronic Commerce, the Global Knowledge Partnership, WSIS, ICC, the Development Gateway Foundation and INfoDev.

The organizational infrastructure for the project of addressing ICT-for-development through multi-stakeholder processes was falling into place. Described as a 'global network of networks' by those involved, this organizational setup catered to the wish for cross-sectoral and regional representation, flexibility and outreach. With multiple levels, the involvement of many social worlds, and strong as well as weak ties, this arrangement was quite different from traditional UN high-level panels and working groups.

At the outset, the Working Group on Internet Governance was a much simpler organizational arrangement consisting only of a core group with 40 members. But as we will see, as discussions about Internet governance developed within the UN, this hybrid forum became even more amorphous than UNICTTF. The 40 members of WGIG were classified as 'government', 'business' and 'civil society', with the latter category including universities, NGOs, and other organizations. As discussed in the previous chapter, WGIG seats were distributed more or less equally between the three stakeholder groups. Furthermore, members were from both developed and developing countries, and the group was regionally balanced. It was planned that there should also be gender balance in the group, but this turned out to be very difficult as most nominees were male (Interview, UNICTTF Executive Coordinator 2005). Most of WGIG's non-state members were consultants, specialists, technical experts and researchers. The government members were primarily directors and managers, although there were also some ministers. As the reliance on self-nominations show, the WGIG process had the construction of non-state actors as important political subjects as one of its key outcomes. But in the case of WGIG, the categorization of different social worlds as civil society, business and government was more difficult than in the UNICTTF because some members had multiple affiliations and did not easily fit the categories.

The group held four meetings at the Palais des Nations in Geneva during 2004–05, and went to a local chateau together to write the final report in the middle of June 2005. Furthermore, the group held four meetings to discuss the question of global Internet governance with the broader group of stakeholders. These different activities were led by the Swiss diplomat, Markus Kummer, acting as Executive Director, and Nitin Desai – a retired Under-Secretary-General for Economic and Social Affairs, who also functioned as the Secretary-General's special adviser for WSIS – acting as Chairman. As observed above, hybrid forums need some distance from the UN system but also ties to the Secretary-General, and Desai provided one such link.

As we have seen, WGIG was a direct outcome of the failure to reach consensus on the question of Internet governance during the final negotiations at the World Summit on the Information Society. But in order to facilitate dialogue between those already in charge of the global governance of the Internet, this hybrid forum had to be placed outside the WSIS process and on the margins of the UN system. Like UNICTTF, the body was structured as a multi-stakeholder forum for dialogue based on equal participation by state and non-state actors. This was an important principle and a pillar of the organizational arrangement, but members stressed that in practice this formal equality was rarely thought about or addressed further within the group. This feature can help us make sense of how hybrid forums rely on principles such as representation and equal footing in order to enrol social worlds, but need to downplay such characteristics in order to move forward. One way of doing this was to invite members to participate as individuals, rather than representatives of the governments, organizations or companies they worked for. To ask members to act as individuals allowed for a higher degree of freedom, particularly for government members who would otherwise have had to check their mandate continuously. The categorization of members as individuals was central to WGIG and the UNICTTF, even if many members acknowledge that in practice, they often spoke as representatives anyway. According to one member of WGIG, who works for an NGO called the Association for Progressive Communication, the principle that people participated as individuals was important, but sometimes difficult to sustain in practice:

> one of the reasons [WGIG] works well is that the group works as a group of individuals – everyone is asked to participate equally. Of course you're going to bring your experience and your expertise based on where you come from, you know, the sector you've been involved in. And so, in that sense you could [. . .] If someone says, 'Who are you in the WGIG?' I'd say, 'Well, I'm one of the Civil Society representatives in the WGIG', but I wouldn't say, 'I represent Civil Society'. And I could probably say that I represent APC's views on this issue. But to be honest, most of us work as individuals – I don't check every other [. . .] I don't check every time with APC before I speak or I write or whatever. You know, the group has a sort of sensible autonomy, I think – an independence – which is very healthy. Even though we all know where everyone's coming from, they try very hard to, even the way they speak, rather than say 'we', which is quite common for someone coming from a government delegation, they try to say 'I', which is not always easy for them. (Interview, APC Member of WGIG 2005)

By categorizing members as individuals rather than representatives, both hybrid forums sought to facilitate dialogue on contentious issues and offer members different ways of engaging in their work. Clearly, to speak as individuals does not mean that members would stop pursuing the goals of the social world to which they were allied, but it did allow them to take up new and unfamiliar positions. For some, however, the offer to participate as an individual was not enough. Coming out of the WSIS process, WGIG could be seen as close to official UN negotiations and decision-making processes. For instance, one of the reasons why the US decided not to become a member of WGIG was that its presence would not allow for dialogue; a representative of the US government would not be able to engage in an amicable and open dialogue about Internet governance, because this could be interpreted as a first step towards the US giving up its central role in this area (Interview, WGIG Executive Coordinator 2005). The US coordinator for international communications and information policy, who was also a member of the UNICTTF, explained the US decision not to become a member of WGIG in the following way: 'The United States Government did not directly participate in WGIG because there were a number of potentially serious legal issues (under US law) that such participation could have raised. We were pleased that a number of private US citizens were asked to participate' (Gross 2005: n.p.). In contrast, the US government had no problem with being a member, and an active one, of the UNICTTF, because

> The UN ICT Task Force has been a very helpful forum for having governments, NGOs, companies and others exchange information and ideas [. . .] The Task Force's purpose of exchanging information is very different than the purpose of WGIG which was to provide a working definition of the term Internet Governance and to identify the 'public policy' issues associated with that term. (Gross 2005: n.p.)

So the very task assigned to WGIG was deemed too politically contentious for the US to be able to take part, and even the invitation to participate as an individual could not do away with this concern.

These negotiations between subject positions, procedures and objects of governance offer a number of insights into the functioning of hybrid forums. Hybrid forums seek to detach actors from their original social worlds by offering them new subject positions. But in practice, such procedures do not offer the kind of interest-free, detached space for dialogue imagined by theorists of deliberation and justice. As pointed out by Callon, Lascoumes et al., hybrid forums may be considered a form of public space, but they are 'not reducible to that imagined by Hannah Arendt, Jürgen Habermas and John Rawls [because] unlike the public spaces described by these three authors, it does not specify that the participants be persons or individuals divested of every particular quality and detached from their networks of sociability, having bracketed off everything they value and everything to which they are attached' (Callon, Lascoumes et al. 2009: 262). But as a governmental technique, the positioning of members as individuals gives the room for manoeuvre on which hybrid forums thrive. As Garsten and Jacobsson (forthcoming) point out, the 'multi-stakeholder model, partnerships, network governance along with notions of trust, voluntarism and win-win games, all illustrate the ideal of consensual relationships'. But in practice, hybrid forums do not seek the kind of consensus that discussions about deliberation and the public sphere tend to idealize (Flyvbjerg 1998). Participation, equal footing and consensus are important ideals, and are used strategically in the attempts to make hybrid forums possible, but at the same time, such principles must remain vague. To make sense of these workings of consensual ideals and practices, we need to explore how hybrid forums deal in practice with questions of equal footing and consensus.

Collaboration without Consensus

In WGIG, the Executive Coordinator deliberately refrained from defining or spelling out more clearly what equal footing would imply in a concrete situation where members disagreed over a particular issue (Interview, WGIG Executive Director 2005). There was, however, a moment when such a situation arose, namely during the drafting of the working papers that were supposed to prepare the ground for the report. Although dubbed a 'fact-finding phase' by the secretariat, the drafting of a paper on intellectual property rights (IPR), written by a civil society member who described himself as critical towards existing IPR agreements, led to a strong reaction from business and other IPR- and WIPO-friendly members. Rather than engaging in a discussion about how to create a better balance between the different positions on IPR in the paper, the latter members simply vetoed its publication on the WGIG website. According to a member of WGIG, private sector members' dislike of the paper meant that it was simply 'canned', while a paper on telecommunications and privatization written by a private sector member, described critically as 'an ode to GATS' by civil society members, was not discarded (IG-Caucus 2004–05). In this situation, the limits of the principle of equal footing were tested. Could some members simply take issues off the WGIG agenda, while others did not have similar privileges? According to the Executive Coordinator, this situation demanded careful navigation and leadership to keep the group intact. By accepting that IPR was treated differently from other questions, he and the Chairman sought to avoid having members vote on one of the most contentious issues:

> That's something we would avoid [because] that would be divisive. There was a phase which was quite tense, what with the papers, you know. As to IPR, some people are not happy with it. Anyway, those who said that it could not be right that some member has the right to veto. Then we said, 'Let's not talk about veto here or after in any phase? Let's accept that you may have major problems in any phase. But don't discuss the procedure – who can veto what or whatever' – you have to move in a way where people are still all on board, you know; it's dangerous moving away [from that and towards] the splitting of the group. There are no hard-and-fast rules, and, you know, some things you have to say privately, and I've had several private exchanges with individual members, to explain. (Interview, WGIG Executive Coordinator 2005)

Hybrid forums aspire to create synergies and consensus, and tend to be very focused on procedures, such as multi-stakeholder participation on equal footing. But as this situation shows, they sometimes need to downplay or circumvent procedures in order to move forward. As we will see in Chapter 5, hybrid forums can only thrive insofar as they stay clear of contentious issues as well as hard-and-fast procedures, such as voting and vetoing, that allow for divisions to come out into the open. Rather than getting bogged down in traditional UN conflicts, such forums seek to carve out spaces for dialogue based on ideals of synergy and consensus. But it is important to note that such ideals of synergy and consensus remain somewhat fuzzy in order to facilitate dialogue between social worlds that may not have compatible goals. As one member of UNICTTF pointed out 'what I mean by consensus is that if people don't agree with it, they don't disagree vehemently with it. So we're not looking for everybody to agree with everything' (Interview, Irish Government Member of UNICTTF 2003). Hybrid networks do not seek the kind of full consensus that traditional UN negotiations demand. Such negotiations take the shape of painstaking compromises about the wording of declarations, and often end in deadlock because no full consensus can be reached. By accepting a weak understanding of consensus, hybrid forums can spur dialogue and networking and stay clear of traditional UN and intergovernmental deadlocks. Similarly, one member of the UNICTTF explained how – over time – members tended to stay clear of contentious issues and focus on areas of consent:

> I think that if you would ask the question around, I mean, in terms of what people, how they position themselves on specific issues, if you have twenty people, you would get at least fifteen different voices, different positions [. . .] Because, I mean, don't forget that we are a group of people who know each other by now. You know, you get a certain club mentality – you know where the borderlines are; you know what you can agree on, and what you definitely [can] not agree on. So why keep on arguing about things that you will never agree on? You don't do [. . .] I don't do that, you know, with the US for instance [. . .] we agree on certain, a few things. So I don't see any point in keeping sort of pushing, punching each other on things that we disagree on, but rather to try to build on something that we are possibly able to agree on and moving that forward [. . .] And then, okay, you can disregard that people have different, you know, own agendas or views – different governments have different views [. . .] So on the one hand I think you can criticize that, 'Okay, you don't take these fights into the [UNICTT]'; [but] on the other hand you can say, 'Okay, that's the strength'; you can try to find the common platform and use that for developing something, instead of as is happening in the normal UN context where you actually get into the conflict immediately, and where you normally end up in the same damned conflict as everybody knows is there [. . .] I mean, you're stuck! And we cannot provide any solution to these things because they're political – they're beyond the reach of what we can even debate. (Interview, SIDA Member of UNICTTF 2005)

Others in the UNICTTF also stressed that this 'club mentality' and a 'common culture' emerged over time (Interview, UNICTTF Acting Executive Coordinator 2004). As we have seen, members were codified and positioned in particular ways, and the resulting orientation towards the least controversial issues allowed for dialogue and collaboration. In this regard, hybrid forums break with the premises that underlie most multilateral negotiations, namely that consensus is about compromise and bargaining. But it also means that there are limits to what can be discussed in hybrid forums and to the outcomes of their efforts. To focus on broad, principles and uncontroversial issues does little to solve existing conflicts and may result in the maintenance of the status quo, or a consensus on the lowest common denominators.

Similarly, the WGIG Executive Coordinator sought to keep a distance from contentious issues by letting the group start its work with what he refers to as a 'fact-finding phase', in which members were asked to map out the issues that could be seen as related to Internet governance. If the group had started with discussions about priorities or proposals, the question of whether ICANN or the ITU should handle the management of the Internet infrastructure, or even the definition of Internet governance, then the group may have come apart before it even got started (Interview, WGIG Executive Coordinator 2005). By focusing on 'facts' first, the group was able to create a collegial and collaborative atmosphere, although the Executive Coordinator realized early on that even 'facts are very touchy' (Interview, WGIG Executive Coordinator 2005). The decision to focus on facts before priorities was intended as a way to make the group work together, and it was an idea that the secretariat came up with and 'felt strongly about' (IG-Caucus 2004–05).

According to the Executive Coordinator, the strategy – to deal with the least contentious issues first – was successful: 'I think the group came out of this exercise – well, okay, we don't agree, there are all these disclaimers, you know – I think as a process it was very useful for the group to come closer together, and to find a common way of working together and of respecting also each other. Of course we don't agree' (Interview, WGIG Executive Coordinator, 2005). By maintaining, at least for a while, a distance from contentious issues, hybrid forums make communication and collaboration between members possible, even where they do not agree. Combined with a very thin definition of consensus and an avoidance of closure, it is possible to create platforms for dialogue in which members can become involved without running into the conflicts that characterize intergovernmental negotiations.

To sum up, the two hybrid networks were structured around formal equality between social worlds and used this feature strategically to facilitate interaction. However, there were times at which they also had to downplay this feature, such as in concrete cases of disagreement where full equality would undermine collaboration and dialogue. Multi-stakeholder arrangements must stay clear of rule-based decision-making processes and closure techniques, such as voting, in order to invite people to do things they would otherwise not have done. The formal equality of members played an important role in the management of the UNICTTF and the WGIG alike, although the practical implications of this principle were different in the two cases. It is another key feature of both forums that they continually invoked the distinction between sectors, such as government, business and civil society, and thus stressed the differences between members. One could imagine that the members were referred to simply as eminent people or experts, in which case the issue of sectoral balance and representation would not be at the forefront to the same degree. But WGIG was presented as 'balanced' and 'triadic' (Interview,

WGIG Executive Coordinator 2005), and the UNICTTF as an 'inclusive', 'representative' and 'globally accepted organization' (UNICTTF 2004a; Abu-Ghazaleh 2002). They were designed to allow for 'real participation' (Interview, UNICTTF Acting Executive Coordinator 2004), to 'have everyone in the tent' (Drake 2005a) in WGIG, and to allow previously excluded non-state actors to sit at the same table as governments, and in governing bodies, such as the Bureau of the UNICTTF.

Inspired in particular by the G8 DOT Force and the light structures developed between Internet specialists and activists, these organizational arrangements clearly sought to infuse the UN system with a 'networking logic' (Castells 1996; Juris 2008). Inside as well as outside the UN, such formations involve a 'confluence of organizational forms, political norms and digital technologies' (Juris 2008: 68). They are driven by the political rationality that digital technologies can propel social (including organizational) transformations and seek to mimic the decentralized, global and networked infrastructure of the Internet. Still, it is not enough to simply describe the two as organizational entities diffusing an already fixed logic. This interpretation misses the important point that such processes always become entangled in multiple translations and negotiations. As this chapter has shown, the positioning and structuring of the two hybrid forums as loosely UN-based, networked, multi-stakeholder arrangements involved many such forms of navigation. Also, as we will see below, the boundaries between hybrid forums and their environment often become so fluid that it is more useful to think of them as assemblages 'composed of various longer or shorter connections' (Kendall 2004: 71) than formal organizations. The point is that we get a better understanding of politics, organization and technology if we start from observations about how organizational forms, political rationalities and objects become entangled. Along these lines, both can be understood as assemblages of networking norms, forms and technologies. But these assemblages also contain humans, and we need to consider how and with what consequences particular social worlds are enrolled and able to act in hybrid forums.

ACTING AS A STAKEHOLDER

The focus on representation and equal footing plays an important role in making multi-stakeholder arrangements possible and attractive. But in order for members and broader groups of stakeholders to influence the work and directions of hybrid forums, a seat at the table is not enough. Becoming a stakeholder involves expectations about how to engage in the process and the honing of a particular set of skills. According to members and staff, particular qualities were needed in order for someone to be able to influence the direction and outcome of the two forums. Starting with the interessement phase and pursued in a much more targeted manner in the enrolment phase, the two hybrid forums were normalizing and encouraging particular ways of acting and contributing. Along these lines, the following discussion shows how multi-stakeholder arrangements work through – and thus discipline – the political subjects they engage (Foucault 1982).

Members had clear ideas about how to act in order to be successful in the context of the UNICTTF; it was driven by people who were able to communicate effectively (Interview, TfDev Member on UNICTTF 2004), who were enthusiastic (Interview, UNICTTF Deputy Executive Coordinator 2004; Jensen 2005) and able to provide administrative backing (Interview, APC Member of UNICTTF 2003; Interview, TfDev Member of UNICTTF 2004). According to one of the civil society members, to be effective and have an impact in the context of the Task Force was:

> not about representation, [but] about being able to be an effective interlocutor, in terms of persuading [. . .] If you can be effective about doing that, you don't need to have the numbers, it is not a numbers game, it's actually a persuasion and influence game [. . .] The same is true of the Task Force, if one can demonstrate, even with few resources or less obvious forms of power that you are effective, then I think you can play a very important role in shaping the direction of the Task Force, and I have seen that in terms of folks, individuals, organizations which are not on the Task Force in an official capacity, who on the margins of the Task Force have been able to insert their particular issues and their particular perspectives and their particular ways of seeing the world in offering those to the Task Force and then getting them to be part of the agenda, just because of the effectiveness of their communication, their effectiveness in terms of process of follow-up – all of these good skills of advocacy that advocacy groups ought to have. (Interview, TfDev Member of UNICTTF 2004)

This conception of an effective and successful member as someone who shows enthusiasm, initiative and commitment – whether in terms of ideas, advocacy or financial backing – was broadly shared by members as well as the secretariat (Interview, APC Member of UNICTTF 2003; Interview, UNICTTF Deputy Executive Coordinator 2004; Interview, UNICTTF Programme Officer 2004; Interview, UNICTTF Technology Associate 2004; Interview, TfDev Member of UNICTTF 2004). When another member explained why she was not able to use her position as effectively as she would have liked, she gave a similar explanation:

> it is a strategic opportunity for us, I recognize that, but I just feel that we do not have the capacity to utilize it effectively [. . .] It is hard to invest in it, I feel really concerned, even now that we have been asked to take on the convening of Working Group 1 that we are not going to be effective in doing it, because we, because there [is] no money that comes with the role, so we have no resources to spend on it, and we are already very overworked, and we are not a big team. (Interview, APC Member of UNICTTF 2003)

When some members were more successful in using the opportunities offered by the UNICTTF, it was because they were able to dedicate more time and effort to the project: 'they put more time and more effort into it than I do, so I respect their right to have more impact on the outcomes, if I really wanted to do that, I could try and be on the Bureau. And I'm sure that if I tried, if I was more active in the process, they would be very open and receptive to me' (Interview, APC Member of UNICTTF 2003). The lack of resources could therefore limit members' ability to pursue their goals and shape the work of the Task Force. The difference between simply participating and actually influencing the process was also stressed by a civil society member, who others (Interview, UNICTTF Deputy Executive Coordinator 2004; Interview, UNICTTF Programme Officer 2004; Interview, UNICTTF Technology Associate 2004) describe as one of the most active and successful:

> I think the main difference is in the de facto power of the different kinds of interventions or the different kinds of contributions or responsibilities, because the Task Force in terms of its membership is very broad and all Task Force members are equal, but I think it is inherent to the nature of the process that the secretariat will respond to the interest of various stakeholders with more, perhaps more urgency, because some stakeholders will be able to put more resources into the ways in which their issues are presented. And I'm not talking just about the formal meetings, I'm speaking about what happens in the period between meetings, and the ability of different stakeholders to have the resources to follow up on activities that they are interested in pursuing or to basically, to pursue the issues we are discussing from their perspective [. . .] I think that the Task Force is very open to initiative, but resources also impact on the, you know, the ability of stakeholders to actually pursue the issue that they might have an interest in, but simply may not have the resources to pursue it, and since the Task Force does not fund those activities, there may be good issues or interesting ideas that are not being pursued because civil society actors or some countries may not have the ability to just go out and pursue those areas of interest [. . .] The ability of different stakeholders to then pursue issues, not at the level of debate or at the level of rhetoric, but then to influence the work program and to carry out the work program or to follow up on interesting ideas is really determined by power and resourcing, that is not a function of the Task Force but a function of structural differences between the resourcing of the different stakeholders in the real world. (Interview, TfDev Member of UNICTTF 2004)

So while good ideas and a seat at the table were important, other resources were also needed. Such insights allow us to reflect on the limits of procedural and organizational attempts to create spaces for dialogue that are detached from what is termed 'the real world' in the quote above. While being proactive, entrepreneurial and enthusiastic were important qualities of a successful stakeholder, multi-stakeholder arrangements are also shaped by resource-based differences between members. So principles such as inclusion and equal footing are an important feature of hybrid forums, but in order to benefit from these, members must also possess strong communication skills and the ability to reinforce ideas with administrative and financial resources. These are important examples of how multi-stakeholder arrangements work through political subjects by encouraging them to act in particular ways (Deetz 1995; Foucault 1982; Alvesson and Willmott 2002).

If one person embodied the political subject envisioned by the UNICTTF it was the first chairman, who also played a central role as the main architect of the body and its approach to development and governance. As a person from a developing country, who had been able to traverse sectoral boundaries by having successful careers in government, the private sector and an international organization, this former president of Costa Rica encompassed not only multiple types of expertise, but also the boundary-crossing competencies that played such an important role in the UNICTTF. Furthermore, he had an approach to leadership and management that fitted perfectly with the UNICTTF wish to break with the UN-style bureaucracy. He had charisma, he set targets, he ended meetings on time and he wanted the UNICTTF to 'deliver' and make a difference. When observing meetings and in the accounts of members, the fact that a multi-stakeholder approach came to play such an important role in the UNICTTF can be tied in directly to the character of the chairman as 'a very, very strong supporter of partnerships, primarily with the business, but is open to seeing and recognizing that civil society organizations play an important role and that you can have input that are coming from outside the governmental sector. I think that was recognized as one of the strengths, one of the essential characteristics of the Task Force' (Interview, TfDev Member of UNICTTF 2004).

In many ways, the chairman embodied the vision that drove the UNICTTF. During his time as president of Costa Rica, he created strong partnerships with telecommunications companies, such as Alcatel, and used these to create a strong momentum for economic growth in the country. However, in 2005, these ties to Alcatel came under close scrutiny by a legislative commission in Costa Rica questioning whether the US$900,000 that he received from Alcatel between 2000 and 2003 was only a 'consulting fee', as he maintained, or part of a string of corruption scandals that have sent two other former presidents of Costa Rica to jail.[7] Even after these allegations forced him step down from his positions as CEO of the World Economic Forum and as Chairman of the Task Force, many members stressed his importance. For instance, the SIDA member described him as,

> extremely important – I think he has been very, very important. And, for two reasons: first of all that he has a background of being from a developing country, and from being a president of a country. And he was very much involved in ICTs, so Costa Rica as a showcase is very important. Secondly, I mean, his former – today former – position as CEO of the World Economic Forum was to have a very strong connection to the private sector. So in a way he has been able to somehow combine development and private sector involvement. I mean, there are pros and cons in that, and that's a tricky kind of balance to get. So, and I don't know what will happen now because he has resigned now from the Task Force. It's basically a question of, or an issue for, the Secretary General of the UN whether he will [. . .] You know, even if he's cleared, which is one assumption; that he's cleared from any corruption, from being involved in anything which is considered corrupt. If he's cleared from that, then the Secretary General has to make a decision whether he wants to reinstate José-María in the Chair or not. But he's a very capable Chair, he's very charismatic, he's bringing in a little bit more of what I think is very healthy, namely a little bit more of sort of a business way of dealing with things. Because if you would just lean on the UN, there's no beginning and no end to anything – everything is an ongoing process – and he's trying very hard to push it, you know, set targets. It doesn't succeed always, but at least he's trying hard, so I'm very positive to him as a Chair. This is a new situation that we have to await the outcome of the process which is going on in Costa Rica, to say whether he could come back. But he needs to be clean to come back. (Interview, SIDA Member of UNICTTF 2005)

Clearly, corruption charges do not fit into the subject position envisioned by the UNICTTF, and even though the chairman was never convicted, he did not return to the UNICTTF. The position as chairman was taken over by the Under-Secretary-General for Economic and Social Affairs, who had a lot of UN experience, but did not embody the entrepreneurial and boundary-crossing qualities that UNICTTF valued.

The need for financial and administrative backing was less outspoken in WGIG, where time, dedication and enthusiasm were the primary resources needed. Members of the IG Caucus, who – more than any other group involved in WGIG – insisted on the importance of multi-stakeholder participation and equal representation, stressed that 'leadership in WGIG will be mostly determined by pro-activity, good proposals, good strategy and good communication, rather than by sheer numbers – especially if governments can't manage to bridge their differences and find a way out on their own' (IG-Caucus 2004–05). Another member stressed that 'WGIG is not about representation, but about connection and facilitation' (IG-Caucus 2004–05), and a third that 'Geographical representation is the wrong approach with regard to multi-stakeholder working groups' (IG-Caucus 2004–05). Although representation and inclusion are central to hybrid forums, members seem to agree that the key to success lies elsewhere. But if representation and numbers are less important than being proactive and strategic, then how are such resources utilized in multi-stakeholder arrangements? According to WGIG members, civil society members had a great impact on the substantive issues dealt with in the report produced by the group, as well as the papers leading up to the report (IG-Caucus 2004–05; Jensen 2005). For instance, it was stressed by the Norwegian government member that even if the group was very balanced in terms of numbers, the 'only sad thing was that there was not a balance in activity levels. Two members were never active, and among the 38 remaining, there was not a good balance. Civil society played an important role due to their activity level, and governments were not able to match the level of activity of civil society' (Jensen 2005). What made civil society members particularly successful was their level of engagement and enthusiasm. Unlike many government and business members, civil society members were able to devote a large amount of time to WGIG activities – throughout the process, and particularly in the final phase where the report was written (Jensen 2005). In his blog, a civil society member wrote about the final WGIG report that:

> the good news is that we have a report, and that it's actually quite reasonable, and, for certain things, even surprisingly good to civil society values (that's also because [two civil society members] and I, the dynamic trio, managed to take over some of the secretariat functions in the last couple of days, drafting and working out the proposed text for the entire group). (Chairman of ICANN At-large Advisory Committee and President and CTO, Dynamic Fun, Italy, quoted from http://hackun.bertola.eu.org/)

This quote gives an insight into the kind of resources that were needed in order to be successful. Just as in UNICTTF, being proactive and devoted was important in order to gain influence, and as a consequence, members were encouraged to act in particular ways. In other words, hybrid forums work through the political subjects they envision and nurture. That multi-stakeholder arrangements discipline political subjects should not be understood in a purely negative manner – as Foucault (1982) stresses, disciplinary power also empowers and enables subjects. For instance, entrepreneurship stood at the heart of both forums, and constituted a valued and useful resource to be drawn upon for those in search of influence and authority.

CONNECTING: COMMUNICATION AND FACILITATION

This chapter has shown how hybrid networks make interactions between actors with different concerns and goals possible. So far, the focus has been on organizational techniques, such as how to distribute seats and structure multi-stakeholder arrangements. In the following, we turn the attention to the practical and strategic ways in which the UNICTTF and WGIG built ties to broader groups of social worlds, other organizations and the political spaces they sought to shape. The Internet offered one way of facilitating links and dialogues outside and in between meetings, but the two forums also relied on other forms of communication, such as book publications. At the same time, to connect and facilitate dialogue between different social worlds, both forums had to navigate carefully, albeit for different reasons. WGIG was set up to address the contentious question of Internet governance. Although less controversial, we have seen how the ICT-for-development agenda created tensions for the UNICTTF and became tied to UN turf wars. To stay clear of such struggles, both forums had to navigate around other projects, other very contentious questions and formal negotiations which would work against the project of facilitating dialogue between all stakeholders.

From the outset, the two forums placed participation, communication and transparency at the centre. In the literature on global networks, the use of the Internet for communication and mobilization is often described as central. For instance, it is regularly claimed that the success of transnational advocacy networks, NGOs and other civil society groups lies in their ability to utilize new media for purposes of agenda-setting, 'information politics' and mobilization (Keck and Sikkink 1998; Deibert 2000; Bach and Stark 2002). Driven by high hopes for the potentials of ICTs, both forums emphasized the importance of using ICTs, particularly the Internet, in their activities and outreach. But in practice, the most important work took place in physical meetings, and in both cases, only parts of their activities were made publicly accessible. Rather than completely open and transparent spaces, both the UNICTTF and WGIG considered carefully the issues of openness and external communication, as well as the balance between transparency and efficiency.

DISCLOSURE AND TRANSPARENCY

Both forums had websites that they used for news, publications of working papers and other types of information. In UNICTTF, a very elaborate communication strategy was developed early on. This stressed that the objective with the website should be two-fold: it should increase 'visibility' and help the UNICTTF 'carry out its outreach and policy objectives' (UNICTTF 2001b). With regards to the former, the website should be used to 'mobilize global public support' and to create networks of public, private and non-profit stakeholders interested in ICT4D activities (UNICTTF 2001a: 5). The website should 'serve as a platform for developing a forum for sharing lessons learned and best practices, and provide local content responsive to local needs' (UNICTTF 2001b), provide hyperlinks to UN and other agencies, NGOs and private industry programmes involved in ICT for development initiatives, and thus function as a 'one-stop shop for this type of information' (UNICTTF 2002: 4). One of the original plans was that the online activities should develop from one-way communication to more interactive or dialogical forms, such as chats (UNICTTF, 2001b). While the UNICTTF sought to spur interaction on the website by creating discussion forums for each of the Working Groups, these never produced more than a few scattered remarks and short exchanges. These discussion forums were later deleted altogether, and interactivity via the website disappeared as an important priority of the UNICTTF.

Primarily, the UNICTTF website was used to post documents and publications, announce upcoming and past events, and provide links to other relevant activities and publications. Looking at the usage statistics, traffic on the website increased considerably every time the UNICTTF held a Global Forum, indicating that these events both created the need for factual information and heightened awareness of the existence of the body. The members of the UNICTTF used the closed, password-protected section of the website primarily for information sharing and to download documents for meetings and the like. In between physical meetings, most communication with the secretariat and between members took place via a mailing list, while the Bureau primarily relied on webcasts (Interview, APC Member of UNICTTF 2003; Interview, Irish Government Member of UNICTTF 2003; Interview, UNICTTF Technology Associate 2004; Interview, TfDev Member of UNICTTF 2004). The UNICTTF also spent a considerable amount of its resources on other types of external communication, particularly in the shape of book-type publications documenting its activities. During its four years of existence, the body published a 12-volume book series documenting its own activities, parts of the WSIS process (Drake 2005b; Stauffacher and Kleinwächter 2005) and other relevant aspects of ICT and development, such as the potential of e-commerce (Wunsch-Vincent and McIntosh 2005), the link between ICTs and peace (Stauffacher, Drake et al. 2005), and information kiosks (Badshah, Khan et al. 2004) and village phones in the poorest parts of the world (Keogh and Wood 2005).

During WGIG consultations, members, particularly those of the IG Caucus, launched the idea that the Internet should play a central role in the management and activities of the group. Unlike in UNICTTF, there was no elaborate communication strategy, but a website and a password-protected mailing list and work space were created. The original idea was that the WGIG website should host a number of online consultations in between meetings, but these were never held. Still, the website and the mailing list played very important roles in the work of WGIG, and were used heavily throughout the process. Over the nine months that the group worked actively, members recount having received more than 3000 emails (Drake 2005a; IG-Caucus 2004–05). The website was used not only to publish the papers and drafts produced by the group, but also as a place for stakeholders to comment. Around each meeting, a large number of documents, together with comments, were uploaded to the website, and throughout the process, the Chairman stressed that papers produced by the WGIG should not be read alone, but continuously related to the comments received in response to them.

Some of WGIG's meetings were recorded and made available for download afterwards. These webcasts were proposed and initiated by a WGIG member from the IG Caucus, and carried out by a small team from an Italian free software project. In later meetings, webcasts were first supplemented, and later replaced by real-time transcriptions, which were projected onto a screen during meetings, and later made available on the website.

While WGIG stressed the importance of transparency and sought to make it possible to participate at a distance, there was also a need to manage the external communication. One of the key arguments for having some closed meetings was that many members would be very cautious when speaking if they knew everything would be made public (Interview, WGIG Executive Coordinator 2005). Government participants in particular stressed that they 'came to brainstorm' (Interview, WGIG Executive Coordinator 2005) and could only do so if meetings were closed to outsiders. According to one member, 'The real problem is that some governmental WGIG members will basically not talk freely in open meetings, because they fear consequences at home if they say something that is not exactly the official view of their government' (IG-Caucus 2004–05). Thus, in order to allow members to speak freely in closed meetings, WGIG members decided to follow the so-called 'Chatham House Rule', which implied that if someone wanted to report on discussions in the closed meetings of the group, they would do so without mentioning the name of the speaker. While some civil society members of WGIG would send reports to the IG Caucus mailing list via email from inside the closed meetings, all members refrained from attributing quotes to individuals (IG-Caucus 2004–05). The potential of ICTs to blur the boundaries between an open and a closed meeting nonetheless inhibited the willingness of some government members in particular to brainstorm and speak freely in the group (Interview, WGIG Executive Coordinator, 2005).

The UNICTTF produced very detailed summaries of meetings and Global Forums, but in most cases, the names of speakers were also omitted. According to the secretariat, this practice evolved because it was impossible to have all speakers review, comment on and accept summaries, a problem which raised the issue of authority. In the words of the UNICTTF Deputy Executive Coordinator (Interview 2004): 'If you do not send [summaries out] for comments, whose authority is the summary issue? Is it the copy writer or the secretary of the Task Force? The Chairman?' The decision to produce non-attributed summaries was presented as a response to a very concrete administrative problem, but it also had the effect of allowing participants to speak more freely. The practice also made it difficult for outsiders to get a sense of possible patterns in the positions of members, with the consequence that arguments, rather than speakers, took centre stage. By foregrounding statements, rather than their origin and source, this practice takes attention away from power differences that could potentially make one statement carry more weight than another. This, in turn, directs our attention to one of the goals of multi-stakeholder arrangements, namely to create spaces for dialogue and deliberation where differences with regards to position and resources can be bracketed off.

Although ICTs did not form the communicative backbone of the two forums, both used the Internet and other ICTs as part of their communication and management strategies and daily operations. Such online platforms are often heralded as central to democratization and novel forms of governance (Cammaerts 2008) because they afford openness, participation and access (Hutchby 2001). But in practice, even hybrid forums focusing on the potential of digital technologies for social and political transformation make strategic choices about the amount and type of information they are willing to make public. None of the closed meetings were webcast, and allowing members to speak freely often weighed more heavily than openness to the broader group of stakeholders. Thus, the strategies and the actual use of ICTs do not play a defining role, neither for the level of openness, nor for the communication approaches or management practices employed. This limited role played by ICTs in the two forums is striking in the light of the global governance and network literature, where the use of ICTs is cited as a key characteristic of, as well as an engine for, new forms of governance, horizontal communication and networked organizations (Bach and Stark 2002; Barney 2000; Brühl and Rittberger 2001; Castells 1996). In the two UN forums, the Internet was used as an add-on or a way to document activities, not as a space where full disclosure or new activities could take place.

FACILITATING DIALOGUE

While the two forums clearly had different goals and mandates, they shared an interest in keeping a distance from the political conflicts and well-worn trenches that mark most UN negotiations (Interview, SIDA Member of UNICTTF 2005). To position themselves as novel spaces for stakeholder dialogues it was important for UNICTTF and WGIG to stress that they did not carry out projects, negotiate agreements or make decisions of any sort. In the case of the UNICTTF, the body also refrained from presenting actual positions or recommendations, although its summaries from meetings clearly foregrounded some questions and concerns at the expense of others. WGIG's mandate was to produce a report, but in order to get the process started the group had to postpone the most contentious discussions until the very end. It is thus a common feature that the two forums sought to facilitate interactions rather than develop policy positions, and to focus on areas of possible consensus rather than disagreement. Thus, we see how facilitation is central to the (fragile) authority of hybrid forums. As noted by Barnett and Finnemore (2005: 175) 'The power of international organizations, and bureaucracies generally, thus lies with their ability to present themselves as impersonal and neutral – as not exercising power but instead serving others.' Although different from traditional organizations, hybrid forums also strive for authority and legitimacy, and do so by offering opportunities for dialogue. The two forums sought to address their matters of concern in ways that would not create tensions among members and broader groups of stakeholders, and would not demand that members actually agreed on a common position. According to the Deputy Executive Coordinator, the UNICTTF as a whole did not have a position on policy questions pertaining to the Internet, just as its purpose was not to make demands. Although it was described as a policy advocacy body by its initiators, it primarily sought to create a platform where different positions and ideas could be aired and discussed. For instance, on the question of Internet governance, the expected outcome of the activities in the Task Force was described in this manner:

> the Task Force doesn't have a ready recipe [. . .] We don't know actually what the ideal situation is. Probably it's going to be different for different situations and different cases, in different countries, and different regions, and different moments of history. What is important is that all of these issues and problems are addressed in a meaningful way, in a participatory manner, in a democratic manner. And this is where the Task Force can actually do something to help bring this about [. . .] There is no future in demands. You can't formulate any kind of demands unless you create an environment in which these demands would be – in the least – in the interest of all stakeholders. Nothing is going to happen; nothing is going to move. You cannot demand that the private sector establishes universal connectivity and universal service for everyone [. . .] It's no point demanding [. . .] and the Task Force just provides a platform, a forum for addressing all these issues. (Interview, UNICTTF Deputy Executive Coordinator 2004)

This way of working gives insights into the role and goal of the UNICTTF, in particular that it did not advocate policy positions, provide solutions or put forward proposals for action. The previous chapter showed how this character as a non-operational body was more or less forced upon the UNICTTF during the worldwide consultations and that it moved some distance from the original vision of its initiators. At the time this was seen as a reduction in the importance and potential impact of the project. But in its later activities this non-operational character actually worked as a way to attract and build ties with particular groups of stakeholders. In a consultancy report on the governance of the UNICTTF, written on a pro bono basis by the vice-chairman, it was stressed that its non-operational character paved the way for the UNICTTF to function as a creator of synergy and cooperation, because it thereby posed no threat to other actors in the field. By refraining from carrying out projects, allocating funds and pushing for implementation, the UNICTTF could emerge as an 'honest broker', rather than a competitor (Abu-Ghazaleh 2002: 11). Clearly, hybrid forums use such features to engage and connect social worlds, and to carve out novel political spaces.

When it comes to WGIG, its non-operational character was specified from the outset by the WSIS Declaration and Plan of Action. Here, and particularly during the consultations and later meetings, it was stressed again and again that WGIG was a forum for dialogue, not a place to negotiate. Its work – the report – should guide negotiations, but neither be a negotiated document nor constitute the language to be negotiated at the Tunis phase of the summit. Stressing that WGIG should not negotiate was used as a way to invite governments in particular, but also other members, to consider and reflect on issues and positions whose discussion would normally need authorization from home. While this approach was described as successful by some WGIG members (IG-Caucus 2004–05) and the Executive Coordinator (Interview 2005), we have also seen that to some, the very creation of WGIG signalled that the issue of Internet governance had moved dangerously close to a degree of institutionalization and formalization that could prove fatal both for the future dialogue about such policies and for the future of the Internet as such. We return to these discussions in the next chapter.

ORGANIZATION AND ENROLMENT

To sum up, hybrid forums can facilitate collaboration and communication without consensus by stressing their roles as forums for dialogue, their distance to formal negotiations and the avoidance of hard-and-fast policy positions and well-known conflicts. As pointed out by Sennett (1980: 17–18) we usually associate authority with qualities such as 'assurance, superior judgment, the ability to impose discipline, the capacity to inspire fear'. But this is far from the kind of authority that hybrid forums seek. To make sense of facilitation as a form of power, insights from actor-network theory and governmentality studies are central. Rather than thinking of authority as a quality or resource, such approaches have a relational conception of authority as a 'matter of connecting' (Bang 2003: 15). This implies that we must see power as the effect of actions and events, rather than their cause (Czarniawska and Hernes 2005: 9). If power is the result of linkages and practices, then we can grasp how facilitation of linkages between social worlds can be used to create authority. Along these lines, an important feature of hybrid forums is their ability to empower and activate stakeholders, that is, to govern through the capacities and authority of the stakeholders involved. We return to a discussion of such forms of entangled authority in the conclusion.

This chapter has provided a thorough examination of the organizational features of the two forums and the governmental techniques used to facilitate and manage interactions between staff, members and stakeholders. In spite of their very different trajectories, UNICTTF and WGIG share a number of organizational traits. Both were positioned as new types of UN bodies that are able to draw on the legitimacy and experience of the UN system, particularly the Secretary-General, without having to operate under traditional procedural and bureaucratic constraints. The formal way of ensuring this careful position vis-à-vis the UN system was for both to be created as advisory bodies to the Secretary-General, to keep a distance from UN agencies, and to rely primarily on external funding. Both were structured according to a networking logic (Juris 2008), and sought to connect and engage multiple social worlds as stakeholders. To this end, they stressed that the composition of members should be representative and balanced with regards to sectors, regions and developed and developing countries, and that all members would participate on an equal footing. Still, members had to mobilize administrative and other resources and develop particular skills in order to make an impact on the direction and work of the two forums. Like other similar bodies emerging from within the UN system, such as the Global Compact, the two forums focused their attention on learning and the facilitation of cross-sectoral dialogue, rather than on regulation, negotiations or policymaking. In subtle ways, they were able to leverage these features and position themselves as spaces where dialogue and collaboration without consensus among very different groupings could be achieved. To further facilitate dialogue, they employed governmental techniques such as the Chatham House Rule, and a careful balancing between open and closed meetings. Finally, both relied on ICTs for communication purposes, but carried out most of their work in physical meetings.

This chapter has focused on the moment of enrolment where the positioning, organization and management of multi-stakeholder arrangements move to the fore. By foregrounding the governmental techniques and processes whereby particular social worlds were enrolled and given 'interrelated roles' (Callon 1986: 211), the chapter has shown the strategies and resources involved in the workings of hybrid forums. What remains to be investigated is how hybrid forums act: that is, how they seek to order and stabilize spaces and relations of governance, in this case the global politics of the digital revolution.

5. Shaping the global politics of the digital revolution

Having defined the scope of their projects, enrolled the necessary allies and developed ways of interacting, the two multi-stakeholder arrangements were now ready to act and mobilize on a larger scale. With techniques, rationalities and organizational arrangements in place, attention could now be shifted to the substantive aspects of the global politics of the Internet. In this phase, they not only mobilized more social worlds and refined their ways of working, but also fleshed out and ordered their matters of concern – ICT-for-development and Internet governance – in new ways. As we will see, non-human actors, such as technological features of the Internet and imaginaires about the potential of ICTs, entered these discussions again and again – and made a difference to the shape of the global politics of the Internet. Chapter 2 launched the discussion about the making of governable objects and Chapter 3 showed how hybrid forums enrol valuable allies. But we have yet to see how hybrid forums can mobilize much larger groups of allies and chains of associations (Callon 1986: 215) and facilitate collaborations without consensus that reconfigure more extensive projects. This chapter digs deeper into the shaping of the politics of the Internet as a transnational policy issue and explores how technological, regulatory and political imaginaires interweave in the mobilizing phase of the project.

MOBILIZATION AND THE ORDERING OF OBJECTS

By problematizing the global politics of the Internet in particular ways, and by attracting and enrolling the allies needed for this project to be successful, the two forums paved the way for the next important step, namely to position themselves as the primary forums for such discussions. Drawing on Callon (1986), we can think of this as the moment of mobilization, where the ordering of positions, allies and matters of concern moved centre stage. Whereas the moment of problematization simply outlined 'a series of negotiable hypotheses on identity, relationships and goals of the different actors' (Callon 1986: 211), the later activities in and around the two forums served to delimit and define these questions, shed light on matters of concern, lock the necessary allies in place and clarify the organizational modalities. Positioned as representatives of the many social worlds they had consulted, excluded or enrolled, the two forums now sought to extend their reach. If these large-scale dialogues could be constructed, positioned and perceived as representative microcosms reflecting the concerns and positions of all social worlds, the UNICTTF and WGIG could act as 'the "head[s]" of several populations' (Callon 1986: 216). In the mobilization phase, the global politics of the Internet was constructed and organized in new ways. Rather than providing or proposing policy substance or solutions to political problems in a traditional sense, the UNICTTF and WGIG created platforms for dialogue, learning and knowledge-sharing. Through mobilizations and dialogues both ICT4D and Internet governance were ordered as matters of concern and objects for intervention.

In UN discussions about the socio-political problems and opportunities of the digital revolution, reconfigurations of the linkage between technology, social transformations and regulation figured prominently. To make sense of these we need to capture the ways in which *objects are made governable*. The kind of attention given to objects, discourses and other nonhuman elements in ANT and governmentality studies directs our attention to the ordering of objects of governance. It is, however, only in recent years and at the very margins of the literature on governance and global politics that such insights have been applied in conceptual and empirical work. Important contributions include Kendall (2004) and Barry (2006), both of which treat humans and nonhumans in a symmetrical manner and shed light on the value of ANT for studies of governance, networks and politics. This attention to the constitution of governable objects allows us to address how objects circulate across social worlds and facilitate the forms of collaboration without consensus on which multi-stakeholder processes thrive.

This chapter explores how hybrid forums construct objects as governable and investigates the making of spaces of governance, without seeing them as already defined and fixed 'policy areas'. This approach helps us capture the sense that 'in many cases it is the constitution of these issues as sites of policy which are at stake' (Larner and Walters 2004: 11). As we will see, the making and ordering of Internet governance and ICT-for-development as UN matters of concern involved a myriad of interactions, mobilizations and subtle forms of control. In particular, the chapter shows how ICT-for-development was positioned as a key component of the governance of the digital revolution, and how Internet governance was constructed as a socio-political, integrated, global, cross-sectoral and visible issue area.

MOBILIZING NEW ASSOCIATIONS

If WGIG and UNICTTF were to position themselves as authorities in their respective issue areas and in relation to the global politics of the digital revolution, they needed not only the insights, actors, procedures and goals they had already assembled, but also to mobilize a much larger number of allies. As Callon reminds us, 'to mobilize, as the word indicates, is to render entities mobile which were not so beforehand' (Callon 1986: 210). All along, the mobilization of stakeholders had been central to the formation and work of UNICTTF and WGIG, but the two hybrid forums had yet to bring the broader social worlds on board, and in the mobilization phase both carried out experiments with multi-stakeholder participation on a much larger scale. At this stage the main question was how many stakeholders – and which ones – they could engage in the attempts at shaping the global politics of the digital revolution.

Establishing Internet governance and ICT-for-development as matters of concern for a much larger group of actors involved a range of meetings and publications. In both cases, large meetings with stakeholders were used to position the two forums as important platforms for discussions about the global politics of the digital revolution. These meetings, forums and consultations are central to the fourth moment of translation – what we may term 'mobilization' – where the two forums sought to increase, facilitate and shape multi-stakeholder dialogues about ICT-for-development and Internet regulation, and, importantly, position these as representative of key discussions about the global politics of the digital revolution. These activities relied on the forms and norms of multi-stakeholder participation already developed in the two hybrid forums, but at this point they were used to mobilize new social worlds and extend the length and breadth of the assemblage. The exploration of the workings and effects of mobilization contributes to the understanding of the organization of multi-stakeholder processes, the consequences for the political spaces under construction and the power of associations.

From their inception, both WGIG and UNICTTF aspired to build their work on principles such as networking, outreach and participation. As previous chapters have shown, this ambition was realized in various forms, such as meetings, workshops, reports, working papers, books and online interactions. At this point, the two hybrid forums sought to position themselves as important platforms for dialogue between stakeholders.

The most significant activities involved in this effort were some so-called Global Forums[8] arranged by the UNICTTF to address different dimensions of the ICT4D issue, and WGIG's Open Consultations, which were designed to address the work of the group and questions about Internet governance.

ORGANIZING MOBILIZATIONS

To mobilize, or 'render entities mobile' (Callon 1986: 216), hybrid forums seek ways to attract social worlds through organizational and procedural innovations, and what the STS literature has referred to as 'boundary objects'. In the original formulation by Star and Griesemer, boundary objects are described as fluid entities that facilitate interaction, associations and translations. They:

> are both plastic enough to adapt to local needs and the constraints of the several parties employing them, yet robust enough to maintain a common identity across sites [. . .] They have different meanings in different social worlds but their structure is common enough to more than one world to make them recognizable, a means of translation. The creation and management of boundary objects is a key process in developing and maintaining coherence across intersecting social worlds. (Star and Griesemer 1989: 393)

In research on boundary objects, this term is used to refer to widely different things, from relatively concrete objects like specimens in a museum (Star and Griesemer 1989) and 'human embryos' (Williams et al. 2008), to more abstract concepts like 'models' (Carlile 2002) and 'reputation' (Power 2007). Star and Griesemer show how the specimens in a museum are interpreted differently by scientists, collectors, administrators and curators, and how the circulation of such constructions of objects facilitates interactions between these social worlds present in the museum (Star and Griesemer 1989). If we want to capture how hybrid forums mobilize social worlds and shape objects of governance, such insights attune us to the possibility that cooperation does not require consensus. In hybrid forums, there is no need for agreement, and heterogeneous actors collaborate without having to accept compromises, develop a common project or change their goals. Boundary objects facilitate such forms of 'collaboration without consensus' and are central to the making and consolidation of multi-stakeholder processes. But boundary objects only facilitate mobilization when they are combined with organizational infrastructures and procedures. The following section shows how the two hybrid forums developed their governmental techniques and organized their mobilization phases.

The most important meetings held by UNICTTF focused on 'Internet governance' (New York, March 2004), an 'enabling environment for ICT4D' (Berlin, November 2004) and 'ICTs and education' (Dublin, April 2005). As with other activities undertaken by the Task Force, the purpose of the forums was not to negotiate a final document or produce policy recommendations. According to members and staff of the UNICTTF, the goal was simply to create a 'platform for dialogue', an open forum where stakeholders could voice their opinions, engage in dialogue, and, hopefully, develop a mutual understanding about how to proceed (Interview, UNICTTF Acting Executive Coordinator 2004; Interview, UNICTTF Deputy Executive Coordinator 2004; Interview, TfDev Member of UNICTTF 2004). The Global Forums consisted of plenary sessions addressing the overall theme of the meeting and break-out sessions focusing on more specialized aspects. The break-out sessions allowed for more interactive discussions and provided opportunities for participants to get to know each other.

In the case of WGIG, the mobilization of stakeholders revolved around four large meetings held at the UN headquarters in Geneva. The WGIG consultations were used for multiple purposes, one of which was to improve the transparency of the process, so that WGIG's work would 'not be a surprise' to the broader groups of stakeholders concerned with Internet governance (Interview, WGIG Executive Director 2005). They also provided an opportunity to follow, comment on, and shape the work of the group, and they made it possible for the different groups and actors involved to become acquainted with each other. These consultations attracted many of the stakeholders involved in Internet governance, and the meetings constitute important pillars in the body's attempts to position itself as an important platform for discussions about the question of global Internet governance. Access to these meetings was restricted to WSIS-accredited entities and UN badge holders, and this clearly narrowed down the number and types of participants considerably. At the outset, most participants were diplomats from the different UN missions in Geneva, but over time, many other groups also took part (Jensen 2005; WGIG 2004–05).

In many ways the UNICTTF forums and the WGIG consultations resembled traditional UN meetings. For instance, the first UNICTTF Global Forum was held in the UN headquarters in New York and even though not everyone wore the black suits or ethnic apparel favoured by UN diplomats and delegations, the format of the meeting did not signal that a novel forum for dialogue was under construction. Most UN conference halls have rows of tables and chairs oriented towards an elevated table or stage where the main speakers are placed. The tables in front are reserved for missions and delegations of member states and representatives from international organizations. These are equipped with microphones, headphones for translations and signs on the table indicating names and country or organization. These signs can be taken out of their slots and are often used to indicate that someone wants to speak. On this particular day, however, new signs had been made. Next to India sat Hewlett-Packard, and many of the signs simply bore the names of UN ICT Task Force members, with no mention of their organizational affiliation. In the conference room where the first Global Forum was held, there were also a number of rows at the far end of the room, where those who did not have a UN sign and a delegation to join were seated. At later Global Forums, members of the UNICTTF and prominent representatives from government, business and international organizations were seated at the front of the room, and all others at the back. Clearly, this made it easier for some participants to catch the attention of the moderator and chairman than others, and during sessions some participants would walk to the front of the room to make sure they were put on the list of speakers.

WGIG's consultations also resembled other UN meetings. Participants were seated at tables in concentric circles in a big wood-panelled room with translation services and single-ear headphones. People would speak on their mobile phones in the room, step out and enter again, and talk to others quietly inside the room. Seated at the table at the centre of the room, the chairman and the executive coordinator of WGIG would present the focus of the meetings and moderate discussions. Most interventions from the floor lasted a couple of minutes, were prepared in advance and they rarely related directly to each other. But as the meetings got started, participants would also make shorter interventions and address the same issues.

Although the point of these meetings was to spur and engage in dialogue, UNICTTF meetings in particular often took the shape of presentations and panel discussions with little room for more spontaneous forms of interaction. Over time, however, some small organizational adjustments and experiments were made to amend this. For instance, at the Global Forum on education, held in Ireland, the Irish government member of UNICTTF asked participants to 'make it a dialogue, not presentations' because 'most people come here for the networking, dialogue, to be active, and not to listen to presentations'. And for the first time in the context of a Global Forum, participants were invited not only to 'pool knowledge and spread views', but also to 'challenge' and react to what they 'do not accept' and 'ask tough questions' (these quotations and those below are taken from notes from meetings). While this signalled an interest in moving beyond broad statements and abstract principles on which disagreement was unlikely, the format of the Global Forums nonetheless tended to eschew controversial issues and open disagreement. When critical questions arose, they were rarely taken up. For instance, at the forum on education, Jeffrey Sachs, then head of the UN Millennium Project,[9] gave a speech which in many ways questioned the founding principle of the Task Force: that private investment and entrepreneurship could solve the problems of development and poverty. While the UNICTTF was founded on the idea that market-based approaches should drive development efforts, Sachs stressed that large and consistent public investments were necessary:

> Don't expect markets to rush in to make these investments. These are public goods and these governments are not credit-worthy because they are impoverished [. . .] Do not look for micro-finance to carry Africa, especially rural Africa, out of extreme poverty – if there is no water, electricity, roads, public health, basic education – it is getting the order wrong. Build the basic infrastructure, which will provide a base for all that goes on in the real economy. (Sachs, in Bracey and Culver 2005: 24)

This call for public, as opposed to private, market-based or partnership-based investment approaches certainly went against the grain of UNICTTF thinking, where market expansion, entrepreneurship and partnerships between public and private actors were central and often repeated proposals. Furthermore, the idea of self-empowerment, so central to the approach to development advocated by the UNICTTF, was also repudiated by Sachs, who said about poor people that 'we should not make them customers, but give them medicine'. After giving his speech, Sachs was quickly escorted out of the room and into a waiting car. The plenary session was ended by the Irish government member of UNICTTF, who apologized that 'unfortunately, there is no time for questions' and, pointing to the directors of the UNICTTF, said that 'these guys here will lynch me' (Secretary-General, DCMNR, Government of Ireland, 2005). While Sachs's tight schedule could have been the reason for this abrupt ending to his talk, the ensuing silence was striking. The official summary from the meeting did not mention Sachs's critical remarks, but simply noted that Sachs 'provided a stark review of progress on the achievement of the Millennium Development Goals (MDGs) and highlighted the need for donor governments to meet the aid obligations to which they have committed themselves. The role of ICT in increasing the likelihood for success in attaining the goals by 2015 was highlighted' (UNICTTF summary, 17 May 2005). As this incident shows, hybrid forums guard their boundary objects – such as the vision of ICTs as a solution to poverty – and rely on organizational arrangements and discursive framings to strengthen mobilization.

While controversies and disagreements were pushed into the background, another feature of UNICTTF interactions was put front and centre: all sessions at Global Forums were divided by what were consistently referred to as 'networking breaks' and 'working lunches'. While most other UN meetings have similarly long breaks, their function is rarely specified. As the chairman noted at one of the meetings, these breaks were 'very important' moments in which to 'get business done' (Chairman, Global Forum on Enabling Environment). With the UNICTTF, the function of such breaks was made visible, and they thereby gained a status as important: they constituted moments where a different – but seemingly equally important – type of work could be carried out. In this respect, the networking breaks can be seen as mundane and low-level expressions of the wider orientation of the UNICTTF towards building linkages and sharing knowledge. Thus, networking breaks may be seen as part and parcel of the particular approach to the making of politics that takes place in hybrid forums.

SHAPING THE GLOBAL POLITICS OF THE INTERNET

So far the focus has been on the organizational infrastructure and governmental techniques at work in the two hybrid forums, but we now turn to the substantive discussions and outcomes of these more extensive multi-stakeholder dialogues, that is, how they ordered and shaped the global politics of the digital revolution. The remaining part of this chapter focuses on the ordering and circulation of ICT-for-development and Internet governance as 'boundary objects', and explores how the activities in the mobilization phase had significant consequences not only for the shape of these issue areas, but also for the consolidation of multi-stakeholder participation.

Ordering ICT4D

The vision that ICTs can propel and contribute to development efforts is one pillar in the construction of the global politics of the digital revolution, and as we will see, the Global Forums held by the UNICTTF sought to connect this vision to a range of other concerns and to mobilize new allies.

As a result of the multiple translations that the project had undergone, the UNICTTF had a sense of the kinds of problems it could engage with, and the kind of allies on which it could rely. The Global Forums and related activities initiated by UNICTTF sought to shape the politics of the digital revolution by fleshing out the ways in which concerns about development, such as those expressed in the Millennium Development Goals, intersect with existing and potential uses and policies surrounding the Internet and other digital technologies. The three Global Forums held by the UNICTTF addressed different aspects of this intersection of ICTs and development and brought together between two and three hundred participants, including high-level government officials, heads of international organizations, private sector leaders, a diverse group of civil society members and a number of academics and experts. Although focused, as we have seen, on Internet governance, an enabling environment and education, each forum gave particular attention to the question of barriers to ICT-driven development.

Like others in the field of ICT-for-development, the UNICTTF posited access as the most important starting point, and concerns about the availability of ICTs – whether perceived in terms of cables, knowledge, skills or connection costs – figured prominently in the activities of the body. But in the UNICTTF access was not addressed by focusing on how more cables could be laid down, on the unwillingness of traditional donor countries to invest in ICT projects, or on whether African villages actually had the electricity needed to make use of Internet access. Rather, the UNICTTF activities revolved around positioning market forces, partnerships and regulatory reforms as the principal solutions to the problems associated with the digital divide. These many discussions and presentations ordered ICT-for-development as a matter of financing, regulating, partnering and building capacities. In the following, we look at how participants at the UNICTTF Global Forums took part in constituting ICT4D around these four features. Taken together, these facets of the boundary object at work offer important insights into the shape and direction that the UNICTTF sought to give the global politics of the digital revolution in the mobilization phase.

Market Stretching

Discussions about financing mechanisms for ICT4D had deadlocked negotiations in the Geneva round of the WSIS negotiations, with some developing countries asking for more aid from developed countries and more resources for infrastructure expansion and other activities. The result of the negotiations in the first part of the WSIS summit was the decision that a Task Force on Financial Mechanisms should be created to assess existing financing mechanisms and investigate possible new approaches to funding (WSIS 2003). So the question of how to fund development activities in the area of ICTs was left unsettled in WSIS, but picked up the UNICTTF. In the three Global Forums and the other activities of the forum, one key discussion was how to create infrastructure and affordable access in those parts of the world where it is not profitable for companies to offer such services. Particularly the Global Forum on an Enabling Environment, held in the impressive white buildings of the Foreign Office in Berlin in November 2004, sought to contribute to these discussions. While the focus of this Global Forum was broader than that of the task force on financing, the meeting was clearly intended to feed into the same process. Keeping in line with its non-operational mandate and lack of financial resources, the Global Forum did not seek proposals on how more computers, cables and connections could be made available in developing countries. Rather, participants were invited to focus on deregulation, tax incentives and other ways of spurring investment and market development, and the resulting discussions revolved around novel ways of creating access and infrastructure.

But as it turned out participants had very different views on the idea of market forces as the solution to development problems. While no one challenged the importance of expanding ICT infrastructure via market incentives, some were uncomfortable with the concept of a 'market-driven' approach and preferred a 'market-friendly' (Interview, TfDev Member of UNICTTF 2004) or 'market-stretching' approach (Interview, SIDA Member of UNICTTF 2005). For instance, what was termed a 'creative middle approach' could combine 'market-driven' and 'indirect market building approaches' with 'donor-driven' and 'direct financing approaches' (Minister, Special ICT Adviser, SIDA, Sweden). Many participants stressed the potential of combining different approaches to financing, such as coupling 'old mechanisms of financing' with new ones, such as 'diaspora funding' and corporate social responsibility (CSR)-oriented initiatives (Secretary and ICT Adviser, Samoan Government National ICT Committee). This speaker pointed out that there was no need to spend more money than at present, but rather to 'use them in smarter ways'. To others, in the context of development, ICTs function as 'multiplication, not subtraction', make it possible to go beyond 'either/or questions' (Adviser, Global ICT Department, World Bank) and make it possible that 'all development goals can be pursued at the same time' (Minister, Ministry of Higher Education, Science and Technology, Mozambique). In support of the argument that there was no need for new resources, one speaker compared the current situation in the ICT domain with the emergence of the telephone system, and explained that as both technologies are 'sources of revenue' they grow by themselves (Coordinator of the Cuban Commission of E-Commerce, Ministry of Informatics and Communications, Cuba).

Other participants suggested that the solution should not be 'money or plans, but partnerships and action' (Minister for Innovation and Technology, Italy). In line with this, it was also stressed that public-private partnerships could be a possible solution, although to 'keep motivation up' it would be necessary to transform 'the idea of industry as donor' into 'industry as partner' (Economic Affairs Officer, ECommerce Branch, UNCTAD). Another participant pointed out how her organization had already developed such collaborations, by saying 'we partner with Nokia in business, and we partner with Nokia in development' (President, Ayala Foundation, Inc., Philippines).

Some suggested a yet more widespread reliance on traditional forms of investment, such as 'overseas direct aid' and donor agencies. According to one, donor money had moved from the ICT sector to other areas such as health and sanitation, particularly because of the impact of the World Summit on Sustainable Development held in 2002 (Adviser, Global ICT Department, World Bank). To this, the chairman replied that he was 'surprised, and not pleasantly so' to hear that ICTs were no longer a donor priority, and that hopefully WSIS would bring the momentum back (Chairman, UNICTTF).

As we have seen, the Global Forums and other activities undertaken by the UNICCTF sought to shape discussions about ICT4D by pointing to investment barriers and proposing new ways of expanding markets and infrastructures. While these were marked by a strong belief in the ability of market forces to solve development problems, many participants also offered alternative perspectives and suggestions.

An Enabling Policy Environment

In the majority of UNICTTF discussions taking place in the mobilization phase, the question of how to develop better and cheaper access intersected with concerns about regulation and policy frameworks in the area of ICTs. As we have seen, the impact of regulation on infrastructure, access and private sector investments had been a topic for discussion in the UNICTTF since its inception, and was one of the four 'priority tracks' on which its members chose to focus. In the so-called Business Plan it was argued that governments should facilitate 'competition by opening markets, eliminating any barriers to competition and encouraging investments in communications infrastructure, and [establish] an appropriate regulatory authority' (UNICTTF 2004a: 5). Along these lines, the main role of governments should be the facilitation of market expansion through deregulation. But rather than talking about deregulation as such, these issues were addressed under the less controversial heading of an 'enabling environment'. Still, the idea was that to harness the potential benefits of ICTs for development, the private sector should be offered a policy environment that would encourage them to build ICT infrastructure and provide low-cost access, particularly in the poorest parts of the world. For instance, at the Global Forum on Internet Governance held in the UN headquarters in New York to discuss the organizational format and mandate of the proposed working group on Internet governance, some participants stressed that regulatory arrangements have consequences for the availability of ICTs because they may encourage or discourage innovation and private sector investments (Deputy Asst. Director-General for Communication and Information, Representative of UNESCO; Chief Technical Officer, Interworking Labs). The argument that an enabling regulatory environment is central to ICT-driven development catered directly to corporate pressure for deregulation expressed during consultations with business in the interessement phase (Chapter 2). But the interactions at the Global Forums showed that participants held different views on the idea of regulatory incentives as a solution to development problems.

The Global Forum on an Enabling Environment was opened by the chairman of the UNICTTF, who highlighted the aptness of holding a meeting on the issue of an enabling environment in Berlin, as this city has 'a history of breaking down walls' (Chairman, UNICTTF). In line with the focus on an enabling environment, some participants argued that market-friendly policies would encourage foreign direct investment and encourage the private sector to build new markets and develop its services and products (Ambassador, United States Department of State; Member of the Corporate Executive Committee, Siemens AG). Others challenged the idea of deregulation as the only remedy, and stressed that unless such measures had 'a long-term perspective', what was meant to be enabling could in fact end up being 'damaging' instead (Professor of International Relations, Syracuse University). Some also stressed that regulatory 'incentives are not enough' and that for change to occur, business would have to show 'corporate social responsibility' and 'go beyond the focus on profits' (Acting Executive Director UNICTTF, DESA), and, as an 'enabling environment means that companies make money', they should 'spend more resources on corporate social responsibility' (Secretary, Ministry of Information Technology, Pakistan). The call for corporate social responsibility was also supported by another speaker, who stressed the importance of projects such as the Global Compact (Representative of Deutsche Telekom).

To others, however, the remedy was neither a market-friendly, liberalized regulatory system, nor more corporate social responsibility, but rather the collection of global taxes that could be used to build infrastructure, to lower access costs and to strengthen capacity-building in developing countries (Mayor of Geneva; Executive Director, ITeM Third World Institute, Congo). The issue of taxation, such as the Tobin tax, spurred a number of interventions, and even some very rare applause from the floor. In his concluding remarks, the chairman of the UNICTTF stated that 'it is my personal belief that like personal taxes, we need global taxes. If we have a global society, we have not internalized it before we accept global taxes also.' The call for global taxation was, however, directly rejected by two speakers, one of whom stressed that taxes 'will make prices go up' and that 'liberalization' and an 'open market' approach would be the only viable solution (Senior Vice-President, NOKIA Group). The US government representative pointed out that his government is 'committed to economic development' and 'spends millions of dollars' on helping developing countries, but that taxation would be 'the wrong way to go' and would 'work against the goals of WSIS' (Ambassador, United States Department of State).

These discussions about the intersection of regulation and ICT4D tied in closely with direction given to the Task Force by business in the early phase of the project. But the interactions with the broader groups of stakeholders did not establish any sort of consensus on deregulation as the key to development. The discursive struggles over the meaning and implications of the idea of an enabling environment show not only the diversity of positions, but also how hybrid forums facilitate associations across social worlds through the circulation and stabilization of attractive and flexible boundary objects.

Education and Capacity-Building

The third Global Forum explored the relationship between ICTs, development and education. Held at a hotel in Dublin, this meeting started from the idea that education is not only a fundamental human right, as spelled out in the Universal Declaration of Human Rights and the International Human Rights Covenants, but is also central to social change in general and development in particular. Despite this, more than 155 million children worldwide do not attend school.

In line with the other activities of the UNICTTF, the forum took the role of ICTs as its focal point. The forum was opened by the UNICTTF member from the Irish government, who was then also vice-chairman of the UNICTTF. He asked participants to ponder the question: 'who are the heroes of today?' and, as his own response, introduced 12-year-old Patrick Dempsey to the meeting. In a pre-planned exchange with a woman sitting in the audience, Patrick explained how the local computer clubhouse had affected his life, which would 'be boring without it' and how the facilities allowed him to make films and Flash animations and to program Lego robots. When asked if there was anything he would like to tell participants at the forum, the boy asked them to build 'more club houses in the poor parts of countries'. Against this backdrop, the host urged participants to keep in mind that 'our task is to explain to others that ICTs are important for the Millennium Development Goals' (Secretary-General, DCMNR, Government of Ireland). Over the following days, participants brought out the different facets of ICT and education, in particular the ties to gender, rights, community, development, capacity-building, partnerships and so on. They discussed how ICTs and education can not only 'transform societies and individuals', but also have far-reaching consequences for other dimensions of development such as 'political engagement' (Under-Secretary-General for Economic and Social Affairs and Chairman of the UNICTTF; Acting Executive Director of the UNICTTF; Representative of Assistant Director-General, UNESCO), 'health' (Acting Executive Director of the UNICTTF; Under-Secretary-General for Economic and Social Affairs and Chairman, UNICTTF) and 'gender' (Capacity Building Manager, Computer for Schools Kenya; Assistant Director-General, UNESCO). Other participants explored questions such as whether teachers or students should be the main targets of education efforts, how education intersects with broader development concerns and how corporate citizenship and private sector involvement may be encouraged to spur development.

It was suggested that education should not just be about schools feeding children facts and information for a finite number of years, but about equipping them with the skills needed in order to continue learning throughout their lives (Minister and Special ICT Adviser, SIDA, Sweden). Along these lines, others stressed the need to 'shift learning processes from teaching to self-directed learning – from one-time to life-long learning' (Assistant Director-General, UNESCO), and 'away from didactic approaches, towards problem-solving, "learning to learn", and independent thinking' (Chairman, ICT in Education, Ministry of Education, Ghana). ICTs were presented as an important aspect of this concern with life-long self-learning, empowerment and capacity-building (Senior Vice-President, Public Communications, SAP AG, Germany). Likewise, a number of participants stressed the importance of combining ICTs with human capacities, and argued that education is about 'individuals and their capacities, not only technology' (Program Manager, Global Teenager Project; Executive Director, Omar Dengo Foundation, Costa Rica), about 'basic literacy skills, not technology' and therefore, giving 'computers to schools is only the first step' (Capacity Building Manager, Computer for Schools, Kenya). But while capacities, and not only computers, were identified as central to education in developing countries, ICTs were seen as ways to help poor people find new ways to learn, produce and think (Representative of Intel).

As with other UNICTTF activities, the Global Forum had an a priori focus on the need for a greater focus on ICTs in education. Participants were encouraged to discuss ways in which this project might be realized, rather than to investigate whether ICTs ought to be the main focus in education efforts in the first place. If the relationship between ICTs and other education efforts were considered from a development perspective, as did Sachs in his speech at the forum (see above), priorities would be different, and ICTs would not necessarily be at the centre. To Sachs, efforts to develop infrastructure should take the shape of 'practical interventions' and 'concrete plans', and he urged participants to 'help, connect, supply' rather than 'talk about how important ICTs are'. From his perspective, infrastructure is only one aspect of development efforts, which should also focus on people's most basic needs, such as health, education and family planning, and give attention to environmental dimensions, such as soil, water and the preservation of eco-systems. For many of the developing countries consulted in the early phases of the process to create the UNICTTF, this focus on discussing new ideas and sharing best practices could be seen as an indication that the initiative would do little to solve the pressing and tangible problems they faced. But according to the subsequent press release, UNICTTF and its forums were not just talking shops: 'The conference did not focus exclusively on rhetoric, rather there were numerous plenary sessions where all participants were invited to contribute so that clarity and tangible next steps could be found for the role that ICT can play in education' (GeSCI 2005). From a developing country perspective, as well as the one presented by Sachs, the distinction between 'rhetoric' and a 'plenary session' – in terms of tangible outcomes – may be murky. Even if hybrid forums primarily seek to spur dialogue, they value whatever decisions and degrees of consensus they identify and consider these to be tangible and satisfactory outcomes.

Synergy through Partnering

Despite the variety of substantive discussions at UNICTTF Global Forums, participation and collaboration were constantly stressed as key to ICT-for-development projects. Not only were meetings framed as invitations to engage in 'cooperation, not conflict' and the need to 'break down walls', but ideals about cooperation also underpinned many of the proposed solutions to the wealth of obstacles to ICT-driven development. Some talked about better ‘international cooperation’ (Acting Director General for Economy and Sustainable Development, German Foreign Office), some stressed that cooperation should take place both during policy development and during implementation phases (Secretary and ICT Adviser, Samoan National ICT Committee), others focused primarily on ‘policy dialogue’ (Under-Secretary-General, United Nations Department of Economic and Social Affairs), and many pointed to the importance of partnering in concrete projects on the ground. Participation and collaboration were discussed using terms such as ‘multi-stakeholder’ and ‘multi-sector’ collaborations (Secretary and ICT Adviser, Samoan National ICT Committee), ‘public-private partnerships’ (Secretary-General, DCMNR, Government of Ireland; Minister for Innovation and Technology, Italy; Executive Chairman, Network Computer Systems, Ghana), ‘collaborative and unified efforts’ (CEO, BITKOM, German Association for Information Technology, Telecommunications and New Media), and simply, ‘inclusion and consultation’ (Secretary and ICT Adviser, Samoan National ICT Committee). While the meanings of these terms were not always spelled out, one speaker argued that ‘we need to move from public-private partnerships to multi-sector collaborations’, as only the latter include civil society (Secretary and ICT Adviser, Samoan National ICT Committee). Participation was presented as the solution to problems such as the lack of investment and financing in the area of ICTs and development (Minister, Special ICT Adviser, SIDA, Sweden), the lack of attention to the ‘e-element’ among governments (Representative of EFAC), the ‘challenging nature’ of the WSIS process (Senior Vice-President, NOKIA Group), and the tendency for developing countries to see developed countries as ‘philanthropists’ rather than ‘partners’ (Executive Chairman, Network Computer Systems, Ghana). Seeking an example of best practice at the end of the second Global Forum, the chairman directly asked the representative of Mozambique to explain what this developing country, which is ‘far from a knowledge society’ (Chairman, UNICTTF) can do to achieve the MDGs, foster development and set new goals for itself. To this, she replied that Mozambique works in ‘multi-stakeholder partnerships on all levels, not only in the creation of policies, but also in the implementation phase’, and takes an ‘integrated approach to technology’, combining different ICTs, in order to ‘connect and inform’ people, ‘stimulate thinking and innovation’ and encourage a sense of ‘global citizenship’. She also stressed the importance of the UNICTTF – with the words ‘we need these people’ as ‘leaders and champions’ – and of meetings such as the Global Forum, which encourage ‘common commitment’ towards the financing of development via ICTs and allow ‘multi-stakeholder participation and networks' to emerge (Minister, Ministry of Higher Education, Science and Technology, Mozambique).

To further stress the importance of collaborations and dialogue, one of the four break-out sessions at the third Global Forum was devoted to the role of partnerships in development efforts. The PowerPoint presentation welcoming participants showed a suggestive equation: $1 + 1 + 1 = 10$?, and in line with this, the presenter argued that 'partnerships are more than the sum of their parts', as they 'maximise complementary strengths'. This session sought to present the necessary components of a successful partnership, such as 'trust', 'commitment', 'strategic approach', 'dialogue', 'communication', 'leadership', 'a winning idea' and 'evaluation of performance' (Executive Director Omar Dengo Foundation, Costa Rica; Special Adviser to the Executive Director, Global Knowledge Partnership, Malaysia). To a few, however, the ideal and practice of multi-stakeholder collaboration was flawed because not everyone can be invited to participate, and even those invited often lacked the opportunities and capacities to participate meaningfully. One speaker criticized the use of civil society as 'tokens' in policy dialogues and multi-stakeholder forums, where one or two civil society representatives may be invited, while 'most are kept out' (Executive Director, Association for Progressive Communications). Finally, one speaker brought up the issue of 'accountability', which he found was brought to the fore by the 'redefinition of public-private' responsibilities (Senior Associate, International Centre for Trade and Sustainable Development).

As we have seen, the UNICTTF meetings identified numerous roads and barriers to the realization of ICT-driven development. These many attempts at ordering ICT-for-development and the global politics of the digital revolution revolved around questions such as financing, regulation and capacity-building. While these three areas came up in most discussions, there was little agreement as to how they might be resolved or weighed against each other. What participants did agree on, however, was that collaboration and dialogue were the way forward. If only governments, the private sector, civil society and other stakeholders would work together, even 'give up old sector labels' and 'take up new roles' (Adviser, Global ICT Department, World Bank), then ICT-for-development could take off. But as we have seen, and will see more of in Chapter 6, there are notable discrepancies between the principled aspirations and practical commitment to collaborating with all stakeholders. As an organizational arrangement in the making, UNICTTF had already experienced the difficulty of finding allies to collaborate with, and as an issue area, ICT4D was in for a new round of ordering.

In the mobilization phase the UNICTTF primarily sought to position itself as the main convener of discussions of ICT4D. Mobilizing old and new allies, these discussions did not result in clear messages or results. Still, the UNICTTF used them as an opportunity to contribute to the construction of ICT4D as a central pillar in the global politics of the digital revolution, and to establish itself as a home for discussions about ICT4D at a time when the G8, the other UN agencies and the broader development community were losing interest in ICTs and the private ICT sector was reconsidering its interest in development efforts. In relation to WSIS, the body took part in bringing development to the centre of discussions about the global information society. Furthermore, as a result of the UNICTTF activities, the shape of ICT4D was reconfigured: it was constructed as a matter of entrepreneurship and knowledge-sharing, not aid and infrastructure; as voluntary and beneficial for business, not a demand; and as dependent on the willingness of policymakers to create regulatory environments that will encourage business to build new markets. While ICT-for-development was not invented by the UNICTTF, the attempts to shape this issue area offer important insights into the ability of hybrid forums to mobilize stakeholders. Taken together, the UNICTTF activities relating to barriers – such as the lack of education, enabling policy environments and financial resources – amount to a wide-reaching attempt at positioning ICT-for-development as a key dimension of the global politics of the digital revolution. We now turn to the activities and discussions which contributed to the consolidation and circulation of Internet governance as a 'boundary object' facilitating 'collaborations without consensus'.

ORDERING INTERNET GOVERNANCE

In the mobilization work of the Working Group on Internet Governance, the ordering of substantive aspects of Internet governance took place in closed meetings of the working group, in consultations with stakeholders and in the final report. The four Open Consultations in particular, held in conjunction with WGIG meetings, shaped and ordered the object of governance in important ways. These meetings often addressed the same issues as in the closed meetings, and gave outsiders a sense of what was going on in the group. Prior to each Open Consultation, lists of issues and documents discussed in the group were made available online, and it was possible to make comments before and after meetings, as well as during consultations. Furthermore, WGIG consultations were accessible to broader groups through various experiments with webcasts, transcriptions of all interventions and other types of online documentation. But WGIG was also challenged from many sides in the mobilization phase.

For instance, many well-established Internet governance bodies, such as ICANN, ISOC and IETF, still questioned the very idea of WGIG and found many of the regulatory aspects of Internet governance that it identified as important to be either technical, uncontroversial or non-political. The phrase 'if it ain't broke, don't fix it' came up repeatedly in these meetings and in the corridors and online spaces where the need for WGIG was debated. Some government delegations, such as those from Syria, China and Algeria, felt excluded and expressed suspicion about the activities taking place behind closed doors at WGIG meetings (consultation 1, WGIG 2004–05). Other, less vocal groups, such as the Patent, Copyright and Trademark Caucus created during WSIS, still felt that their concerns about intellectual property rights and open source software were not represented adequately and expertly in WGIG. Accordingly, this hybrid forum had to establish its merits and legitimacy in the face of multiple critics.

The Open Consultations attracted many of the social worlds involved in Internet governance, and the report submitted to WSIS played an important role in the construction of this issue area as central to the broader discussions about the 'global information society'. Increasingly, Internet governance is a concern to national governments, international organizations, the business community, technical groups and civil society organizations alike (DeNardis 2009; Drake and Jørgensen 2005; Mueller 2010). This part of the chapter shows how Internet governance was shaped by these activities, and has been ordered in the following manner: this issue area is *socio-political*, not just technical; it is *global*, and not only of concern to a few national governments; it is *cross-sectoral*, involving state and non-state actors; it is *integrated*, rather than being an isolated set of concerns; and it is *visible* as an emergent and important issue in global politics.

In existing accounts of the principles underpinning Internet governance and other types of telecommunications policy, the focus is often on broad, foundational principles such as public interest, diversity, pluralism and universal service (Napoli 2001, 2008) or on historical policy trends such as deregulation and social concerns (Napoli 2001; Siochrú and Girard 2002; Braithwaite and Drahos 2000). These and other specific principles, such as the 'free flow of information', an 'enabling environment', 'human rights', 'freedom of expression', 'transparency', 'accountability', 'democracy and 'inclusion' were also discussed in the context of WGIG. But rather than extending existing approaches to regulation by settling on a particular combination of these, the many discussions ordered Internet governance as a socio-political, global, cross-sectoral, integrated and visible matter of concern in need of novel regulatory and organizational arrangements.

While this ordering is ongoing and in flux, it is worth pondering on the five features of Internet governance mentioned above, particularly because they tell us something about the ability of WGIG to position itself as an 'obligatory passage point' at a crucial stage in the ordering of the global politics of the digital revolution. At this moment of translation when mobilization moved to the fore, WGIG constituted *the* place in the UN where those concerned with Internet governance would get together and exchange views on current and future developments within the field.

Internet Governance as Socio-Political

During the Geneva phase of WSIS, in the UNICTTF forum on Internet governance and in the early discussions in WGIG, technical bodies and expert groups, such as ICANN, ISOC and IETF, argued that many of the issues brought together under the heading of Internet governance were matters of technical coordination rather than concerning governance or politics. For instance, the chairman of ICANN responded to critical inquiries about ICANN's role in Internet governance in the following manner: 'ICANN does not "aspire to address" any Internet governance issues; in effect, it governs the plumbing, not the people. It has a very limited mandate to administer certain (largely technical) aspects of the Internet infrastructure in general and the Domain Name System in particular' (Chairman of ICANN, 1999).

During the WGIG process, such descriptions of the management of the Internet as 'plumbing, not politics' would come up repeatedly, and be used to portray WGIG as unnecessary and the very idea of Internet governance as misguided. Such attempts at ordering the object of governance as a technical matter with no political ramifications constituted a major obstacle to the acceptance of WGIG as a necessary and useful forum – because why fix the plumbing if it is working fine?

One of WGIG's tasks was to come up with a working definition of Internet governance, and this question was also a key concern of those involved. At the outset of the WGIG consultations, many participants invoked a distinction between a broad and a narrow conception of Internet governance. The broad conception included issues such as access, rights, development and gender, while the narrow one posited issues such as root servers, domain names and numbers as the core issues to be dealt with under the heading of Internet governance. As the process unfolded, the list of issues considered relevant to Internet governance grew steadily. By the first WGIG consultation the distinction between broad and narrow Internet governance started to dissolve and gave way to a more complex mapping of the relevant issues and the links between them.

The construction of Internet governance as a socio-political matter of concern implied a very broad and encompassing list of issues that could be addressed under this heading. During its meeting on the day before the first Open Consultation, WGIG created a lengthy list of public policy issues with potential relevance for discussions about Internet governance. This 'Inventory of Public Policy Issues and Priorities' was conceived by members with inspiration from a paper prepared by the then vice-chairman of UNICTTF (Abu-Ghazaleh 2004). The list included 46 issues, ranging from infrastructure and developmental aspects through IPR and cybercrime to technical standards and administration of names and IP addresses.

To the surprise of some participants, the definition was not yet ready by the second consultation, although there were indications that it would be broad and encompassing. By the time of the third consultation, the group had divided its object of governance into four 'clusters of key issues': (1) management and infrastructure issues, such as domain names, IP addresses, and root servers; (2) uses of the Internet, including spam, cybercrime and security; (3) broader issues with relevance to, but not limited to, Internet governance, such as IPR and trade; and (4) developmental issues, such as gender, capacity-building and access. In line with the earlier production of working papers, the group prepared papers on these different clusters and their specific character, current governance arrangements, and ability to live up to the WSIS principles. While the positions of business representatives that WGIG should not be concerned with IPR and ICANN-related issues remained in place, most other participants accepted the broad agenda developed and implied in the division of Internet governance into four equally important clusters.

At the third Open Consultation, discussions about governance arrangements and the distribution of roles and responsibilities addressed whether some aspects of the Internet should be considered relevant to questions about global governance and others should be excluded because of their overly technical nature. For instance, South Africa asked WGIG to engage with the question of what constitutes a public policy issue, because some issues would be described as technical by the private sector and as public policy issues by governments, and this conflict 'is the crux of the matter'. And to one member of WGIG, 'the main reason for the establishment of this group and for asking the Secretary-General of the UN to establish this group is because the issue is not technical. I think the issue is political' (Director-General Department of Communications, South Africa).

The work to define and scope Internet governance was a central aspect of the WGIG process. If plumbing could be constructed as politics, the call for institutional reforms would carry more weight. But if the goal was a better understanding of the need for better infrastructure and access in the developing world or more coordination among stakeholders, WGIG's task was a very different one. At the first consultation, these choices were up for grabs, and participants used Internet governance to argue for everything from an international treaty to maintaining the status quo.

In between the first and the second consultation, WGIG's members produced working papers on the many different public policy issues on the inventory list prepared for the first consultation. The goal of these papers, which were written by two members and circulated to all members for comment, was not to prioritize the different issues, but to describe the state of affairs. The production of working papers was presented by the secretariat as a matter of 'fact-finding' (Interview, WGIG Executive Coordinator 2005). Both internally in the group and in relation to the external stakeholders, this strategy was used as a way to move the WGIG process beyond the conflicts which stalled the WSIS negotiations and to postpone conflicts over issues such as institutional reforms, public policy priorities and the distribution of roles and responsibilities. In this manner, WGIG sought to provide an alternative to traditional UN negotiations. But describing these activities as a simple matter of fact-finding turned out to be more difficult than expected. As noted in Chapter 4, the working paper on intellectual property rights created so much tension in the group that the secretariat decided not to publish it, and only post a summary on the website. But even this two-and-a-half page document spurred a number of reactions, for instance from the International Federation of Film Producers' Association and the International Video Federation, both of which – in written contributions – called the paper 'misleading' and asked for it to be revised so as not to do 'damage to the credibility and neutrality of the WSIS Internet Governance process'. During the consultation, a similar organization argued that the summary of the paper was 'not fair' because it did not mention 'existing treaties' (Representative of Motion Picture Association, Brussels). The publication of this short summary not only mobilized a new stakeholder – the film industry – but the reactions to the summary also show how the distinction between facts and politics was difficult to sustain. At the second consultation the conflicts over IPR dealt not only with the question of whether the paper treated the issue in a balanced manner or not, but also with the question of whether IPR belonged on the WGIG agenda at all. To some, there was 'no need to worry too much about' IPR, since this could be discussed at WIPO and 'will not be overlooked in WSIS' (Representative of India). In an attempt to move discussions forward, the chairman stated that there was 'a certain amount of consensus, I sense, that there are a whole class of policy matters which are salient to the Internet, but where the real locus of action is elsewhere, somewhere else in the international system', such as IPR. Stressing that 'we are not going to be able to solve the IPR issue in the Internet governance system', which 'is a much larger problem', he then suggested that this matter should not be addressed by WGIG. But members of the IG Caucus challenged this immediately, and argued that the chairman had 'called a consensus on taking IPR off the agenda', even though no such consensus had emerged during discussions. From the perspective of civil society, WGIG was the appropriate, even the only, place for discussions about the 'intersection between IPR and Internet governance' to take place, because WGIG is the 'only agency that can take a holistic view, and is not encumbered by bureaucratic special interests' (members of IG Caucus). This situation sheds light on the efforts made to scope the work of WGIG, and how the forum dealt with controversies, long-standing conflicts and attempts to narrow down the agenda.

After the second consultation, WGIG left the 'fact-finding phase' and entered the 'analytical phase', where proposals moved to the fore. Still, there was little agreement as to how the different issues should be weighed, and a number of discussions about whether they could or should be dealt with in the same way. For instance, both India and Syria argued that the Internet should be posited as part of telecommunications, because it is not 'very different from all the other media'. According to the Indian government, 'there is nothing uniquely different about the Internet that dictates a completely different oversight mechanism at the global level compared to various other fields of human activity' (Representative of India), and this implied both that Internet governance should be regulated by governments and that the issue would fall under the authority of ITU (Representatives of Syria and India). These descriptions of the Internet were, however, opposed by a member of WGIG who stressed that the Internet 'cannot be reduced to telecommunications', and therefore should operate in a 'regime' of its own (Director of Computing Academic Services, Universidad Autonoma de Mexico and Vice-Chairman of the Board of ICANN, Mexico). Thus, considerations about the nature of the object of governance become directly tied to choices about the type, location and control of possible, future governance arrangements. Widespread agreement that the Internet is different from other ICTs served as a way to avoid a situation in which Internet governance could be subsumed under the heading of telecommunications, which would pave the way for more intergovernmental control, for instance under the auspices of ITU.

The final report, produced by WGIG in the three days following the fourth consultation, defined Internet governance as 'the development and application by Governments, the private sector and civil society, in their respective roles, of shared principles, norms, rules, decision-making procedures, and programs that shape the evolution and use of the Internet' (WGIG 2005: 4). According to the group, this definition was broad enough to encompass all the activities identified as relevant to and part of Internet governance, and descriptive, not prescriptive, with regards to policy proposals and institutional arrangements. The report discussed the four clusters of issues – management and infrastructure issues, uses of the Internet, IPR and trade and development – and pointed to 13 issues of particular importance and in need of solutions. These were: administration of the root zone files and system; interconnection costs; Internet stability, security and cybercrime; spam; meaningful participation in global policy development; capacity-building; allocation of domain names; IP addressing; IPR; freedom of expression; data protection and privacy rights; consumer rights; and multilingualism (WGIG 2005: 5–8). But the report also stressed the need to discuss and flesh out the 'higher-level, cross-cutting' or 'horizontal' issues relevant to Internet governance, such as 'the economic and social aspects of the Internet' and the 'capacity of existing Internet governance arrangements to address governance issues in a coordinated manner'. Finally, the document recounted the importance of addressing the WSIS principles for Internet governance, namely that it should be 'multilateral, transparent and democratic, with the full involvement of Governments, the private sector, civil society and international organizations' (WGIG 2005: 12). Captured in a document, an important ordering of the global politics of the internet was in place. But the process of ordering Internet governance shows how important and controversial the definition of objects of governance can be: how the elements, scope and ramifications of a definition are about the assembly and making of a governable object (Gottweis 2003), and how definitions and fact-finding activities call the very activity of governing into question (Dean 1999). But out of these many interactions taking place during the mobilization phase, Internet governance was constructed as a *socio-political*, not just a technical, matter of concern.

Internet Governance as Integrated

A main outcome of WGIG was that it established Internet governance as an issue that could not be limited to the technical management of core Internet resources, names and numbers, but included development, rights, gender and other broad socio-political concerns. But the process did not just expand the list of potentially relevant issues, it also sought to establish the need to approach these in an integrated manner. As pointed out by Drake and Jørgensen (2005), a wide range of policy issues are collated under the heading of the global information society. This term is used to cover:

> telecommunications and media regulation, digital convergence, radio frequency spectrum management, technical standardization, Internet governance, trade in networked goods and services, competition policy, intellectual property, privacy and consumer protection, freedom of speech and censorship, network security and cybercrime, cultural and linguistic integrity, development and the global digital divide, e-commerce, e-government, e-education, e-everything. (Drake and Jørgensen 2005: 2)

In a similar fashion, Internet governance emerged as an umbrella term for an increasingly wide range of issues related to the Internet and its global spread. As we will see in Chapter 6, many very broad discussions about development and the global information society are increasingly transformed into questions of Internet governance. In this section, we see how the integration of multiple, scattered issues into a common matter of concern was central to the mobilization phase in WGIG.

During WGIG consultations some participants proposed that the issues to be addressed should span 'root servers', 'domain names and IP addresses', as well as newer issues such as 'spam' and 'security', 'multilingualism' and 'internationalized domain names' (Government Representatives of Brazil, Switzerland, China; Representative of UNESCO). Some argued that the WGIG process should be used for a closer inspection of access-oriented aspects, such as 'international interconnection costs' (Government Representative of Brazil, Representative of ITU), while others stressed broader principles, such as 'freedom of expression' (Representative of UNESCO) and 'human rights' (Government Representative of El Salvador). A member of WGIG presented IPR as 'the biggest problem right now' (IG Caucus member and President and CTO, Dynamic Fun, Italy), but according to the delegation from the Swiss government, the fact that this issue had not been resolved at WSIS I made it 'too complex' to address in the context of WGIG, suggesting that it should 'be addressed in the appropriate framework', that is, WIPO. Another participant stressed the importance of seeing Internet governance as closely tied to the attempt to reach the MDGs (Director, MacLean Consulting, Canada), and one stressed the importance of addressing 'content and the issue of the "digital divide"', rather than only the domain name system (President, NTIC Commission, Dakar Regional Council, Senegal).

What WGIG's members did, however, was to organize the rapidly growing list of potentially relevant issues into a model of Internet governance that divided the issues into vertical and horizontal dimensions. While the vertical dimension concerned the substantive issues to be addressed, such as domain names, use, security and access issues, the horizontal dimensions contained criteria proposed by WSIS, such as transparency, multilateralism and democracy, that could be used to evaluate existing institutional arrangements. During consultations, this approach was not explained in a very detailed manner, but participants were asked to comment on whether WGIG should only focus on vertical dimensions, because the evaluation of existing governance arrangements would likely result in the same kind of conflict which brought about WGIG. This request for input, however, spurred no reaction from participants. But as the following will show, the proposed ordering of Internet governance came to play a crucial role in the work of WGIG by structuring many of the following discussions. Also, we see how classifying and sorting (Bowker and Star 1999) are important forms of ordering that – in this case – integrate seemingly disparate discussions into one entity.

In the multi-stakeholder dialogues facilitated by WGIG, technical, social and policy issues related to Internet governance were treated not only as potentially relevant, but also as tied to one another. Domain names, root servers, spam, content, human rights, multilingualism, access, funding, education, IPR, trade and other facets came together under the heading of Internet governance, but this did not mean that they should all be treated in the same manner, by the same social worlds or in the same place. What WGIG facilitated was an opportunity to discuss these facets of Internet governance in an integrated and comparative manner. Like discussions about the global information society, Internet governance too emerged as an increasingly integrated issue. Both areas are marked by 'a growing tendency to view these issues in a more holistic manner – as elements of a single overarching policy space rather than as a random assortment of disconnected topics that are somehow related to ICT' (Drake and Jørgensen 2005: 2). Thus, 'sorting things out' (Bowker and Star 1999) is a central part of mobilization.

Internet Governance as Global

The work of WGIG also contributed to the positioning of Internet governance as a global issue area, that is, one that cannot be solved by individual nation-states or by groups of Western, developed countries. The entire WSIS process sought to engage all UN member states in discussions about how to shape and benefit from the digital revolution, and the summit offered a rare occasion where national governments, civil society groups, industry and technical associations and international organizations could address this emergent issue. But WGIG contributed in particular to a related, but more specific concern, namely the need to enhance global participation in Internet governance and policy discussions.

In many ways, Internet governance was always transnational. While many areas of what was considered Internet governance in WGIG and WSIS involve nation-states and are subject to the principle of national sovereignty, the technical and administrative underpinnings of the Internet involve multiple sites and cross-border flows. What the UN process brought out was a widespread dissatisfaction with US-based Internet governance bodies, particularly ICANN, and the growing demands for global participation in these governance activities. Developing countries in particular, but many EU countries as well, saw WGIG as an opportunity to push for the internationalization of Internet governance (Mayer-Schonberger and Ziewitz 2007), and this question remains central. Particularly to developing countries the main problem was that 'the Internet is governed by American law and managed by an American business', and they therefore proposed that these activities should be transferred to 'an international organization which can guarantee [. . .] all their rights' (Government Representative of Syria), such as the ITU. As the oldest such intergovernmental institution ITU's procedures and activities are well-established and well-known to developing countries. Especially in comparison to the specialized Internet governance organizations, such as ISOC, IETF and ICANN, the ITU would allow less technically savvy government representatives to participate in discussions about Internet governance in the same ways as they would approach the regulation of other media technologies. Along these lines, the Chinese government argued that 'Internet public policy-making shall and should fall within the authoritative and legal entities under the UN framework', as a way to solve the problem that 'the position and role of governments have been ignored, even in the danger of being marginalized, rather than being strengthened. This, however, goes against the basic principles of Internet, namely, openness, fairness, and democracy and freedom.' Interweaving political and technical lines of reasoning, such statements not only point to the dissatisfaction with existing arrangements, but also show how the object to be governed continuously entered and shaped discussions. Finally, even the EU, which until then had not been explicit about its position, stated that there was a need for 'the internationalization of the management of the Internet's core resources', and this call was also supported by the Norwegian government.

However, as the WGIG process unfolded, many of these participants acknowledged that the cross-sectoral dialogue facilitated by WGIG was also worthwhile. Increasingly, multi-stakeholder dialogues are recognized as acceptable alternatives to the kinds of intergovernmental negotiations national governments are most familiar with. Nonetheless, countries like China, Syria and India continued to complain about the dominance of the US in this area, and called for more direct attempts at changing the landscape and division of labour in Internet governance. On the other hand, many technical Internet groups resisted intergovernmental approaches and the governmentalization of Internet governance spurred by these UN processes and argued that such forms of traditional regulation would halt the innovation and creativity that made the Internet possible. With time, and in particular at the fourth Open Consultation and after the Tunis phase of WSIS, many of these groups acknowledged the value of a forum for discussion about the gamut of Internet-related governance issues. In particular, this acceptance among technical groups must be understood in the light of the realization that the discussions were non-binding and without formal ties to the existing or future governance arrangements pertaining to the Internet. The mobilization of these groups was only possible if they could be certain that these dialogues would not add to or interfere with existing forms of governance, particularly relating to the infrastructure, names and numbers and other core resources of the Internet.

Thus, in line with the making of Internet governance as a socio-political, integrated issue area, these discussions also sought to order this matter of concern as *global*. And similarly, the reliance on multi-stakeholder processes facilitated the construction of Internet governance as a global issue area, as well as the growing acceptance of the need for Internet governance to involve participation on a global scale. The lack of agreement about institutional arrangements and anchorage contributed to the realization that such discussions can take place in hybrid forums such as WGIG without affecting more everyday forms of steering directly or negatively. Unlike at the outset of WGIG's activities, the later discussions were less about developing a new regulatory framework or finding a home for Internet governance and more about identifying and promoting a set of principles to shape interactions relating to existing and future forms of governance in this area. The positioning of Internet governance as a global issue area ties in closely with the next outcome of dialogues in WGIG, namely the insistence on cross-sectoral participation.

Internet Governance as Cross-Sectoral

One of the driving forces behind the WSIS process and the main stumbling block in the Geneva negotiations was the dissatisfaction with the unilateral approach to Internet governance pursued by the US government and ICANN. But as we saw in the problematization phase, there was also a growing wish for a space where broader information society issues could be discussed by all stakeholders, and during the mobilization phase this goal became central again. As the first UN-based multi-stakeholder forum addressing Internet governance, WGIG catered to these concerns. By bringing together stakeholders and inviting them to reflect on the future shape of substantive and procedural aspects of Internet governance, this forum contributed to the reconfiguration of this matter of concern as *cross-sectoral*. Looking back, the increasing and almost unanimous acceptance of multi-stakeholder arrangements as the most appropriate mechanism for the UN discussions about Internet governance constitutes one of the most significant outcomes of WGIG's activities. Historically, and in the vast majority of the UN system, member states are the primary actors – taking the floor, deciding the rules of procedure and making policy proposals. So, particularly in an intergovernmental context, participation by non-state actors – on equal footing – breaks with established practice. But the growing acceptance of this approach did not take the shape of a clear-cut break. Rather, it emerged through the kinds of associations, negotiations and translations that this book seeks to capture. Discussions and controversies over the practical and political consequences of multi-stakeholder arrangements recurred throughout the WGIG process. So rather than simply addressing the substantive questions, participants spent a lot of time discussing multi-stakeholder participation as a principle for WGIG processes, as well as for existing and future Internet governance arrangements, and the relationship between 'intergovernmentalism' and 'multi-stakeholderism' as forms of governance and decision-making.

The attempt to transpose the multi-stakeholder format to the world outside WGIG constitutes a key element of the mobilization phase. Would this hybrid forum be able to position itself as a model for other forms of multi-stakeholder governance and create a wider acceptance for this principle and approach in Internet governance? From the perspective of many of the civil society groups involved, WGIG constituted best practice when it came to involving non-state actors in UN affairs. But there was also resistance to the project. Many governments saw multi-stakeholder participation as a threat to national sovereignty, representative democracy and intergovernmental decision-making, because processes such as WGIG gave too much voice and influence to civil society, and paved the way for (illegitimate) forms of 'governance by enthusiasm' (Jensen 2005). At the same time, business and the existing Internet governance institutions saw no need for new governance arrangements – multi-stakeholder or not. Still, the quest for a wider acceptance of multi-stakeholder participation went on.

The primary focus of WGIG's third Open Consultation was to discuss a preliminary report and four clusters of public policy issues identified as relevant by the group. But discussions also revolved around procedural and institutional aspects of Internet governance, and revisited the long-standing conflict between those seeking a UN-based intergovernmental mechanism and those wishing for the maintenance of the status quo when it came to institutional anchorage. But over time, the simple demand for a transfer of authority from existing organizations to an intergovernmental UN mechanism gave way to discussions about 'better coordination' and new 'multi-cross-organizational, multi-stakeholder governance processes' (Director, MacLean Consulting, Canada), where the appropriate roles for the different stakeholders could be defined. This WGIG member asked 'those who see the need for an intergovernmental mechanism involving other stakeholders' to consider and explain whether they imagined 'a single answer, one sort of arrangement, one organization that would cover everything that the Internet touches' or 'differentiated mechanisms in each of the areas' identified by WGIG in its classification of the four clusters. To another participant, the way the papers presented the distribution of roles and responsibilities as different from cluster to cluster made 'a strong argument against a single institution handling all the different issues'. From this perspective, the clustering of issues pointed to the need for different mechanisms, and an 'interoperation mechanism' to coordinate these (Director of WSIS Online.net, member of IG Caucus). Similarly, one member suggested that there was a need for a 'broad multi-stakeholder body', with 'no decision-making capacity', where all the issues relevant to Internet governance could be discussed and recommendations made (IG Caucus member, Lecturer, University of Aarhus, Denmark/Germany). This structuring of potential issues to be addressed under the heading of Internet governance ordered discussions about the kinds of governance arrangements that could be developed. The EU proposed that 'a new cooperation model is needed in order to confer the WSIS principles regarding the crucial role of all actors within Internet governance'. In this 'new public/private cooperation model' governments should play a role in 'issues of public policy' but not in the 'day to day operations' of the Internet (Representative of EU). Another participant found that a number of interventions focused on 'shared responsibilities', and stressed that one of the most important contributions of WGIG was to map the different actors and their respective contributions to the development and governance of the Internet (Director of WSIS Online.net, member of IG Caucus). This need for coordination and division of labour among the actors involved was also stressed by the representative of Switzerland who said that depending on which one of the many dimensions of Internet governance one looked upon, the roles and responsibilities of the different stakeholders could vary, so that 'when we have public policy issues, governments prefer to be more involved in comparison with other perhaps more technical matters which are not within their sphere of expertise'.

These returns to the distinction between technical and political aspects of the Internet spurred a discussion about the need for 'making clear the distinction' between technical and public policy matters (Representative of Internet Governance Task Force, Japan).

The norms and forms of multi-stakeholder approaches were also explored towards the end of the second day of WGIG's second consultation. Here, the debate over the kind of governance to which the Internet should be subject led to a debate about the meaning of the words 'multilateral' and 'multi-stakeholder'. It was spurred by an IG Caucus intervention, which expressed support for the 'multi-stakeholder approach' of WGIG and stressed the 'fundamental difference between multilateral and multi-stakeholder processes', saying that it:

> should be remembered at all times that the WSIS Declaration of Principles states that Internet governance decision-making should be pursued on multi-stakeholder basis, reflecting the full participation of civil society. The governments who agreed to this new international norm should now take positive steps to ensure its full implementation. As a first step, conformity with this norm should be carefully assessed with respect to existing arrangements at the intergovernmental level, like the ITU, OECD, and WIPO, and also private sector arrangements like ICANN, and to any new emerging mechanisms. (GLOCOM representative and Caucus coordinator, on behalf of IG Caucus)

This attempt to establish multi-stakeholder participation as a 'new international norm' to which all existing and future Internet governance arrangements should adhere spurred a lengthy discussion. In fact, the WSIS Declaration contained no mention of the term multi-stakeholder, using instead the term multilateral. This led the WGIG chairman to ask 'particularly governments' to react to the distinction between multilateral and multi-stakeholder, stressing that so far 'the word we have been using is multilateral', particularly in the WSIS context. India responded that in a UN-led process, the concept of multilateral has a 'very specific meaning' and should be used to 'refer to the intergovernmental process, rather than an issue which has many different types of participants, which is probably better referred to using the multistakeholder concept'. But according to the IG Caucus, it was 'not enough to just look at one word' in the Declaration of Principles, because right after the word multilateral comes the sentence 'with the full participation of governments, the private sector, civil society and international organizations', so the sentence 'reads like multi-stakeholder' (IG Caucus coordinator, Executive Research Fellow, GLOCOM, Japan). A member of WGIG, who took part in the Geneva negotiations on the very paragraph under scrutiny, explained that in the context of the Declaration, 'multilateral' should not be understood in 'its traditional sense as inter-governmentalism', and was rather used as a way to 'avoid a situation where something is managed, coordinated or governed single-handedly'. So rather than the opposite of multi-stakeholder, multilateral was used 'against the concept of unilateralism'. It is worth noting that the paragraph in question is more concerned with the narrower aspects of Internet governance, and not the broad range of issues that WGIG addressed, which may explain why, during the WSIS negotiations, multilateral came to be used as a somewhat concealed attack on perceived unilateral US control, with the technical, infrastructure and core resources of the Internet overseen by ICANN. The member then clarified that the words 'full participation, etc.' were added as an 'interpretation of multilateral', precisely so that multilateral would not be understood as referring to an intergovernmental process (Counsellor, Permanent Mission of the Islamic Republic of Iran to the UN Office in Geneva). What he did not explain, however, was the reason for not choosing the term multi-stakeholder instead.

These attempts at capturing the exact meanings of, and relationships between, the terms 'multi-stakeholder' and 'multilateral' are important not only because they give insight into the importance of the specific language in documents such as the Declaration, and the context-specific, seemingly haphazard way the language in the Declaration came about, but because it shows the fluidity of such terms and the problems that arise when this fluidity is sought to be stabilized. Before this discussion took place, 'multi-stakeholder' covered both developing countries' wish for an intergovernmental process and civil society's hopes for a governance arrangement where all stakeholders could work on equal footing.

With the ground-clearing discussed here, an ordering of the boundaries between multilaterialism and multi-stakeholder approaches took place. Thus, participants were asked not to conflate 'multilateral' and 'multi-stakeholder', since 'those two terms are in fact mutually exclusive because if a governance mechanism is multi-stakeholder, our definition of it is that it contains representatives on equal footing from civil society and the private sector and governments. On the other hand, an intergovernmental governing mechanism is one of governments only.' Based on this distinction, participants were invited to make clear which one of the two models they would find 'acceptable' (Executive Director, World Information Technology and Services Alliance, USA). Clearly, these interventions sought to limit the ambiguity and invite participants to be more specific about their preferences. But such ordering was rarely stable for long. As an example, Syria argued that 'we are not asking for an international organization that will be solely intergovernmental, and we already have the ITU', where 'as far as standardization goes, the private sector is also involved, as [are] international operators'. By positing ITU as a multi-stakeholder mechanism, 'which is open to all' (Government Representative of Syria), and not an intergovernmental one, Syria tried again to dissolve the distinction between the terms. Similarly, India argued that in asking for an intergovernmental organization, it was 'certainly not excluding the role for all stakeholders', just as the Publishers' Association presented WIPO as 'animated by a desire to achieve a balance between stakeholders and users'. But, clearly, the definition of multi-stakeholder offered by the WGIG member would not fit the ITU – an international organization, formed by governments, where the highest decision-making body, the Plenipotentiary Conference, only allows governments to vote, although the private sector is consulted and involved in many other activities (Siochrú and Girard 2002: 47). Neither would it fit WIPO, which according to its critics is dominated by the interests of rights holders and has, for instance, 'denied accreditation to some NGOs of intellectual property users' (IG Caucus Member, Chairman of ICANN At-large Advisory Committee, President and CTO, Dynamic Fun, Italy). Also ICANN presented itself and its 'current evolution' to 'be consistent' with the importance that the WGIG papers assigned to 'a successful multi-stakeholder model' with ample attention to 'community input' (General Manager, Global Partnerships, ICANN). The attempts at establishing multi-stakeholder participation as a baseline principle of Internet governance sought to move beyond intergovernmental mechanisms which consult with non-state actors, but do not involve them on equal footing with states, and beyond purely private sector mechanisms that do not allow for meaningful participation by governments, civil society groups and other stakeholders. Even if contested, momentary and fluid, these attempts at fixing the meaning of multi-stakeholder also shaped interventions by countries like China, which said that a new 'intergovernmental organization under the UN', should 'be multi … should have multiple participation' and that 'governments of sovereign states representing common interests of stakeholders, including private sector, civil society and mass Internet users should play a leading role in global Internet policy-making, while private sector, civil society and other stakeholders will continue to play an active and promoting role in this process'. The wording is important because it sought to fuse 'intergovernmental' with 'multiple participation', while still arguing that governments represent all stakeholders and should be in charge of public policymaking. While these discussions paved the way for a widespread acceptance of multi-stakeholder participation as a central – even if somewhat fuzzy – feature of Internet governance, there was still considerable resistance. Obviously, full-fledged multi-stakeholder participation challenges the very foundation of the UN system as an intergovernmental institution where states make collective decisions, and raises questions about the legitimacy of multi-stakeholder arrangements. Participants in the WGIG process discussed these questions at length. One of them argued that 'governments that are elected have public accountability in their countries', while the private sector could be 'one person or a number of people that are accountable to [. . .] shareholders', and that she was 'not sure what the accountability to civil society is', although there 'are some stakeholder accountabilities there'. In order for a new mechanism to be 'legitimate', she argued that it had to be rooted intergovernmentally, preferably in the UN system, as the 'only intergovernmental [. . .] or legitimate mechanism that we know that represents the will of the peoples of the world'. But still, she did not wish to abandon the multi-stakeholder principle, and suggested that maybe – in a reformed UN – 'it is not inconceivable that we would have an intergovernmental structure that is actually multi-stakeholder, within which, then, the different roles would be agreed to' (Director-General, Department of Communications, South Africa). This questioning of the sustainability of the composition of the UN system as a collection of states ties in with the other calls for reforms discussed in Chapter 2.

These discussions show how WGIG members and participants at the Open Consultations grappled with the meaning and implications of different approaches to governance, such as multilateral and multi-stakeholder arrangements, and how the ordering of these terms helped establish multi-stakeholder participation as an increasingly central and accepted procedural principle in the UN-led reconfiguration of Internet governance. Linking questions of legitimacy, the nature of the Internet and multiple social worlds, this norm and form of organization made dialogue and mobilization possible: it was flexible and abstract enough to appeal to most participants, yet solid and concrete enough to be a path worth exploring. Taken together, these discussions contributed significantly to the construction of multi-stakeholder arrangements as central to the global politics of Internet governance.

Internet Governance as Visible

UN conferences have come to be known as well-meaning and laudable initiatives that address – but rarely solve – the major challenges facing the so-called 'international community'. Previous summits have taken up issues such as the environment, development, human rights and gender equality, and while they certainly draw attention to these matters of concern, their tangible political and policy outcomes are difficult to assess. Pondering on this question, Klein provides an institutional analysis of WSIS and argues that such summits provide 'opportunity structures' that may be realized if other factors – such as a suitable topic, jurisdiction, legitimacy and timing – are in place (Klein 2006). However, such analyses still struggle to assess the effects of events like WSIS, and lack methodological tools for establishing causal links between UN summits and changes in world politics. It is not clear what the parameters or success criteria could be, just as it is impossible to isolate UN summits from other driving forces and political developments. Even when UN summits seem to lead to new international institutions, conventions or political watersheds, it is not feasible to see them as the sole cause. As Klein points out, although at times summits produce more concrete results, 'it is in the realm of words that they have perhaps the greatest effect', because they are able to construct and broadly diffuse discourses and visions (Klein 2006: 158). A similarly cautious way of approaching this question is to identify and trace the different ideas which have been launched or nurtured by the UN (Emmerij, Jolly et al. 2001). Such intellectual histories posit ideas as powerful in their own right and seek to capture how they are picked up by others, institutionalized at national and international levels, and brought into use in decisions on future priorities. Other approaches study not the conferences as such, but the preparations for them and the later follow-up activities, as well as the role played by non-state actors, such as the NGOs that sustain and implement visions conceived in UN summits (Schechter 2001). Such analyses arrive at cautious conclusions about impacts and focus instead on the advocacy, contributions and added value of civil society groups in UN conferences. When ITU and other UN agencies take stock of the impact of WSIS, it is also by measuring the amount of input by different stakeholders, the types of policy reforms carried out in national contexts, the current number of cell-phone users in developing countries and other criteria, which say little about either tangible consequences or the relationship between such developments and WSIS (ITU 2008). So while we may only be cautiously optimistic about the long-term tangible impact of UN summits on political decisions and social transformations, they certainly make the issue areas under scrutiny *visible* for a period of time. By drawing thousands of participants to preparatory meetings, national and regional meetings and the actual summits, and by animating press coverage of these activities, UN conferences construct these issue areas as important. This also goes for the two phases of WSIS. The object of this intervention, 'the information society', was constructed as a socio-political opportunity (Kooiman 2003) rather than as a problem (such as global warming, poverty and the like) to be solved, and the agenda was broad, even fuzzy, throughout the process. Nonetheless, the theme appealed to a wide range of actors and provided an opportunity to address central concerns within the UN system, such as development, education and technology transfer.

The growing interest and number of attendants at WGIG's consultations and, more recently, at the Internet Governance Forum's meetings increased the visibility of Internet governance as an important matter of concern in national and international contexts.

ICANN and other existing Internet governance bodies were consistently opposed to the idea of UN activities in this area. But the WSIS process also made their work and position in Internet governance more visible. Early on, for instance, technical groups found that the call for increased legitimacy was caused by the fact that 'people and governments, sometimes, they don't understand the work that we do or they don't even know we exist [. . .] So it's important that there is more education toward United Nations and the governments of the planet to the understanding of the work that we do' (Representative of World Wide Web Consortium, W3C, at the fourth WGIG consultation). As the process unfolded, the work and responsibilities of existing arrangements were made visible to governments, international organizations and the wider public. Furthermore, and unexpectedly, the lack of consensus at the Tunis negotiations in relation to institutional arrangements and concrete regulation and management of Internet core resources can be seen as a stamp of approval on ICANN. Whether more people – and the right people – now know what ICANN does, or care about where the root servers are located and how top-level domain names are allocated is an open question. But certainly, as the sheer number of participants, the analyses in this book and other publications about WSIS show, the summit came to function as a meeting place for a wide range of issues somehow related to the growth of the Internet, development and global governance.

Another tangible way in which WSIS and WGIG made the global politics of the digital revolution visible was through media coverage. Particularly in the Tunis phase of WSIS, Internet governance appeared in the headlines in major international newspapers.[10] While never 'high politics' on the scale of terror, climate change or the financial crisis, the WGIG process and the final negotiations over Internet governance certainly contained enough of the ingredients necessary to make an otherwise opaque and technical issue newsworthy. Most news reports revolved around the sensationalist question of whether the UN and the US were at war over Internet governance, and many of those involved in the final negotiations willingly contributed to this story. In a widely publicized statement, the US negotiator, Ambassador David Gross, added to the fire by saying that the 'United Nations will not be in charge of the Internet. Period' (Gross 2005: n.p.). That the tasks and concerns of WGIG – and the Internet itself for that matter – were much more complex tended to evade these news stories. But the fact that the discussions about Internet governance could be cast as a war between well-known adversaries certainly made the issue more visible in the media landscape, particularly in newspapers, technology-oriented journals and in blogs and other online resources. Furthermore, the growing literature on the global politics of Internet governance (Chadwick 2006; Goldsmith and Wu 2006; DeNardis 2009; Zittrain 2009; Mueller 2002, 2010) clearly contributes to the visibility of this issue area.

To sum up, the WGIG activities contributed to the ordering of Internet governance as a socio-political, integrated, global, cross-sectoral and visible matter of concern. This ordering did not imply traditional negotiations or agreement about substantive or institutional aspects of Internet governance. Rather, the WGIG process created a better understanding of the multiple questions involved in Internet governance and a more nuanced mapping of the existing and potential forms and levels of involvement of the different social worlds. At the same time, the process provided a home for discussions about Internet governance within the UN, and helped pave the way for an organizational and institutional ordering of Internet governance in and around the UN system.

THE POWER OF MOBILIZATION

It is a defining feature of hybrid forums that they facilitate sustained and organized interactions and negotiations between very different social worlds *without asking them to agree*. Multi-stakeholder processes allow for what I have termed 'collaboration without consensus', and 'enable challengers and defenders to substantively collaborate by building a bridge between divergent worlds that allows collaborators to preserve their competing interests' (O'Mahony and Bechky 2008: 426). To understand this feature, which cuts against prevailing conceptions of negotiations and governance based on dichotomies such as conflict versus consensus, we need to capture two important traits of hybrid forums, namely their ability (1) to introduce and circulate shared, but fluid matters of concern and (2) to develop organizational practices that allow social worlds to engage without having to agree. Let us look at these two in turn. To make sense of the ability of hybrid forums to facilitate dialogue between very different social worlds, discussions about objects and the associations they facilitate are valuable. Engaging the concept of 'boundary objects' (Star and Griesemer 1989; Santos and Eisenhardt 2005; O'Mahony and Bechky 2008; Trompette and Vinck 2009), such studies have brought out how objects may be recognized as important by many social worlds and still be interpreted differently. In the words of Stark:

> boundary objects are not objects at the boundary or objects that make boundaries. Instead, they circulate across the boundaries of different social worlds sharing the same territory. To contribute to the work of coordination, boundary objects must be stabilized enough to circulate across sites, yet plastic enough to adapt to the local constraints and needs of the disparate parties deploying them. Robust enough to be recognizable in different settings, boundary objects are recognized by the different communities in distinct ways. (Stark 2009: 194)

This combination of relevance and flexibility means that boundary objects can bring actors together and allow them to maintain their differences. In the two hybrid forums, their matters of concern needed to be robust and concrete enough to appeal to broader groups of stakeholders involved in Internet governance and ICT4D, but plastic and abstract enough to allow these groups to maintain their particular focus and identity. But the mobilization of heterogeneous social worlds cannot only be seen as the result of the creation and management of boundary objects, it is also the outcome of 'methods standardization' (Star and Griesemer 1989: 392). Nonetheless, most studies drawing on discussions about boundary objects tend to ignore the importance of organizational infrastructure. As noted by Trompette and Vinck (2009), most research drawing on insights from ANT has concentrated on the analysis of 'fact stabilization' through boundary objects, at the expense of capturing and conceptualizing the 'work of coordination, alignment mechanisms and translation chains between the different actors and worlds involved' (Trompette and Vinck 2009: e [5]).

Throughout this book, the everyday practices and governmental techniques involved in multi-stakeholder processes have been a key concern, and the ability of hybrid forums to develop organizational and managerial practices that allow for collaboration without consensus is an important feature of multi-stakeholder processes that deserves closer scrutiny. In order for collaboration without consensus to be possible, a set of regularized practices, shared principles and ways of managing work have to be in place and accepted by those involved. In this moment of translation in the UNICTTF and WGIG, these governmental techniques took the shape of a number of meetings, consultations and forums for discussion with a more extensive range of social worlds, in effect mobilizing a much larger group of stakeholders to take part in UN-based discussions about a wealth of issues relating to ICT4D, Internet governance and the politics of the digital revolution more broadly. The Global Forums and Open Consultations utilized many of the techniques developed in the formative phase of the UN ordering of global Internet politics, and used these to engage and mobilize multiple social worlds. But the two hybrid forums also needed to develop these governmental techniques to position themselves as *the* UN hubs for such discussions. Testing the limits of the power of multi-stakeholder dialogue, the mobilization phase involved not only a stabilization of the objects of governance, but also a refinement of the organizational practices making hybrid forums possible. In particular, this moment of translation positioned multi-stakeholder participation as the primary mechanism and principle for the global politics of the Internet. But it is important to note the fragility of such arrangements, and mobilization also involves the question of how the 'representativity of the spokesman is questioned, discussed, negotiated, rejected' (Callon 1986: 219). During the moment of translation explored in this chapter, the two arrangements sought to position themselves as platforms for dialogue between all those involved in ICT4D and Internet governance, but were also met with some resistance. In fact, these two arrangements were transient and fragile, and as we will see in the analysis of the moment of displacement, organizational setups and objects of governance are always under reconstruction in hybrid forums. Thus, the next chapter shows how the global politics of the Internet has given rise to multiple new organizational arrangements with varying degrees of stability and links to the UN system.

6. Displacement as ordering

Ordering is always partial and in-the-making, and all attempts to act on the world must compete with other, equally possible modes of ordering (Kendall and Wickham 2001; Law and Mol 2008). As we have seen in previous chapters, the organization of the global politics of the Internet has in this way been marked by constantly shifting alliances, ongoing organizational experiments and recurring contestations of attempts at ordering. So far, however, we have observed a stabilization and consolidation of organizational techniques, subject positions and issue areas. Focusing on the relationship between stability and transformation in hybrid forums, this chapter will show how ordering also takes the shape of dissidence and instability and will substantiate the somewhat counter-intuitive claim that 'instability and multiplicity actually contributes to the continuity of the program' (Singleton 1998: 86). This concern with instability as a form of ordering ties in with discussions about longevity in STS, and particularly more recent calls for a closer scrutiny of difference, instability and looser networks in what has been termed the post-ANT literature (Law and Singleton 2005). While the emergence of ANT was driven by a discomfort with categories and explanations based on conceptions of order, and sought to pave the way for a sociology of association and ordering (Law 1994; Latour 2005a), much of the work in this tradition actually ended up only focusing on successful stabilizations, or what have been termed 'macro actors' (Czarniawska 2008: 21). But ordering also involves messier and more fluctuating configurations.

This chapter captures the ways in which displacements and radical reconfigurations do not necessarily lead to anarchy or failure, but may contribute to ordering. As pointed out by Bach and Stark (2005: 37) 'forms of social organization trade on the illusion of permanence while constantly renegotiating their relationships; their stability rests in part on their ability for transformation'. In the case of the UNICTTF and WGIG hybrid forums, stabilization through displacement involved a wide range of new experiments with multi-stakeholder processes. For instance, when UN member states, business and civil society groups reconvened for the second part of the World Summit on the Information Society in Tunis in November 2005, the goal was to settle some of the many discussions about the relationship between technology, development and regulation around which the process had come to revolve. At the same time, this event marked a moment of transition for the organizational arrangements developed to address two of the most central themes. With the end of WSIS, questions about ICT-for-development and Internet governance had to be pursued in new organizational settings if they were to remain a UN priority. While this fifth moment of translation is marked by dissidence, dispersion and displacement, it still contributes to the ordering of the global politics of the Internet in important ways, thus giving weight to the argument that organization always involves disorganization (Cooper 1986; Hassard, Kelemen et al. 2007).

Compared to previous chapters, this one zooms out (Nicolini 2009) and seeks to capture how the global politics of the Internet has come to involve an increasing number of organizational arrangements and emergent questions about governance. The chapter focuses on the moment of translation where the stability of the UNICTTF and WGIG was unsettled once again, and gave rise to new organizational arrangements as well as evolving more extensive ties to other forms of multi-stakeholder participation within and beyond the UN system.

THE GLOBAL ALLIANCE

In 2005, the UNICTTF mandate was expiring and a new arrangement to perpetuate the ICT-for-development project was under construction. The majority of those involved in the UNICTTF found it to have been an innovative attempt to engage multiple social worlds in discussions about an issue that was gaining momentum in a number of spheres at the time. By attracting many of the major players in the ICT domain, in particular business, governments and international organizations, the UNICTTF had established itself as an important convener of these discussions and contributed to the WSIS process. In this respect, the body provided a platform for a broad-based and transnational dialogue on ICT4D that had not existed before. But as the analyses have also shown, the body was challenged all along: at the outset because it sought to coordinate and compete with existing UN development agencies; later when it was turned into a non-operational forum for dialogue that some feared would only be a 'talking shop'; and finally because it invited too few civil society people to become members, thus primarily enabling business and governments to voice their concerns.

Seeking a way to continue their work on ICT4D, the directors and members proposed that a UN-based 'Global Alliance on ICT and

Development' (UN-GAID) should be created to replace the UNICTTF after its mandate expired in late 2005. In early discussions about this Global Alliance, some members expressed concerns over the wish to perpetuate activities at all, because they saw the limited life span of UNICTTF as a strength. But DESA went ahead with the plan, and with the decision to establish the Global Alliance and to appoint the former director of the UNICTTF as Executive Coordinator, the Secretary-General confirmed his commitment to keeping ICT4D issues on the UN agenda. In many respects, the process of getting the Global Alliance off the ground resembled the consultations leading up to the creation of the UNICTTF. But at the same time, it is worth noting that the process was considerably more open and inclusive. For example, stakeholders were invited to nominate members in a transparent process that contrasted strongly with the selection of members for the earlier body. Responding to some of its critics, the UNICTTF experimented with a more open and participatory approach when setting up the UN-GAID. In this sense, the creation of the Global Alliance is testament to the emergence of multi-stakeholder participation as an increasingly accepted norm and form of organization and steering.

The consultations about the Global Alliance also enabled the venting of some critical assessments of the approach and accomplishments of the UNICTTF. For example, the Director of APC, who was a member of the Task Force, used the WSIS Plenary mailing list to stress that while she supported the idea of a new body, she also had a number of concerns about problems that had been visible in UNICTTF all along, but that were never addressed. One of her objections was to the idea that business would step in as a major donor in development activities: 'what has to be abandoned is the idea that if we woo the private sector it will invest millions in IC[T4]D. That is simply not how it works. We can influence the private sector, and learn from it, and partner with it, but it is not the magic bullet that so many misguided ICD champions never stop looking for' (Director, APC, 2005). She also questioned the portrayal of such bodies as representative and accountable: 'In fact, can such bodies be accountable at all? Even if civil society participation on the TF should triple or quadruple in size (which it should) can we say that those CSOs [civil society groups] are representative of CSOs globally. I don't think so' (Director, APC, 2005). Finally, she stressed the need for more than one body, arguing that 'to have impact at broader level we need more such bodies, representing a diversity of specialties, political perspectives, languages, regions, etc. etc.', and that this could not be achieved by 'one that sets itself up as the "mother of all multi-stakeholder alliances"' (Director, APC, 2005). Taken together, such critical remarks point to some of the shapes taken by the moment of dissidence, where even the most basic assumptions and practices of UNICTTF were questioned. The UNICTTF initiators still went ahead with the Global Alliance project, but also – as we saw in the formative phase of the earlier body – made sure to exclude critical social worlds, such as APC, who had otherwise been closely involved in the Task Force activities.

The UN-GAID was launched in 2006 as a way to continue discussions about ICT4D and to build ties between these ideas and the Millennium Development Goals. The forum was presented as an 'open and inclusive platform that can broaden the dialogue on innovative ways of harnessing ICT for advancing development' (UN-GAID 2010), and was organized much like the UNICTTF. Many of the people from UNICTTF remained involved as members and employees and the secretariat was located in the same place in the UN headquarters in New York. Instead of a Bureau, the body had a Board composed of 20 members, including government ministers (particularly from developing countries), CEOs and directors of big telecommunications companies such as Intel and Ericsson, and high-level representatives of international organizations and UN agencies, as well as a few NGOs. Much like the UNICTTF Bureau, the Board guided the direction of the UN-GAID. The organization also involved a Strategy Council composed of 74 members from government, international organizations, the private sector and civil society providing advice and outreach in relation to the project. Finally, the body invited a group of close to 150 specialists, practitioners and policymakers to act as 'High-Level Advisers' and created a 'Champions Network' consisting of 43 members working in the field of ICT4D.

In line with some of the other moments of translation, this one involved the mobilization and categorization of new social worlds. In order to achieve its goal, the UN-GAID needed to keep some social worlds on board, exclude others and mobilize new ones. The UN-GAID held its inaugural meeting in Kuala Lumpur in 2006, bringing together more than 500 participants to discuss the focus and organization of the initiative as well as the project of using ICTs to address poverty and education. Continuing the tradition developed in the UNICTTF, in 2008 the body held its first Global Forum in Malaysia, focusing on the topic of 'Access and Connectivity in Asia-Pacific and on Innovative Financing Mechanisms for ICT for Development'. Since then, the body has held multiple Strategy Council meetings, as well as meetings for all members. Furthermore, UN-GAID held Global Forums in Monterrey, Mexico, in 2009 on the topic of 'ICT and Innovation for Education' and in Abu-Dhabi in December 2010 on the topic of 'ICT for MDGs: Moving from Advocacy to Actions'.

While UN-GAID still advocates the ICT4D agenda at the level of policies, principles and the sharing of best practice, recent changes in the orientation of the body show a growing concern with more tangible results and projects. For instance, a press release stressed the 'intention to re-focus the work of the Alliance in 2010 on the paramount objective of fostering effective use of ICT for achieving the Millennium Development Goals' (GAID 2010). Recently, the most visible activity in the UN-GAID has been the creation of a so-called 'e-enabler'. Built much like a database with information about national achievements and best practice, the tool is intended to help not only the UN, but also national governments and business to 'transform the policy and operational environment and accelerate the implementation of MDGs by all stakeholders' (GAID 2010). Other recent initiatives include a 'Declaration on Rights in the Information Age', and attempts to forge stronger and more visible ties to the UN Secretary-General. Notably, in early 2010, the UN-GAID asked the Secretary-General to lead the body. As we have seen, the UNICTTF also operated under the patronage of former UN Secretary-General Kofi Annan, who demonstrated his support for the initiative by opening or otherwise addressing many of the events. According to the first chairman of the UNICTTF, Annan characterized it as 'the most successful task force in UN history' (UNICTTF Chairman 2004, personal note; SIDA member 2005), and in his speech to the Strategic Council in September 2006, he stressed the importance of both the IGF and UN-GAID in attempts to 'translate the vision of a truly global information society into reality' (Annan 2006). Contrasting the Task Force and GAID, he stressed the need to engage and include more participants and welcomed the strategy of the GAID to 'develop a decentralized "network of networks" on a global scale' and the promise to 'turn the spirit of WSIS into action' (Annan 2007; Barrett 2007). The UN-GAID has continued to pursue such close links to the new Secretary-General, Ban Ki-moon, who in February 2010 accepted the invitation to act as an Honorary Chair of the Alliance. While stressing its close relationship to the Secretary-General, the UN-GAID also sought 'administrative, budgetary and thematic autonomy' (UNICTTF 2005), thus continuing the balance between proximity and distance to the UN system that we saw in the case of UNICTTF. This balance between a close affiliation with the Secretary-General and a degree of autonomy also appears to be a distinguishing feature of other UN-based hybrid forums, in particular the Global Compact (Rasche and Kell 2010). While ICT4D relied on high-level support from the UN, the Secretary-General, or other UN leaders such as the Under-Secretary General, rarely participated in the meetings on Internet governance.

Taken together, these attempts at emphasizing the ties to the

MDGs and the Secretary-General are an important facet of the UN-GAID, and show how this hybrid forum has sought to strengthen its legitimacy and sense of direction and purpose. ICT-for-development is still on the agenda in parts of the UN system, among business actors and civil society groups, but elsewhere, it seems that other matters of concern have moved centre stage. For instance, one of the key business actors in the WSIS process, the computer giant Hewlett-Packard, has now replaced its concern with development and the global information society with a new problem in the process of being assembled, ordered and translated – the environment. At the same time, ICT-for-development does not have political support from key players like the US (IGF 2008), and there are also other indications that the global politics of the Internet is moving elsewhere.

NEGOTIATING THE GLOBAL POLITICS OF THE INTERNET

While the UNICTTF was being displaced by a new organizational arrangement, the WSIS process was also coming to an end. The final summit meeting was held in Tunis in November 2005, and brought together almost 20,000 people. The long, straight road from the city centre to the Kram Palexpo conference centre looked as though it had just been built, and the lush, newly planted palms and flowers lining the route were a sharp contrast to the dry, dirty and dusty surroundings. The industrial-looking conference centre housed not only plenary sessions and negotiations in smaller rooms over the final wording of the declaration, but also the so-called 'ICT Village', with product stands and project exhibitions by companies and organizations. While many of those social worlds positioned as stakeholders were still taking part, the event also marked a break with the multi-stakeholder approach. Rather than open-ended panels and consultations, the goal was now to determine the final wording of the agreement, or what is usually referred to as the 'language', and then to celebrate the completion of the WSIS process.

As noted in the previous chapter, the report from WGIG was intended to lay the foundation for more nuanced and productive negotiations about global Internet governance. The 24-page report included a broad definition of Internet governance, discussions of relevant public policy issues, and reflections on the roles and responsibilities of different stakeholders. On the question of institutional arrangements, the report 'identified a vacuum within the context of existing structures, since there is no global multi-stakeholder forum to address Internet-related public policy issues', and argued that there would be 'merit in creating such a space for dialogue among all stakeholders'. This forum should be linked to the UN, allow for participation for all stakeholders 'on equal footing' and should be 'modeled on the WGIG open consultations, supported by a very lightweight structure and guided by a multi-stakeholder coordinating process' (WGIG 2005: 1). The need for this space for dialogue was presented as a WGIG consensus. But with regards to the creation of new institutional arrangements that could replace, oversee and/or coordinate the existing system of governance, the group had not been able to reach consensus, and instead presented four different options, some of which were proposals made by individual WGIG members, and not the outcome of collective work in the group (Jensen 2005). The first option was to create a UN-based Global Internet Council that would be made up of governments and replace ICANN's Governmental Advisory Committee (GAC). A second model was to allow existing organizations to reform themselves, and refrain from creating any new oversight bodies. Third, a non-UN-based International Internet Council could be created to replace ICANN's GAC, as a place where governments could address issues of national interest, with advice from other stakeholders. Finally, it was proposed that a reformed and non-US-based ICANN, a new government-led Global Internet Policy Council and a coordination-oriented, multi-stakeholder Global Internet Governance Forum based in the UN could handle Internet policy governance, oversight and global coordination in a collective manner (WGIG 2005: 12–16). The argument in the report that 'no single Government should have a pre-eminent role in relation to international Internet governance' (WGIG 2005: 12) paved the way for none of these options to leave the unilateral US control over key aspects of Internet governance untouched. Also ICANN would be affected by all four, although the second model only proposed a slight reform of the GAC. Finally, the three other models posited governments as the key authorities in relation to Internet governance, with other stakeholders acting merely as advisers (Afonso 2005).

The final negotiations leading up to the summit in Tunis were the ultimate test of the viability and appeal of these suggestions. And the result of this second attempt at agreeing on a way forward was, if not surprising, at least sobering. The Tunis Commitment was a comprehensive list of the many facets of UN discussions about the global politics of the digital revolution stressing just about everything – from access, the digital divide, diversity, human rights, development, education, public policy, funding and gender equality to the need for cross-sectoral collaboration while respecting the 'key role and responsibilities of governments' (WSIS 2005a). But except for a promise to keep 'focusing on financial mechanisms for bridging the digital divide, on Internet governance and related issues', the central Internet governance controversy was missing from the document. By contrast, inside Palexpo, Internet governance was *the* main topic. It was what most journalists were there to cover, and it was on most participants' lips. In one of the smaller rooms in the temporarily partitioned and noisy conference centre, a mixed group of participants were busy constructing an important object – the language on Internet governance to be contained in another, more action-oriented document, the Tunis Agenda. Crafting such language is a honed skill among diplomats and government representatives and revolves around seemingly endless revisions and rewordings of a piece of text. Beamed onto a screen, the 'language' being negotiated contains first attempts at wordings provided by the chairman, suggestions for changes and new additions in a confusing soup of coloured text, underlining and other attempts to keep track of changes. Participants can simply ask for new words to be added, while agreeing on wordings and deleting words demands consensus among participants. So most of the time, the text gets messier and longer as the day passes, leaving the chairman with the task of preparing a new version that everyone will agree to work on the following day. In the case of Internet governance, the disagreements stalling the Geneva negotiations two years earlier were still visible. What was different was the positioning of these questions. From its position at the margins of the UN process to address the global politics of the digital revolution, Internet governance had moved centre stage. But the composition of the group in the room was also different – unlike in Geneva, non-state actors were not asked to leave the room, instead they could follow the negotiations first hand. Apart from that, the procedures were familiar and the conflicts as fierce as ever. As a result, and in contrast to most UN summits where heads of state simply meet to sign an already agreed-upon document, the final wording for the Tunis documents would not be agreed upon until the last minute.

What came out of the negotiations was neither a new institutional setup nor an international agreement for global Internet governance, but a decision to let the discussion proceed, without interfering with the existing governance arrangements. The Tunis Agenda discarded most of the suggestions in the WGIG report, but picked up on the proposal to initiate a forum for further discussion. So out of the various WGIG proposals about potential models and mechanisms for a new Internet governance framework – ranging from governmental oversight, through reforms of existing institutions to continued dialogue – the only agreement possible in Tunis was to ask the Secretary-General to set up an 'Internet Governance Forum' with no regulatory teeth, where this matter of concern could be discussed by all stakeholders. A new hybrid forum was born.

THE INTERNET GOVERNANCE FORUM

The Internet Governance Forum (IGF) was launched in 2006. It shared a number of characteristics with WGIG, such as its location in the same office in Geneva and a small secretariat run by the same people. The purpose was not to create another organization, but rather to facilitate further and more extensive discussions about the multiple facets of global Internet governance, in what the mandate refers to as a 'new forum for multi-stakeholder policy dialogue' (WSIS 2005b: para 72). In line with this, the IGF was organized as a light structure containing the secretariat, an advisory group with 56 members referred to as the 'Multi-Stakeholder Advisory Group' (MAG) and a small number of advisers to the chair. As pointed out by the Executive Coordinator of the IGF, Markus Kummer, it was 'not an organization, [it was] a loose platform for dialogue', and the role of the secretariat was 'to provide the space making it possible to get together and discuss' (Interview, IGF Executive Director 2009). Thus, we see a clear continuation of aspirations that were also shared by the UNICTTF and WGIG, namely to create platforms that facilitate dialogue.

Since its inception, the IGF has arranged yearly meetings that have attracted a steadily increasing number of participants. Starting in Athens in 2006, IGF meetings have become important occasions for transnational, cross-sectoral and participatory dialogues about global Internet governance. Understood as a moment of ordering, the emergence of the IGF has both contributed to the stabilization of global Internet governance as a matter of concern, and involved a notably different configuration of the assemblage – both in terms of the elements and in the relationship between them. As we will see in this chapter, the annual IGF meetings – held in Athens (2006), Rio de Janeiro (2007), Hyderabad (2008), Sharm el Sheikh (2009) and Vilnius (2010) – have not only given new momentum and suggested new angles for discussions about the global politics of the Internet, but have also strengthened the link between Internet governance and hybrid forums under the auspices of the UN, and mobilized new social worlds. Furthermore, the IGF has sought to make its work more accessible and transparent for actors that cannot participate physically by web-casting from meetings, allowing for remote participation, and by publishing transcripts of interventions made during the meeting.

Exploring New Issues and Procedures

The Internet Governance Forum has not only addressed the issues identified as relevant by WGIG, but has also explored new aspects of Internet governance. IGF meetings include sessions on core themes, such as security, openness, diversity, access and security, as well as sessions on emerging issues, such as youth participation, social media and cloud computing. The meeting in Rio in 2007 added the controversial theme of critical Internet resources to the list. In later IGF meetings, in Hyderabad (2008), Sharm el Sheikh (2009) and Vilnius (2010), the object of governance has been divided into similar themes. One development has been the decision to address questions of security, openness, and privacy collectively, stressing that these cannot be discussed separately as they impact each other directly, because more security will mean less privacy and so on. By dividing its meetings into sessions on core themes and emerging issues, the IGF has sought to keep up with technological and regulatory developments. And the emergence of new issues on the agenda shows how technological developments – such as the emergence of cloud computing, IPV6 and social media – become integrated under the ever-expanding umbrella of Internet governance (DeNardis 2009). But there are also other, less obvious themes that seem to flow over from other policy discussions, such as 'green-tech' and the relation between ICTs and climate change, both of which have been taken up in recent IGF and national meetings. However, what is particularly interesting in the context of this investigation is that the issue of development has gained an increasingly central role. For instance, the overall theme of the meeting in Rio was 'Internet Governance for Development', and all meetings have involved workshops on the question of development. In many ways, the multiple facets of what used to be referred to as ICT-for-development, such as questions about access, infrastructure, rights, policies, education and so on, are now discussed under the heading of global Internet governance. Culminating with a main session titled 'IG4D (Internet Governance for Development)' in Vilnius, it seems that the ICT-for-development project may slowly be being absorbed by Internet governance.

Looking at organizational and procedural processes, it is noticeable that the IGF has continued the experiments with multi-stakeholder arrangements initiated in UNICTTF and WGIG. But rather than formalizing its operations, this hybrid forum has explored the value of continuously developing its organizational setup and procedures. With a very open mandate, activities in the IGF have only been shaped by some broad parameters about its status as non-operational, its role as a platform for dialogue and the demand that its proceedings are made public (WSIS 2005b: para 72; Interview, IGF Executive Director 2009). As with other UN-based hybrid forums, the decision to start out with no or few rules and procedures has made it possible for multiple social worlds to engage in dialogue. In the words of the Executive Director the 'process would have collapsed early on' if rules of procedures had been the starting point, particularly because 'governments would never accept that everyone in the room had a vote' (Interview, IGF Executive Director 2009). Rather, the approach has been to address the concerns of participants as they arise. One issue has been to find ways of making differences between participants less visible. For instance, some participants have pointed out that the different colours used on IGF badges to distinguish between participants from business, civil society and governments create unnecessary divisions between stakeholder groups (Interview, IGF Participant, 2008). As a result, all IGF badges are now the same colour. Nonetheless, categorization into stakeholder groups remains in place in lists of participants and in plenary sessions, where moderators may call on 'the private sector' or 'governments' to voice their opinion.

However, in the plenary sessions too, the IGF has sought to downplay differences between participants. Early on it was decided not to rely on the 'usual format where you have [. . .] panels and [. . .] PowerPoint presentations and in the end, there's little time for discussion' (Interview, IGF Executive Director 2009). Instead, the yearly IGF meetings are used as test beds for novel ways of discussing and engaging with both technical and regulatory aspects of Internet governance. Access to these meetings is largely unrestricted, and participants are invited to propose and arrange panels on topics they find pertinent. From meeting to meeting, the MAG and the secretariat rely on feedback and suggestions in the attempt to develop new ways of organizing and running the process (Interview, IGF Advisor 2009; Interview, IGF Executive Director 2009). In the beginning, most IGF sessions took the shape of panels, and 'because we couldn't agree on who should be on the panel, we ended up with enormous panels with 10–12 people' (Interview, IGF Executive Director 2009). Later meetings have experimented with more open formats, such as three-hour plenary sessions addressing broad themes, led by one or two moderators. At the outset, some feared that if you have such 'freewheeling, open discussion it might get out of hand, people might start shouting and whatever' (Interview, IGF Executive Director 2009). But in practice, these sessions resemble other discussions in the IGF, and the job of the moderators is primarily to encourage and manage contributions from the floor, and not to stop people from shouting at each other. A case in point was the open session on 'managing the critical Internet resources' in Vilnius in 2010. Whereas questions about domain names, root servers and the role of ICANN used to be the most controversial topics during WSIS meetings and were kept off the agenda in the first IGF meetings, no one in Vilnius seemed to disagree on very much at all. At the beginning of the meeting, participants were asked to be 'active', but also 'very polite' to one another. But rather than being monopolized by accusations of US dominance and lack of transparency, these discussions took the shape of practical considerations about technological developments, such as the emergence of the new protocol system IPV6, the growth of cloud computing, and new top-level domain names. As noted in the summary at the end of the meeting, the 'level of outright disagreement, the acrimony has reduced, and the level of information exchange, real world examples, has increased. A great deal of the heat has gone out, the dialogue is more wide ranging' (IGF summary 2010). What used to be the most controversial item on the list of Internet governance issues seems to have become yet another opportunity to share best practices and stress the importance of collaboration in IGF. For instance, during the WSIS process, China was one of the most outspoken critics of existing Internet governance arrangements and constantly stressed the need for intergovernmental control and national sovereignty. In Vilnius, the statement by the representative of China took a very different approach. He said: 'the management of the critical Internet resources is critical for, critically important for China, and if we talk about the actual management of the critical Internet resources, well, China's cooperating with many countries around the world. We have the same common position. We're prepared to communicate with other countries to resolve problems that arise in connection with the Internet all over the world' (IGF transcript 2010). It seems that the IGF is no longer a battleground when it comes to questions about the governance of the Internet infrastructure, and that what was cast as 'high politics' during WSIS is now treated as a set of relatively practical and technical concerns. That discussions about the governance of Internet resources and infrastructure are no longer controversial – but almost boring, as one of the moderators noted afterwards – can of course be explained in multiple ways. To some, this could be seen as evidence that IGF discussions have contributed to a better mutual understanding and have convinced everyone that dialogue is a better way forward than deadlocked negotiations. Some may argue that it is because a growing number of social worlds, including governments from developing countries have realized that after all, ICANN really only does Internet 'plumbing'. Or it could be that the really important discussions and decisions about Internet governance have moved elsewhere. While all these explanations are feasible, it is clear that the IGF and other hybrid forums increasingly distance their work from formal politics and policy decisions. At the same time, many find that the legal and political consequences of the current governance arrangements are multiplying rapidly, and remain unresolved. For instance, at the national IGF in Denmark in 2009, representatives from multinational companies voiced their frustration with ICANN's reluctance to listen to their concerns about the threats to their corporate brand posed by new top-level domain names – such as for instance .ibm or .lego – for which ICANN plans to invite applications. Neither ICANN's open meetings nor the IGF are useful for companies pushing for regulation and governance arrangements that will prevent abuses of their brands and counterfeiting of their products. What they can do is to take such cases to court one by one. Clearly, multi-stakeholder processes were never intended to be able to solve such problems, but still it is worth keeping in mind that while such softer forms of regulation are spreading, so are demands for more hard forms of governance of Internet-related activities.

Hybrid forums can only solve some kinds of problems, and this recognition of their possible limitations is currently visible in the IGF. One example is when moments of conflict arise. As we have seen, multi-stakeholder arrangements seek to foreground broadly framed questions, issues and challenges, rather than particular organizations, positions and proposals for action. Although it rarely happens, there are moments when these tacit principles are violated. For instance, the IGF meeting in Athens involved a direct questioning of Cisco's role in supplying Internet filtering equipment to the Chinese government. And in Sharm el Sheikh, a direct mention of Chinese filtering practices at a book launch was seen as a violation of UN protocol by the Chinese delegation. Provoked by the wording 'the first generation of Internet controls consisted largely of building firewalls at key Internet gateways; China's famous "Great Firewall of China" is one of the first national Internet filtering systems', the Chinese delegation persuaded UN staffers to pull down the poster promoting the book. Situations such as this, in which the stabilized ordering of multi-stakeholder arrangements breaks down because particular companies or governments are criticized, are telling: they help us to understand what ordering and disordering is, and how those involved seek to restore some sort of order. As the Acting Executive Director of the IGF said in his press conference addressing the incident at the book launch, the situation arose because the poster lacked 'political sensitivity', and he therefore urged participants to remember that 'one principle we developed fairly successfully over the years [is to] focus on the issues, not engage in naming and shaming of countries or companies, but rather discuss the principles. This is one of the ways in which IGF can actually reach progress and engage in dialogue' (IGF Press conference 2009). This incident shows how hybrid forums and multi-stakeholder dialogues can fall apart if particular problems and practices are tied to specific actors, and interactions take the shape of naming and shaming rather than discussions about broad principles or practical concerns.

Another way to explore the limits of hybrid forums is to look at what they produce. In the case of the IGF, the outcomes of its meetings are not recommendations, because that 'would be divisive' (Interview, IGF Executive Director 2009), but rather full or slightly edited transcripts of interventions (IGF proceedings 2006, 2007, 2008, 2009). The decision to publish transcripts from IGF meetings certainly caters to principles of participation and transparency, but being accessible and transparent does not mean that hybrid forums are also able to achieve their ambitions. Reading these book-like publications containing up to 500 pages of transcripts does not give participants or outsiders a clear idea about the purpose or potential achievements of such meetings, and the line between transparency and invisibility, and between disclosure and information overload, is a fine one. Thus, the IGF can help us think about the limits of multi-stakeholder dialogues: making a mark on global politics, such as global Internet governance, might take more than bringing everyone together and publishing everything they said, and this realization seems currently to be shaping attempts to develop the IGF and its ways of organizing multi-stakeholder processes. While some call for the IGF to produce recommendations and pursue decision-shaping activities, others stress the value of learning and the sharing of best practices, and thus worry less about whether their work impacts on the practices of outside actors and regulatory activities taking place elsewhere. In the IGF, one plan is to explore the possibility of offering recommendations while stressing that they are not recommendations *by* the IGF, but rather recommendations made *at* the IGF (Interview, IGF Executive Director 2009).

In sum, the IGF stands out as a remarkable experiment in multi-stakeholder dialogue. Constantly addressing barriers to participation and relying on as few organizational structures as possible, with no formal membership, and constant attempts at refining its procedures, the IGF has sought to perfect and stabilize the principles and practices of multi-stakeholder participation in the context of the UN.

EXTENDING AND NORMALIZING MULTI-STAKEHOLDER PROCESSES

Looking at the current shape of the domain of Internet politics in and around the UN, it is striking how hybrid forums become *the* defining feature. All along, the various UN arrangements to address these matters of concern have used the idea of multi-stakeholder participation as a way in which to engage, enrol and mobilize social worlds and gain authority and legitimacy. In retrospect, the movement has been toward increasingly stabilized multi-stakeholder processes in more and more open and loosely organized arrangements. For instance, UN-GAID stresses that it is now a fully open, inclusive multi-stakeholder body, implicitly contrasting it with the UNICTTF, which was a close-knit group of carefully selected participants (Annan 2007; Barrett 2007; UN-GAID 2009). Similarly, since its inception, the IGF has sought to refine the practice of multi-stakeholder participation, to include more and new social worlds, and to continuously develop its procedures and formats. In contrast to WGIG, the IGF has sought to dissolve the boundary between members and stakeholders by holding only open meetings and keeping the organizational infrastructure as minimal as possible.

From being a highly contested and fragile principle advocated primarily by civil society groups, multi-stakeholder participation is now cherished and demanded by all those involved, including those who used to argue against the very idea of addressing Internet governance and those who used to call for intergovernmental control. Across the board, the social worlds involved in these UN activities stress that they respect and seek to develop practices and principles of participation and inclusion. This broad-based allusion to multi-stakeholder participation goes beyond descriptions of the IGF and UN-GAID as they are offered during meetings and in calls for the continuation of this form of organization, and increasingly, many representatives of other organizations stress the multi-stakeholder character of their own organizations. In particular, ICANN has sought to dissolve the opposition between IGF (as open and accessible) and itself (as closed and exclusionary) by stressing that it practises multi-stakeholder participation in all its processes. This book has sought to capture the many associations and steps that have made this stabilization of a norm and form of steering possible. Still, to fully understand how hybrid forums have emerged as the primary mechanism for addressing the global politics of the Internet, we need to investigate how recent and ongoing activities in and around the UN have contributed to the forging of this strong link between a form of organization, an emergent issue area and an intergovernmental institution.

The current ordering of the global politics of the Internet around hybrid forums is visible in a number of ways, but the position gained by the IGF is particularly illustrative of the way in which this domain seems to be shaping up. The following examines a number of different indications, such as the growing number and diversity of participants at IGF meetings, the growing financial support for the initiative, the spread of the IGF model, and the growing normalization of this form of organization and interaction in the wider UN system. Whereas WGIG and UNICTTF meetings would be attended by between one hundred and three hundred people, the Internet Governance Forum draws around 1500 people to its yearly meetings. Accordingly, the IGF involves much more extensive activities, including up to 100 workshops proposed and arranged by groups of stakeholders. These workshops address both well-known and emergent facets of Internet governance, and are used to take stock of both procedural and substantive developments. The ability to attract such large numbers of participants from multiple social worlds – and to rely on them to develop, organize and execute most activities – testifies to the attraction and stabilization of the IGF as a primary platform for discussions about global Internet governance.

When it comes to the financial support that the IGF receives, many of the problems faced by earlier organizational arrangements seem to be waning. Whereas the UNICTTF in particular struggled to source funding from the private sector and even changed its orientation to appeal to the private sector, the IGF has been able to attract a number of public and private sources of funding, and still retain principles such as not allowing businesses to use their affiliation with the IGF for direct marketing and PR purposes. While all hybrid forums seem to struggle to mobilize non-UN funds, it seems that the work and approach of the IGF is attractive to a wide range of public donors – ranging from Finland, Switzerland, the UK and Japan to the EU Commission – who have chosen to channel some of their resources earmarked for development purposes into the IGF. The IGF gets a growing number of private donations – from ICANN, the Number Resource Organization (NRO), Verizon, AT&T, Nokia Siemens and national service providers – without giving any of them the visibility and legitimacy that charitable donations are usually intended to yield. According to the Executive Coordinator, many of these donors stress that they want to contribute because they have realized and experienced the value of taking part in the kinds of dialogue made possible by IGF. It is particularly striking that ICANN, one of the most outspoken critics of the idea of addressing the question of Internet governance, now contributes financially to the work of the IGF.

There are other indications that the link between hybrid forums and the global politics of the Internet is getting stronger. Following the first IGF meetings, a number of similar meetings have taken place across the world. Modelled on the IGF, these regional and national meetings address more specific and local questions and seek to create links between national, regional and transnational discussions of Internet governance. Regional meetings have been held in East Africa, West Africa, Latin America, the Caribbean region, Asia and Europe. Some of these meetings have been one-off events, while others have become organized as more permanent arrangements. The most visible of these is a European platform for discussions about Internet governance. Created in 2008, this 'European

Dialogue on Internet Governance' (EuroDIG) seeks to facilitate discussions, identify common ground and highlight European experience and best practice in this area. Also, EuroDIG works to 'raise awareness in Europe and among European stakeholders about the relevance of the issues discussed in the IGF context and also to raise awareness of the value of the new multistakeholder discussion format developed by and around the IGF' (www.eurodig.org/about-eurodig/what-about).

Besides these regional meetings, a number of national meetings under the auspices of the IGF have been held in India, the US, Bangladesh, Germany, the UK, Finland, Portugal, Italy, Denmark, Russia, Spain, Sweden, Côte d'Ivoire and Ukraine. Like the regional meetings, these events are used to prepare for and raise awareness of the yearly IGF meeting. But they do not only address the same questions, they also tend to rely on the same procedures and organizational arrangements as IGF. In particular, this implies experiments with the mobilization of multiple social worlds, combinations of plenary sessions and workshops, and discussions on both well-established and emergent Internet governance issues. The links between these national and regional meetings and the annual IGF event are not formalized, but take the shape of presentations by the IGF Director or other high profile participants, in the same way as the annual global IGF meetings have slots for presentations of results from regional and national meetings. These meetings often address the topics on the IGF agenda, but they are also tied closely to national concerns and discussions, and often held in the local language. Clearly, these multiple configurations extend the length and breadth of the assemblage, and contribute to the ordering of the global politics of the Internet as a multi-stakeholder process. These national and regional meetings indicate a growing awareness not only of Internet governance issues, but also of the potential value of relying on hybrid forums as the primary form of organization for these activities. But while such meetings are inspired by the IGF, they are neither initiated nor coordinated by the IGF secretariat. Rather, they seem to come about through initiatives taken by national governments, agencies and other actors involved in Internet governance. In the case of the US, the decision to hold a national meeting was made after the US administration had participated in the global IGF. So while the US government refused to be part of WGIG, it now stresses that the national IGF has been a 'great thing' and allowed for useful dialogues with stakeholders on questions about national policies in relation to the Internet. According to the Executive Director of the IGF, the case of the US is one example among many that national governments are realizing that since 'ministries don't have brainstorm sessions', multi-stakeholder processes can be useful also for governments (Interview, IGF Executive

Director 2009). But this does not mean that national IGFs are necessarily used to shape national policies or bring out what the priorities or ramifications of particular policy choices may be. For example, in the case of Denmark, the government agency arranging the national IGF has not made any attempts to link discussions at the Danish IGF to past, existing or future Internet governance policies in the country, but rather used the occasion to invite various groups to propose and organize workshops and thematic discussions about issues related to Internet governance. As pointed out many times in this book, multi-stakeholder processes addressing the politics of the Internet are made possible by, and thrive on a degree of distance to formal policy- and decision-making.

HYBRID FORUMS IN GLOBAL POLITICS

The emergence and consolidation of hybrid forums is not only visible in discussions about Internet governance. While most UN bodies remain intergovernmental when it comes to their procedures and composition, calls for and experiments with multi-stakeholder participation are visible in a number of places. For instance, the UN Commission for Science and Technology for Development increasingly invites business to observe and make statements at its meetings, and such interventions are often used to encourage bodies like ECOSOC and the General Assembly to 'take into account and reflect the multistakeholder spirit of the Tunis Agenda' (ICC statement 2010) when addressing questions of ICTs and governance. Also a number of UN secretariats and initiatives are increasingly open to multi-stakeholder collaborations. Most famously, the UN Global Compact brings together public sector organizations, business associations, corporations, labour and civil society organizations, and – more recently – cities and universities around a set of principles for corporate citizenship. As a multi-stakeholder forum, the Global Compact seeks to facilitate learning and the sharing of best practice, while also advocating reporting and seeking to monitor progress in this area (Ruggie 2001, 2002; Therien 2004; Rasche and Kell 2010). Such multi-stakeholder schemes are often lauded as solutions to a wealth of problems, such as the inability of national politics to solve global challenges, the recurrence of deadlocks in international negotiations, the gap between citizens, corporations and policymakers, and the questioning of the legitimacy of existing regulatory bodies (Deng and Reinicke 2000). In contrast, many governments remain uncomfortable with multi-stakeholder processes. In particular, some developing country governments fear that hybrid forums will undermine national control and give developed countries with strong civil society structures and highly professional business lobbyists new opportunities to shape decisions and policy choices. In describing these concerns about accountability and transparency, which underpin developing countries' preference for 'strong governments' over hybrid forums, the IGF Director argues that 'if you don't believe in democracy you do not believe too much in multi-stakeholder cooperation' (Interview, IGF Executive Director, 2009). Thus, hybrid forums are seen both as a threat to democracy, and as a solution to the lack of democracy.

The growing acceptance of multi-stakeholder processes is not only visible in and around the UN. Multiple forms of transnational governance are currently marked by an upsurge of attempts to develop soft and voluntary forms of global business regulation through multi-stakeholder participation (Utting 2001; Fransen and Kolk 2007), particularly in the shape of codes of conduct, standards and social responsibility schemes (Brunsson and Jacobsson 2000; Djelic and Sahlin-Andersson 2006; Tamm Hallström and Boström 2010). A myriad of policy arenas and issue areas are currently marked by this 'shift to dialogue' (Goven 2006) or a 'participatory turn' (Bäckstrand 2006). National policies, regulation, codes of conduct and global politics in such different sectors as apparel, labour, forests, business ethics, cut flowers, water and the environment (Utting 2002; Bäckstrand 2006; O'Rourke 2006; Fransen and Kolk 2007) are increasingly developed and discussed in hybrid forums and multi-stakeholder processes. Also anti-corruption activities increasingly take place through multi-stakeholder arrangements, initiated by international organizations like Transparency International and various UN agencies. Multi-stakeholder initiatives to combat corruption bring together business, NGOs, regulatory bodies and government representatives around a shared concern with the negative socio-economic effects of corruption, an attempt to monitor and measure corruption and the wish to develop new forms of global governance to tackle bribery (Hansen 2009).

These different examples make it clear that that multi-stakeholder dialogues and governance initiatives occur in a wide range of issue areas and policy domains. Such experiments with multi-stakeholder processes take many shapes, and include at least all the forms captured in this book – from brief consultations over formalized, long-term interactions to full-fledged organizations. Depending on the issue area, hybrid forums bring together scientists, governments, shareholders, employees, customers, suppliers, international organizations, NGOs, communities and other groups. In some cases, multi-stakeholder arrangements are used to pave the way for more formal negotiations, in other cases, they develop standards and principles, and at times they are used as ways to stimulate dialogue and learning.

DISPLACEMENT AND THE POLITICS OF THE INTERNET

Trying to capture the intensification of associations between multi-stakeholder processes and the global politics of the Internet, this chapter has pointed to some of the many new arrangements and developments emerging at the nexus of techno-political visions and hybrid forums. The chapter has captured some of 'the manifestations by which the representativity of the spokesman is questioned, discussed, negotiated, rejected, etc.' (Callon 1986: 219) and brought out how such forms of displacement may contribute to ordering. Such moments allow controversies and alternative forms of ordering to move centre stage, and the chapter has shown how the ordering of the global politics of the digital revolution into two organizational arrangements and two issue areas has been unsettled. These findings point to the fragility of mobilizations in hybrid forums, and offer important insights into the ways in which assemblages break apart and reconfigure in attempts to keep their momentum and strengthen their attraction and authority.

The moment of displacement built upon, but also unsettled, some of the ordering that was in place, particularly the positioning of the UNICTTF and WGIG as representatives of the wider social worlds and the shape of the global politics of the Internet. This issue area is marked by continuous experiments with multi-stakeholder processes, and we now have a growing number of hybrid forums addressing national, regional and transnational questions about Internet governance. The IGF in particular is driven by a willingness to try out new formats and procedures, and let these develop through the active engagement of its stakeholders, although the MAG still has an important say in defining the focus and themes to be addressed. Meetings have become much more loosely structured, and a number of ways have been developed to allow participation from a distance. The meetings held by and inspired by IGF also attract a growing number of social worlds, and they are valued even by those who started out arguing against the very idea of addressing Internet governance. If one thing has made this development possible, it is the reliance on and perfection of multi-stakeholder processes as a norm and form of governance and organization. The value attached to open multi-stakeholder processes shows how stabilized and normalized this practice and principle is becoming in and around the UN. By engaging and mobilizing non-state actors and developing new ways of organizing and interacting, hybrid forums play an increasingly important role in the reconfiguration of the UN and the broader 'multilateral system's formal, hierarchical way of operating' (Bull 2010: 194).

The issues addressed by the IGF are also developed on a rolling basis, for example, to address technological changes or to respond to issues that particular stakeholders find relevant. This has contributed to the overall configuration of the global politics of the Internet as a socio-political, transnational, cross-sectoral, integrated and visible issue area, but has certainly added new facets to the debate as well. In particular, it seems that discussions at the IGF increasingly address practical problems, such as those encountered by service providers preparing to shift from IPV4 to IPV6. This orientation to concrete challenges and best practices stands in stark contrast to the heated discussions about principles that marked discussions at WSIS and in WGIG. Another important development is the apparent absorption of the waning ICT-for-development agenda by the increasingly solidified Internet governance project, with many of the questions about the digital divide recast as Internet governance issues. While the UN-GAID still focuses on ICT-for-development, concerns about the global digital divide have largely been taken up under the heading of global Internet governance, for instance in the shape of 'Internet governance for development' (IG4D). There are a number of indications that Internet governance is where the global politics of the Internet will play out in years to come. While UN-GAID has no official time limit, the mandate of IGF expired with the meeting in Vilnius in 2010. As recommended by the UN Secretary General (UN General Assembly 2010) and many participants at IGF meetings, the UN General Assembly has renewed IGF's mandate for another five years, from 2011–15. The UN resolution asks the Secretary General to convene IGF's 'multi-stakeholder policy dialogue on Internet governance issues according to its mandate as set out in paragraph 72 of the Tunis Agenda for the Information Society', but also stresses the need to 'improve the Forum, with a view to linking it to the broader dialogue on global Internet governance' (UN General Assembly 2011: para 17).

The changing configuration of the boundaries between ICT-for-development and Internet governance as two previously separable issue areas also ties in with the emergence of new social worlds as stakeholders. Not only do we see more actors taking part, but new groups seem to find the IGF particularly valuable as a place where practical concerns and technological developments can be discussed. Service providers, business and technical groups in particular increasingly rely on the IGF as an annual opportunity to discuss and reflect on the current status of their occupation and to call for particular standards to be developed and adopted (Senior Consulting Engineer, Cisco Systems, 2009). The diversity of participants and discussions at the IGF and the lack of tangible output means that it takes more the shape of a social movement than a 'standards developing organization', and the range of topics addressed in workshops and plenary sessions increases and changes from year to year. Finally, when it comes to political rationalities at work, UN-GAID, the IGF and other hybrid forums addressing the global politics of the digital revolution may still be driven by the hope that technology will produce social, political and cultural transformations, for instance in the shape of development. But as noted above, the approach is much more practical than at the outset and, more than ever, networking and dialogue seem to be the driving force of these multiple activities to address the global politics of the Internet. However, this also implies that some of the urgency seems to have disappeared from discussions about the global politics of the Internet. There is no formal, political negotiation to contribute to, no decisions to make or funds to distribute and less and less disagreement within the hybrid forums to address the global politics of the Internet. When asked what he sees as the ultimate goal of the IGF, the Director mentions 'organizing the next meeting', 'to have discussions', 'networking', 'running the process', as his main concerns. Rather than offering recommendations, solutions or other closures, the objective is to provide a platform for dialogue about Internet governance issues as they emerge: 'As long as there is an Internet there will be problems emerging all the time [. . .] We don't know yet what tomorrow's problems will be. But I don't think, that whatever the problems are, there won't be immediate solutions to emergent problems, so there will be a need to have this kind of forum to accompany the growth and maturing of the Internet in years to come. Not to provide solutions, but just to have debate and discussion, and maybe also prevent the wrong solutions or quick fixes that can make the problem worse than it actually is, or stifle further developments' (Interview, IGF Executive Director, 2009). The aim of simply letting the process run is also expressed in other ways. For instance, having opened the IGF meeting in Vilnius by singing the Louis Armstrong song 'What a Wonderful World', the Latvian chairman closed the session on 'Internet Governance for Development' by pointing to another 'great song' by Armstrong, and promised that 'if we meet again next year', he would perform 'We Have All the Time in the World'.

Conclusion: the power of networks

Hybrid forums are attractive and increasingly accepted ways of addressing emergent issues and controversies in global politics because they bring together the multiple actors involved in or affected by governance activities in a given domain. Operating at the margins of formal politics and intergovernmental institutions, such organizational arrangements open up new sites of contestation, unsettle boundaries between the technical and the political, and forge links across social worlds. Although multi-stakeholder processes hold a number of promises, we still know little about their inner workings and effects in global politics. This book has captured how hybrid forums are used to reduce the increasingly visible gap between national politics and global problems (Bauman 1999; Benner, Reinicke et al. 2002). They constitute innovative spaces for dialogue, participation and collaboration without consensus, and contribute to the emergence of novel forms of policymaking and governance beyond the nation-state (Held 1995; Risse 2000; Castells 2008). But hybrid forums also have more mundane effects. To capture these, this book has explored the entanglement of hybrid forums and the global politics of the digital revolution under the auspices of the UN. Following assemblages as they have been stabilized in five different moments of translation the analyses have contributed to our understanding of the practical and often painstaking ways in which orderings are crafted, how they start to travel and circulate, and how they act on the world. While hybrid forums do not change policies, priorities or governance arrangements in any direct manner they do provide new avenues for decision-shaping, and they do so in more transparent and participatory ways than traditional forms of lobbying and negotiation. But the ordering of this political domain has neither taken the shape of institutional integration nor of an attempt to coordinate existing activities and bodies already involved in Internet governance and ICT-for-development. Such coordination would imply that hybrid forums were able to position themselves as obligatory passage points (Callon 1986) through which others had to pass. Rather, they allow for interactions, associations and orderings with more intricate effects. Through dialogues within hybrid forums and with broader groups of stakeholders, positions, concerns and conflicts become visible; new groups, practices and principles emerge, and new roles and responsibilities are proposed and acted upon. As the analyses have shown, the result is that the global politics of the digital revolution has been reconfigured and ordered in numerous, but subtle ways. Even though many groups and organizations go about their business in the same way as before these multi-stakeholder dialogues were initiated, they have shed new light on existing governance arrangements and their possible flaws, and the institutionalized continuation of these problematizing interactions signal that they have gained a momentum that cannot easily be brought to a halt. Thus, the findings show that power and authority are not only about 'hard' governance, decisions and clear-cut victories, but also about the ability to foster and steer dialogue, to make regulatory issues and activities visible, to organize processes that allow and encourage the involvement of different social worlds, and to circulate and stabilize such new forms and norms of governance and entangled authority across multiple domains.

Based on these findings, this chapter takes stock of the effects of organizing global politics around multi-stakeholder processes. In short, it proposes that the resultant ordering has not only shaped – in significant ways – the objects, subjects, techniques and rationalities populating this emergent space of governance, but that it also offers important lessons about power and authority.

THE MAKING OF A POLITICAL DOMAIN

The Internet is not only an important medium, technology and social space (Cavanagh 2007: 4), it is also an emergent space of governance and politics marked by a number of distinctive features. First and foremost, it has become organized around multi-stakeholder processes. As we have seen throughout this book, the making of this issue area has involved multiple and consistent experiments with multi-stakeholder processes, and there are no indications that we will see less experimentation in the future. The stabilization of this mode of organization and steering as unanimously accepted is striking, in particular when we keep in mind that these hybrid forums have emerged in and remained affiliated with an intergovernmental institution such as the UN.

Hybrid forums have been used for a number of different projects and taken multiple shapes. At the outset, the UN ICT Task Force hoped that engaging with stakeholders would make it possible to mobilize financial resources from the private sector and foundations in the attempt to bridge the digital divide. When this did not work out, the multi-stakeholder approach became a way to engage and enrol important allies and to position the project as innovative, legitimate and central to UN development efforts. In the preparations for WSIS, stakeholders were invited to discuss and help set the agenda for the future governance of the 'global information society', but excluded from the actual negotiations at crucial moments. With WGIG, multi-stakeholder participation emerged as a response to the deadlocked UN negotiations about Internet governance, and as a way to engage important actors – such as ICANN and the US – that could otherwise choose to ignore these UN efforts and proceed as before. Moreover, we are witnessing a widespread acceptance of this organizational format as central to the politics of the digital revolution, indicated for instance by the ability of the IGF to engage thousands of practitioners, policymakers and experts in ongoing discussions about the intersection of technical, regulatory and socio-political questions pertaining to the Internet. These examples bear witness not only to the ordering of the politics of the digital revolution around multi-stakeholder processes, but also to the multiple problems to which this approach is seen as a possible solution. In practice, hybrid forums may not be a panacea to the financial, regulatory and organizational challenges facing the UN, but as we have seen, they have been used to address all these and others. In this regard, the findings of this book contribute to the emerging literature on the spread and effects of multi-stakeholder dialogues, or what has been termed the 'dialogization' of relations of government, in national (Goven 2006; Karlsen and Villadsen 2008) as well as transnational settings (Gössling, Oerlemans et al. 2007; Tamm Hallström and Boström 2010).

The turn to dialogue captured in this book has taken multiple organizational forms. The various hybrid forums examined have been organized and positioned in very different ways. We have seen a formal working group with a clear mandate positioned as an advisory body to the UN Secretary-General, because this would allow for non-state participation. We have also encountered a group of mostly high-profile leaders from business, international organizations, government and a few civil society organizations seeking to become a UN-based 'network of networks' linking public and private actors and developmental and regulatory agendas. And we have seen slightly revised versions of these organizational arrangements and more wide-reaching attempts to refine and develop multi-stakeholder processes. These variations remind us of the fluidity of hybrid forums – they may be more or less formalized, organized and ambitious, and bring together some groups while not mobilizing or inviting others. Some hybrid forums have clear organizational borders and explicit rules about membership and procedures, while others thrive by having fluid boundaries between the inside and the outside, and very few guiding principles.

TOOLS AND TARGETS OF HYBRID FORUMS

Following Foucault, power is an effect not only of the ability to use resources, positions or institutions to shape conduct, but also of the ordering and stabilization of multiple elements into something we take to be given (Foucault 1977a, 1982, 1985). Such forms of normalization setting our 'conditions of possibility' take the shape of, for instance, boundary drawing, systems of control, rationalization and institutionalization. Along these lines, to make sense of the power effects of hybrid forums we need to examine and conceptualize their tools and targets of ordering, that is, how they rely on and shape human and non-human elements in processes of ordering. Let us look briefly at the subjects, objects, rationalities and techniques at work in and shaped by hybrid forums.

When it comes to the social worlds involved in these hybrid forums, we have seen not only that the stakeholders have increased considerably in number and diversity, but also that this categorization allows for a large variety of actors to enter UN-based dialogues about the digital revolution. If we simply go by the categories circulating in this domain, it seems to be populated by 'business', 'governments', 'civil society', 'international organizations' and, increasingly, 'youth'. But these categories cover a much more diverse mixture of actors, including diplomats, technical experts, lobbyists, activists, researchers, and many others with fluctuating and entangled aims. Furthermore, as we have seen, actors may not even be physically present to make a mark: in many cases the implied actors (Clarke 2005) – such as the 'school child in sub-Saharan Africa', the 'ICT entrepreneur' or the 'philanthropic CEO' – play very important roles in shaping the work of hybrid forums. This book has brought out that such subject positions and categorizations are not given, and play important roles in the mobilization and positioning of social worlds as stakeholders. That is, stakeholders are enacted and produced through categorizations (Hallström and Boström 2010) that posit dispersed social worlds as allies in the project of ordering the global politics of the Internet. Such categorizations are central to hybrid forums. The IGF in particular seems to bring together technical groups and practitioners that were less involved in the early attempts to address the broader questions about the digital divide, the 'information society' and development. Increasingly, Internet service providers, technical developers and different administrative bodies take part in IGF dialogues and pull these discussions in the direction of technical questions and standards that may also be taken up in other standards developing organizations.

Reflecting on the objects that these hybrid forums seek to make governable and shape in particular ways reminds us just how much has happened to the UN engagement with the politics of the digital revolution over the past decade. The problematization of this domain started as an attempt to secure private funding for initiatives to bridge the digital divide, particularly by expanding infrastructure in the poorest parts of Africa. But as the associations and allies changed, so did the object of these interventions. For instance, significant associations and translations made new matters of concern emerge as central to the UN ICT Task Force, such as deregulation in the ICT sector, UN reforms through digital and public-private networks, and education as a key component of the ICT-for-development project. With the emergence of Internet governance as a highly contentious question during the WSIS process, the global politics of the digital revolution was shaped in new ways. Furthermore, we have seen how a technical object, such as the Internet, becomes inscribed into organization and politics in surprising ways. And with the invention of 'Internet-governance-for-development' (IG4D) as a new project in need of attention – in effect turning the stranded ICT-for-development agenda into yet another sub-theme under the heading of Internet governance – we have ample evidence that politics are not about the diffusion of particular ideas or regimes, but the assemblage, entanglement and translation of surprising configurations of human and non-human elements. As we have seen, moments of translation transform and reconfigure assemblages, and in the process, organizational arrangements and the various shapes of the issues addressed tend to become entangled in new ways.

The global politics of the Internet is also marked by shifting boundaries between the political and the technical. While the majority of the findings in this book show how this issue area has been constructed as socio-political, there are also some indications of a return to an understanding of Internet governance as a matter of technical concerns. The return to technological aspects of Internet governance is particularly visible in the IGF, where, for instance, discussions about 'critical Internet resources' are now really concerned with technical and practical issues relating to the transition from IPV4 to IPV6, and no longer with contentious discussions about ICANN and the internationalization of Internet governance. But it is important to stress that these discussions are not technical in the way they were at the outset: the argument that Internet governance is simply a misnomer for what is actually just 'plumbing' has vanished. But so have the very aggravated calls for intergovernmental control and the propositions that Internet governance is 'high politics'. Increasingly, technological developments and logics seem to become inscribed into and drive the process. In sum, the multiple translations of this techno-political assemblage captured in this book have involved orderings not only of the object, but also of the relations and boundaries around it.

The techniques and rationalities at work in hybrid forums have also become entangled and stabilized in significant ways. The analyses have distinguished between the political rationalities that 'render reality into the domain of thought' and the technologies of government that 'seek to translate thought into the domain of reality, and to establish "in the world of persons and things" spaces and devices for acting upon those entities of which they dream and scheme' (Miller and Rose 1990: 8). But like other assembled and translated elements, organizational techniques and political rationalities become tied in surprising and shifting configurations in hybrid networks. When it comes to the techniques used to organize and manage activities and relations in hybrid forums, we have seen well-known and stabilized methods, like consultations, but also novel devices, such as stakeholder self-nominations. Once established, such arrangements rely on a suite of organizational techniques to position, structure and communicate their work, while at the same time keeping their allies engaged in the project. One important insight is that hybrid forums revolve around circulating and malleable 'boundary objects' and flexible organizational infrastructures that make 'collaboration without consensus' possible. Furthermore, we have seen a need for constant innovation when it comes to organizational techniques, such as when the IGF makes procedural innovation a defining feature of its operations and appeal. All these organizational techniques do important work such as enrolling, excluding and categorizing different social worlds. At the same time, they become entangled with other elements in the assemblage, such as the objects made governable, for example, when the first UNICTTF consultations made it clear that the target of these efforts had to be something less tangible than funding ICT-for-development projects.

Also, the book has sought to capture the intricate and shifting mixture of political rationalities shaping the global politics of the Internet. Propelled by a sanguine belief in the transformative potential of technology, the early attempts to bridge the digital divide involved a kind of technological determinism that many ICT-for-development projects seemed to inherit more or less blindly from much earlier attempts to encourage development by simply transferring technologies to developing countries. While less emphasized in more recent activities to foster and govern the digital revolution, this political rationality still underpins the various hybrid forums we have encountered in this book. The view of the Internet as an engine of social change seems to give direction to multiple facets of the global politics of the digital revolution. For instance, this political rationality drives the economic argument that the Internet facilitates new forms of trade and markets. Socially speaking, it posits the Internet as the backbone of what has been termed the network society (Castells 1997) where knowledge becomes a key resource and horizontal relationships prevail. And politically, the Internet is seen as an engine of emergent forms of governance allowing new actors to take part in decision-making processes and new forms of democracy to emerge. But this optimism also intersects with another political rationality, namely what we may term a 'trust in numbers' and classifications (Porter 1995; Bowker and Star 1999). Rather than simply transferring technology, the UN hybrid forums we have examined in this book seek to 'sort out', quantify and circulate indexes of best practice as a way to shape and act on this issue area. But if one political rationality underpins all the activities examined in this book it is what we may term a 'networking logic' (Juris 2008). The global politics of the digital revolution is all about networks. Hybrid forums are (organizational) networks that seek to shape (electronic) networks, and propose (regulatory and resource-based) networking as the solution. In more mundane ways as well, this political domain is saturated by references to networking, such as when the UNICTTF labelled the time between panel discussions as 'networking breaks' and its organizational setup as a 'network of networks'. Taken together, these findings show UN-driven dialogues about global Internet politics can be seen as a perfection of the networking logic identified in more abstract, structural terms in theories about the 'network society' (Castells 1996, 1997, 1998). Finally, it is worth noting that political rationalities do important work in relation to categorizations of actors. For instance, ICT-for-development casts poor people as entrepreneurs and consumers rather than aid recipients, and the entire project as a matter of empowerment, rather than donation. And by positioning particular social worlds as stakeholders, hybrid forums mobilize and professionalize actors and make them act in similar and compatible ways.

Against this backdrop, we can sum up that the entanglement of hybrid forums and the global politics of the digital revolution can be understood as a dynamic techno-political assemblage revolving around four elements – rationalities, techniques, objects and subjects – all of which have, in turn, been reconfigured and shaped by the process. The ability to capture such entanglements shows the value of a research strategy focusing on the ordering of techno-socio-political assemblages. By examining assemblages and translations very closely, this book has shown how the nexus linking hybrid forums and the politics of the digital revolution was made possible by such different human and non-human elements as organizational techniques, existing regulatory arrangements, a rapidly growing technology, technological visions and networking logics, calls for organizational and political innovation, entrepreneurial subjects, negotiation deadlocks, ICT companies, and many others. In contrast to conventional studies of global governance and networks, which set out to classify organizational arrangements – as epistemic communities (Haas 1992), transnational advocacy networks (Keck and Sikkink 1998) or associative clusters (Mueller 2010) – a practice-oriented, relational and agnostic research strategy helps us examine how processes of classification and boundary-drawing play out, and to reflect on the performativity and effects of such attempts at ordering. The findings also foreground the value of the agnostic research strategy: had we settled on the defining features of an organization in advance, we would miss this diversity and fluidity of the organizational arrangements created to make multi-stakeholder participation durable in and around the UN system.

POWER AND ENTANGLED AUTHORITY

So far, this chapter has summarized the ways in which hybrid forums operate and reconfigure, and how they order relations and boundaries of government. But we still need to consider what the effects of this linking between hybrid forums and political domains may be in terms of power and authority. Reflecting on the effects and costs of ordering for the subjects, objects, techniques and rationalities involved, these questions pave the way for a better understanding of how the ability to mobilize resources and engage social worlds is about power, how dialogue and participation may be conceived as forms of steering, and how we may conceptualize hybrid forums as entangled forms of authority.

This book set out from a conception of power as an effect of associations, not their cause. In other words, power is 'composed here and now by enrolling many actors in a given political and social scheme, and is not something that can be stored up and given to the powerful' (Latour 1986: 264). Having followed the numerous successful and unsuccessful attempts to engage important allies in the project – through problematization, interessement, enrolment, mobilization and displacement – we can now summarize the multiple power effects of hybrid forums. For one, power takes the shape of 'subjectification', that is, the codification and positioning of particular social worlds through stakeholder categorizations. But power also plays out as implicit expectations about how stakeholders are expected to act and contribute when taking part in the work of hybrid forums. Such organizational arrangements invite social worlds to organize in particular ways, signal enough unity and agreement to constitute a stakeholder group, develop procedures such as choosing their representatives, and mobilize intellectual, financial and administrative resources. In this respect, we can think of subjectification and resource-based power as part of the same codification of social worlds as stakeholders.

Power is also inscribed in objects, such as when 'things strike back' (Latour 2000) and technological developments such as cloud computing, social media and IPV6 become important actors shaping the direction of discussions on the global politics of the Internet. Notably, this domain is an odd techno-political assemblage where technological traits are constantly invoked as arguments for particular regulatory approaches. This implies, for instance, that the networked, decentralized, global makeup of the Internet is used as an argument that governance arrangements in this area should also be equally networked, decentralized and global, or that this technical 'network of networks' should be governed using organizational 'networks of networks' or regulatory 'mechanisms of mechanisms'. The study of ordering is particularly well-suited to capturing such an entanglement of politics, technology, organization and society, because it gives substance to the claim that technology plays an increasingly important role in the invention of politics and the reconfiguration of spaces and relations of government (Foucault 1997; Barry 2001).

Finally, we can think of power as discursive. One effect of the ordering of this political domain is that it is no longer possible to refer to Internet governance as a simple matter of technical coordination of networks. The kinds of closures produced around this political domain, captured particularly in Chapter 5, show us how discursive orderings also have important effects. This implies that the ability to facilitate and perpetuate dialogue between social worlds constitutes a form of power, and points to another power effect of these dialogues: it is worth noting that those who preferred the discussions about Internet governance to go away – such as ICANN, the US and other existing authorities in this area – were unable to bring the reconfiguration of Internet governance to a halt, neither during, nor after WSIS.

As Barnett and Finnemore (2005: 179) stress, power is not only about the ability to regulate, but also about being able to constitute the world in particular ways and define the problems to be solved. This is one kind of power at work in attempts at problematizing, constructing and organizing the global politics of the digital revolution. By engaging these insights in an investigation of very mundane and subtle forms of steering, this book reminds us how the ability to construct and organize spaces for dialogue and to define the identities of different actors as stakeholders and make them work together constitutes important but often overlooked forms of power.

So hybrid forums certainly produce power effects. But this tells us little about their ability to position themselves as authorities by creating 'some form of normative, uncoerced consent or recognition of authority on the part of the regulated or governed' (Hall and Biersteker 2002: 4–5). In other words, how do hybrid forums put connections and stabilizations to work when seeking to make a mark and achieve the kind of legitimacy that makes it possible to turn power into authority? Because hybrid forums rest on 'procedures of consultation that do not sit easily with the idea of sharp, clear-cut decisions' (Callon, Lascoumes et al. 2009: 191), it is not obvious that they are also about power and authority. They do not seek to make stakeholders agree, or allow conflicts to move to the fore, but seek actively to avoid such closures altogether. As a result, conventional conceptions of power and governance tend to write off hybrid forums as insignificant 'talking shops' that are unable to change policies or control the actions of others. But this misses an important effect of such organizational arrangements, namely that they allow for collaboration without consensus, thus making novel and potentially significant interactions possible. Hybrid forums are able to build linkages and associations across multiple domains and social worlds and thereby connect multiple forms of legitimacy and commitment. To think of this as a source of authority, we must develop a more nuanced understanding of power, and look beyond the 'most visible and destructive dimensions of power' (Barnett and Duvall 2005: 3). In particular, insights from governmentality studies and ANT allow us to bring out the ways in which spaces for dialogue become attractive – and mobilizing forces – for multiple social worlds. Multi-stakeholder arrangements offer opportunities for interaction, learning and collaboration between stakeholders, and invite different actors to construct objects as governable and devise solutions. And this ability to facilitate ordering constitutes an important form of authority. Thus, we can think of the authority of hybrid forums as the ability to facilitate novel forms of 'institutionalized cooperation' (Cutler, Haufler et al. 1999: 334) across political, social and technological boundaries. Furthermore, by constituting platforms for the creation and organization of new forms of political and regulatory contestation and ordering, hybrid forums gain authority because they are able to enrol and entangle multiple forms of authority. To capture the significance of this form of entangled authority, Porter's (2008) distinction between four different types of authority is useful. Firstly, we can think of a state-created *public authority*, which 'draws upon traditional respect for the law' and 'democratic practices'; secondly, business-created *private authority*, which is based on the 'widespread belief in the inherent superiority of the market and other private-sector ways of doing things'; thirdly, expert-created *technical authority*, which 'draws on respect for the scientific method'; and finally, civil society-created *popular authority*, which 'evokes the inherent righteousness of a populace mobilized to create its own future' (Porter 2008: 29). Rather than setting out to establish whether one form of authority wins out in a given political or regulatory domain, a practice-oriented, relational and agnostic approach allows us to capture the ways in which authority is produced by building linkages and associations across multiple domains, social worlds and forms of legitimacy and commitment. This book has shown that the power of hybrid forums lies in their ability to engage and stabilize multiple forms of authority, and the production of such forms of entangled authority through associations deserves more attention in future studies of power, governance and global politics.

Notes

1. It should be noted that the ambition is neither to investigate how the Internet, or the digital revolution more broadly, is currently governed at the global level, nor to determine whether the UN activities in this area have been effective or not. Rather, the purpose is to explore how this global, socio-political space has been ordered and organized, and to bring out the effects of these activities for political rationalities, organizational techniques, subjects and objects – and, ultimately, questions about power and authority. Neither does the book claim that all parts of the UN are changing in similar ways. Experiments with multi-stakeholder arrangements seem to occur primarily in the parts of the UN addressing issues like media, culture and development, and remain very much at the margins of the system – far away from the Security Council and 'high' politics.
2. In other contexts, Bill Gates has also argued that ICTs should come in when all other problems have been solved. For instance, at a conference he said, 'come on, these people don't have medicines, they're dying, they don't have electricity. Why are we just sitting here talking about computers?' (http://www.microsoft.com/billgates/speeches/2000/10-18digitaldividends.asp (accessed 7 March 2011)).
3. Members from governments were not asked to nominate themselves, but were picked by the Secretary-General on the basis of informal consultations, which made a number of governments complain that the process had not been transparent enough.
4. The mailing list was started during the preparations for the Geneva phase of WSIS and had approximately 150 subscribers, but only 10–15 very active members. The archive is no longer available.
5. These two functioned as the authoritative bodies for the 30 thematic and regional WSIS caucuses and working groups referred to as civil society.
6. These groups were redefined in line with the UNICTTF Business Plan of 2004, which sought to focus and narrow the activities of the UNICTTF. Thus, the five original working groups, which focused on the following themes: (1) ICT Policy and Governance; (2) National and Regional e-Strategies; (3) Human Resources Development and Capacity Building; (4) Low Cost Connectivity and Access; and (5) Business Enterprise and Entrepreneurship were reduced to four, redefining regional and national e-strategies as Enabling Environment, removing low-cost connectivity and access and business enterprise and entrepreneurship altogether and adding a focus on ICT mapping/MDG indicators, in the attempt to show that ICT4D has tangible and measurable outcomes. These changes must be understood in the light of the activities of the UNICTTF – each of the four new working groups was linked to an earlier UNICTTF activity, whether in the shape of a Global Forum, a book or a commissioned study.
7. See for instance, http://insidecostarica.com/dailynews/2005/march/09/nac03.htm, and http://www.businessweek.com/magazine/content/04_49/b3911066_mz054.htm (accessed 7 March 2011).
8. The idea of holding open meetings emerged as early as 2003, and the UNICTTF held the first of these in conjunction with its fifth meeting at the WIPO headquarters in Geneva in September 2003. This first meeting, which included a broader group of stakeholders, had no overarching theme and had considerably fewer participants than later ones. Unlike the later ones, it was designed more as a way to interact with those actors already identified as 'partner organizations' than with the broader group of stakehold-

ers concerned with ICT and development. Furthermore, participants were invited and handpicked. As for myself, I had to tag along with someone who was formally invited. For these reasons, I have chosen not to make this meeting part of the following analyses, and instead focus on the later three, full-fledged forums. This decision also corresponds to the decision of the UNICTTF to only refer to the last three meetings as Global Forums, and to only publish the proceedings from these.

9. The UN Millennium Project (2002–06) was initiated by the UN Secretary-General with the purpose of spelling out how the Millennium Development Goals might be reached. The initiative included ten task forces involving more than 250 experts, and resulted in a number of action plans, recommendations and publications (see http://www.unmillenniumproject.org/).
10. See for instance, 'Compromise Reached in Tunis on Internet Control', *International Herald Tribune*, 16 November 2005; 'A Compromise of Sorts on Internet Control', *New York Times*, 16 November 2005; and 'Tunis Talks Find Internet Stalemate', *The Times*, 16 November 2005.

References

Abbate, J. (1999), *Inventing the Internet*, Cambridge, MA: MIT Press.

Abu-Ghazaleh, T. (2002), 'Organization and governance', UN ICT Task Force Archives, New York.

Abu-Ghazaleh, T. (2004), 'Internet governance without a governance body', UN ICT TF meeting, Berlin.

Afonso, Carlos A. (2005) 'Internet governance: a review in the context of the WSIS process', paper prepared for Instituto del Tercer Mundo (ITeM), June 2005, available at: http://wsispapers.choike.org//papers/eng/carlos_internet_governance.pdf (accessed 1 March 2011).

Ahrne, G., N. Brunsson et al. (2007), 'Organizing organizations', *Organization*, **14**, 619–24.

Alvesson, M. and H. Willmott (1992), *Critical Management Studies*, London: Sage.

Alvesson, M. and H. Willmott (2002), 'Identity regulation as organizational control: producing the appropriate individual', *Journal of Management Studies*, **39** (5), 619–44.

Annan, K. (2000), 'We the peoples: the role of the UN in the 21st century', Executive Summary, available at: http://www.un.org/millennium/sg/report/summ.htm (accessed 2 March 2011).

Annan, K. (2006), GAID meeting in New York, available at: http://www.unis.unvienna.org/unis/pressrels/2006/sgsm10662.html (accessed 28 February 2011).

Annan, K. (2007), 'Message to steering committee of the Global Alliance for ICT and Development', in A. Celik (ed.), *Foundations of the Global Alliance for ICT and Development*, UN GAID Series, vol. 1, New York: UN GAID.

Bach, J. and D. Stark (2002), 'Link, search, interact: the co-evolution of NGOs and interactive technology', COI working paper, Columbia, New York.

Bach, J. and D. Stark (2005), 'Recombinant technology and new geographies of association', in R. Latham and S. Sassen (eds), *Digital Formations: IT and New Architectures in the Global Realm*, Princeton and Oxford: Princeton University Press.

Badshah, A., S. Khan et al. (eds) (2004), *Connected for Development: Information Kiosks and Sustainability*, UN ICT Task Force Series, New York: UNICTTF.

Bang, H. (ed.) (2003), *Governance as Social and Political Communication*, Manchester: Manchester University Press.

Barker, J.R. (1993), 'Tightening the iron cage: concertive control in self-managing teams', *Administrative Science Quarterly*, 38, 408–37.

Barlow, J.P. (1996), 'Declaration of the independence of cyberspace', available at: http://homes.eff.org/~barlow/Declaration-Final.html (accessed 1 February 2006).

Barnett, M. and R. Duvall (eds) (2005), *Power in Global Governance*, Cambridge: Cambridge University Press.

Barnett, M. and M. Finnemore (2005), 'The power of liberal international organizations', in M. Barnett and R. Duvall (eds), *Power in Global Governance*, Cambridge: Cambridge University Press.

Barney, D. (2000), *Prometheus Wired: The Hope for Democracy in the Age of Network Technology*, Chicago: University of Chicago Press.

Barrett, C. (2007), 'Preface', in A.P. Celik (ed.), *Foundations of the Global Alliance for ICT and Development*, UN GAID Series, vol.1, New York: UN GAID.

Barry, A. (2001), *Political Machines: Governing a Technological Society*, London: The Athlone Press.

Barry, A. (2006), 'Technological zones', *European Journal of Social Theory*, **9**, 239–53.

Bauman, Z. (1999), *In Search of Politics*, London: Polity Press.

Beniger, J.R. (1986), *The Control Revolution: Technological and Economic Origins of the Information Society*, Cambridge, MA: Harvard University Press.

Benner, T., W.H. Reinicke et al. (2002), 'Shaping globalization: the role of public policy networks', *Carl-Bertelsman Award 2002: Cooperation – Responsibility – Transparency*, Gütersloh: Bertelsman.

Bevir, M. (2003), 'A decentred theory of governance', in H. Bang (ed.), *Governance as Social and Political Communication*, Manchester: Manchester University Press.

Bevir, M. (2004), 'Governance and interpretation: what are the implications of postfoundationalism?' *Public Administration*, **82** (3), 605–27.

Bevir, M. and R.A.W. Rhodes (2003), 'Decentring British governance: from bureaucracy to networks', in H. Bang (ed.), *Governance as Social and Political Communication*, Manchester: Manchester University Press.

Bigo, Didier and R.B.J. Walker (2007), 'Political Sociology and the Problem of the International', *Millenium: Journal of International Studies*, **35** (3), 725–39.

Blau, P.M. and W.R. Scott (1962), *Formal Organizations: A Comparative Approach*, San Francisco: Chandler.

Blumer, H. (1969), *Symbolic Interactionism: Perspective and Method*, Englewood Cliffs, NJ: Prentice-Hall.

Bowker, G.C. and S.L. Star (1999), *Sorting Things Out: Classification and its Consequences*, Cambridge, MA: MIT Press.

Bracey, Bonnie and Terry Culver (eds) (2005), *Harnessing the Potential of ICT for Education – A Multistakeholder Approach*, UN ICT Task Force Series 9, New York: UN Publications.

Braithwaite, J. and P. Drahos (2000), *Global Business Regulation*, Cambridge: Cambridge University Press.

Bratich, J.Z., J. Packer et al. (2003) 'Governing the present', in J.Z. Bratich, J. Packer and C. McCarthy (eds), *Foucault, Cultural Studies and Governmentality*, Albany: SUNY.

Brinkerhoff, J.M. (2002), *Partnership for International Development: Rhetoric or Results?* London: Lynne Rienner.

Brühl, T. and V. Rittberger (2001), 'From international to global governance: actors, collective decision-making, and the United Nations in the world of the twenty-first century', in V. Rittberger (ed.), *Global Governance and the United Nations System*, Tokyo: United Nations University Press.

Brunsson, N. and B. Jacobsson (2000), *A World of Standards*, Oxford and New York: Oxford University Press.

Bull, B. (2010), 'Rethinking multilateralism: global governance and public-private partnerships with the UN', in M. Ougaard and A. Leander (eds), *Business and Global Governance*, London: Routledge.

Burawoy, M. (2000), *Global Ethnography: Forces, Connections, and Imaginations in a Postmodern World*, Berkeley: University of California Press.

Burchell, G. (1991), 'Peculiar interests: civil society and governing "the system of natural liberty"', in G. Burchell, C. Gordon and P. Miller (eds), *The Foucault Effect: Studies in Governmentality*, Chicago: University of Chicago Press.

Burchell, G., Colin Gordon and Peter Miller (eds) (1991), *The Foucault Effect: Studies in Governmental Rationality*, Hemel Hempstead: Harvester-Wheatsheaf.

Bäckstrand, K. (2006), 'Multi-stakeholder partnerships for sustainable development: rethinking legitimacy, accountability and effectiveness', *European Environment*, **16**, 290–306.

Çalişkan, K. and M. Callon (2010), 'Economization, part 2: a research programme for the study of markets', *Economy and Society*, **39** (1), 1–32.

Callon, M. (1986), 'Some elements of a sociology of translation: domestication of the scallops and the fishermen of St Brieuc Bay', in J. Law (ed.), *Power, Action and Belief: A New Sociology of Knowledge?* London: Routledge and Kegan Paul.

Callon, M., P. Lascoumes et al. (2009), *Acting in an Uncertain World: An Essay on Technical Democracy*, Cambridge, MA: MIT Press.

Cammaerts, B. (2008), *Internet-Mediated Participation beyond the Nation State*, Manchester and New York: Manchester University Press.

'Cardoso Report', Report of the Panel of Eminent Persons on United Nations–Civil Society Relations (2004), 'We the peoples: civil society, the United Nations and global governance', UN General Assembly, New York (document A/58/817).

Carlile, P.R. (2002), 'A pragmatic view of knowledge and boundaries: boundary objects in new product development', *Organization Science*, **13**, 442–55.

Castells, M. (1996), *The Rise of the Network Society*, Oxford: Blackwell.

Castells, M. (1997), *The Power of Identity*, Oxford: Blackwell.

Castells, M. (1998), *End of Millennium*, Oxford: Blackwell.

Castells, M. (2008), 'The new public sphere: global civil society, communication networks, and global governance', *Annals of the American Academy of Political and Social Science*, **616**, 78–93.

Cavanagh, Allison (2007), *Sociology in the Age of the Internet*, Maidenhead, Berkshire: Open University Press.

Chadwick, A. (2006), *Internet Politics: States, Citizens, and New Communication Technologies*, Oxford: Oxford University Press.

Chairman of ICANN (1999), Esther Dyson letter, 15 June 1999, available at: http://www.icann.org/en/correspondence/dyson-response-to-nader-15jun99.htm (accessed 1 March 2011).

Charmaz, K. (2003), 'Grounded theory: objectivist and constructivist methods', in N.K. Denzin and Y.S. Lincoln (eds), *Strategies of Qualitative Inquiry*, 2nd edn, Thousand Oaks, CA: Sage.

Clarke, A. (2005), *Situational Analysis: Grounded Theory after the Postmodern Turn*, Thousand Oaks, CA: Sage.

Clarke, A. and C. Friese (2007), 'Grounded theory using situational analysis', in Kathy Charmaz and Anthony Bryant (eds), *The Sage Handbook of Grounded Theory*, London: Sage.

Clarke, A.E. and S.L. Star (2008), 'The social worlds framework: a theory/methods package', in E.J. Hackett, O. Amsterdamska, M. Lynch and J. Wajcman (eds), *The Handbook of Science and Technology Studies*, Cambridge, MA and London: MIT Press.

Clegg, S. (1998), 'Foucault, power and organizations', in A. McKinlay and K. Starkey (eds), *Foucault, Management and Organization Theory: From Panopticon to Technologies of Self*, London: Sage.

Clinton, B. (2000), Address by Bill Clinton at Johns Hopkins University, 8 March: available at http://www.techlawjournal.com/cong106/pntr/20000308sp.htm (accessed 2 March 2011).

Commission on Global Governance (1995), *Our Global Neighborhood: The Report of the Commission on Global Governance*, New York: Oxford University Press.

Consultation team, UNICTTF (2000), 'Report on African consultations on the ICT TF and Trust Fund', 15–29 November, UN ICT Task Force Archives, New York.

Cooke, B. and U. Kothari (eds) (2001), *Participation: The New Tyranny?* London: Zed Books.

Cooper, R. (1986), 'Organization/Disorganization', *Social Science Information sur les Sciences Sociales*, **25** (2), 299–335.

Cruikshank, B. (1999), *The Will to Empower: Democratic Citizens and other Subjects*, Ithaca, NY: Cornell University Press.

Cunningham, H. (1999), 'The ethnography of transnational social activism – understanding the global as local practice', *American Ethnologist*, **26** (3), 583–604.

Cutler, A.C., V. Haufler et al. (eds) (1999), *Private Authority and International Affairs*, Albany: State University of New York Press.

Czarniawska, B. (2007), *Shadowing: And Other Techniques for Doing Fieldwork in Modern Societies*, Malmö: Liber.

Czarniawska, B. (2008), *A Theory of Organizing*, Cheltenham, UK and Northampton, MA, USA: Edward Elgar.

Czarniawska, B. and T. Hernes (eds) (2005), *Actor-Network Theory and Organizing*, Copenhagen: Liber and Copenhagen University Press.

Dean, M. (1999), *Governmentality: Power and Rule in Modern Society*, London: Sage.

Deetz, S. (1992), *Democracy in an Age of Corporate Colonization: Developments in Communication and the Politics of Everyday Life*, Albany: State University of New York.

Deetz, S. (1995), *Transforming Communication, Transforming Business: Building Responsive and Responsible Workplaces*, Cresskill, NJ: Hampton Press.

Deibert, R.J. (1997), *Parchment, Printing and Hypermedia – Communication in World Order Transformation*, New York: Columbia University Press.

Deibert, R.J. (2000), 'International plug 'n play? Citizen activism, the Internet and global public policy', *International Studies Perspectives*, **1**, 255–72.

Dekker, H.C. (2004), 'Control of inter-organizational relationships: evidence on appropriation concerns and coordination requirements', *Accounting Organizations and Society*, **29** (1), 27–49.
Deleuze, G. and F. Guattari (1998), *A Thousand Plateaus: Capitalism and Schizophrenia*, London: Athlone.
DeNardis, L. (2009), *Protocol Politics: The Globalization of Internet Governance*, Cambridge, MA: MIT Press.
Deng, F. and W.H. Reinicke (2000), *Critical Choices – the United Nations, Networks, and the Future of Global Governance*, Ottawa: International Development Research Centre.
Digital Partners Consultant, UNICTTF (2000a), 'Foundation and corporate consultations', draft in-progress report, UN ICT Task Force Archives, New York.
Digital Partners Consultant, UNICTTF (2000b), 'Considerations for establishing an ICT Task Force', first draft, UN ICT Task Force Archives, New York.
Digital Partners Consultant, UNICTTF (2000c), 'Ideas guiding possible revisions to design of ICT document', UN ICT Task Force Archives, New York.
Director, APC (2005), available at: http://mailman-new.greennet.org.uk/pipermail/plenary (accessed 28 February 2011).
Djelic, M.-L. and K. Sahlin-Andersson (2006), *Transnational Governance: Institutional Dynamics of Regulation*, Cambridge and New York: Cambridge University Press.
Dossal, A. (2002), 'Digital partnerships', available at: http://www.un.org/unop/Docs/Digital%20Partnerships%20WSIS%202003.pdf (accessed 2 March 2011).
DOT Force (2000), 'Bridging the digital divide: on-going activities', Tokyo.
DOT Force (2001), 'Digital opportunities for all: meeting the challenge', Genoa, G8.
Doty, R.L. (1997), 'Aporia: a critical exploration of the agent-structure problematique in international relations theory', *European Journal of International Relations*, **3** (3), 365–92.
Drake, William (2000), 'The rise and decline of the international telecommunications regime', in C.T. Marsden (ed.), *Regulating the Global Information Society*, London: Routledge.
Drake, William (2004), 'Reframing Internet governance discourse: fifteen baseline propositions', in D. MacLean (ed.), *Internet Governance: A Grand Collaboration*, New York: United Nations Information and Communication Technology Taskforce.
Drake, William (2005a), 'On the creation of a new IG forum', public

meeting on Internet Governance Ministry of Science and Technology, Copenhagen, 14 September.
Drake, William (ed.) (2005b), *Reforming Internet Governance: Perspectives from the Working Group on Internet Governance (WGIG)*, UN ICT Task Force Series, New York: UNICTTF.
Drake, William and R.F. Jørgensen (eds) (2005), *Human Rights in the Global Information Society*, Cambridge, MA: MIT Press.
Easton, D. (1971), *The Political System: An Inquiry into the State of Political Science*, New York: H. Wolf.
ECOSOC (2001), 'Information and Communication Technologies (ICT) Task Force: Report of the Secretary-General', New York: UN ECOSOC.
Emirbayer, M. (1997), 'A manifesto for relational sociology', *American Journal of Sociology*, **103** (2), 281–317.
Emmerij, L., R. Jolly et al. (2001), *Ahead of the Curve? UN Ideas and Global Challenges*, Bloomington: Indiana University Press.
Escobar, A. (1995), *Encountering Development: The Making and Unmaking of the Third World*, Princeton, NJ: Princeton University Press.
Eriksson, J. and G. Giacomello (2008), 'Who controls the Internet? Beyond the obstinacy or obsolence of the state', *International Studies Review*, **11** (1), 205–30.
Ferenz, M.N. (2002), 'Multi-stakeholder dialogues: learning from the UNCSD experience', Consensus Building Institute, Cambridge, MA.
Fleming, P. and A. Spicer (2007), *Contesting the Corporation: Struggle, Power and Resistance in Organizations*, Cambridge and New York: Cambridge University Press.
Flichy, P. (2007), *The Internet Imaginaire*, Cambridge, MA: MIT Press.
Flyvbjerg, B. (1998), 'Habermas and Foucault: thinkers for civil society?' *British Journal of Sociology*, **49** (2), 210–33.
Flyvbjerg, B. (2001), *Social Science that Matters: Why Social Inquiry Fails and how it can Succeed Again*, Cambridge: Cambridge University Press.
Flyverbom, M. (2011), 'On/off the agenda: intellectual property rights, the UN and the global politics of the Internet', in K. Gherab-Martin and P. Kalantzis-Cope (eds), *Emerging Digital Spaces in Contemporary Society: Properties of Technology*, Basingstoke: Palgrave Macmillan.
Flyverbom, M. and H.K. Hansen (2006), 'Technological imageries and governance arrangements: global networks in the service of development', in H.K. Hansen and J. Hoff (eds), *Digital Governance, Networked Societies: Creating Authority, Community, and Identity in a Globalized World*, Copenhagen: Samfundslitteratur.
Foucault, M. (1965), *Madness and Civilization: A History of Insanity in the Age of Reason*, New York: Vintage Books.

Foucault, M. (1973), *The Order of Things: The Archaeology of the Human Sciences*, New York: Vintage.

Foucault, M. (1977a), *Discipline and Punish: The Birth of the Prison*, Harmondsworth: Penguin.

Foucault, M. (1977b), 'Truth and power', in J. D. Faubion (ed.), *Power: Essential Works of Foucault 1954–1984*, Harmondsworth: Penguin.

Foucault, M. (1980), *Power/Knowledge: Selected Interviews and Writings 1972–1977*, New York: Pantheon Books.

Foucault, M. (1982), 'The subject and power', in J. D. Faubion (ed.), *Power: Essential Works of Foucault 1954–1984*, Harmondsworth: Penguin.

Foucault, M. (1985), *The History of Sexuality, vol 2: The Use of Pleasure*, New York: Pantheon.

Foucault, M. (1991a), 'Politics and the study of discourse', in G. Burchell, C. Gordon and P. Miller (eds), *The Foucault Effect: Studies in Governmentality*, Chicago: Chicago University Press.

Foucault, M. (1991b), 'Governmentality', in G. Burchell, C. Gordon and P. Miller (eds), *The Foucault Effect: Studies in Governmentality*, Hemel Hempstead: Harvester-Wheatsheaf.

Foucault, M. (1991c), 'Questions of method', in G. Burchell, C. Gordon and P. Miller (eds), *The Foucault Effect: Studies in Governmentality*, Chicago: Chicago University Press.

Foucault, M. (1991d), 'A concern for truth', in S. Lotringer (ed.), *Foucault Live: Interviews, 1961–84*, New York: Semiotext(e).

Foucault, M. (1997), 'Ethics as the concern for self as a practice of freedom', in *Ethics: Subjectivity and Truth: Essential Works of Foucault 1954–1984*, Vol. I, ed. P. Rabinow, New York: The New Press pp. 281–301.

Foucault, M. (1998a), *The History of Sexuality, vol. 1: The Will to Knowledge*, Harmondsworth: Penguin.

Foucault, M. (1998b), 'What is an author?' in *Aesthetics*, Harmondsworth: Penguin.

Fransen, L.W. and A. Kolk (2007), 'Global rule-setting for business: a critical analysis of multi-stakeholder standards', *Organization*, **14** (5), 667–84.

GAID (2010), 'Chairman's press release: Secretary-General Ban Ki-moon's meeting with GAID', UN, New York, 19 February: available at http://www.un-gaid.org/About/Howdoesitfunction/GAIDChairman/GAIDChairmansPressReleases/tabid/1199/mctl/ArticleView/ModuleId/3286/articleId/21181/Default.aspx (accessed 28 February 2011).

Gal, U., K. Lyytinen et al. (2008), 'The dynamics of IT boundary objects, information infrastructures, and organisational identities: the introduction of 3D modelling technologies into the architecture, engineering, and construction industry', *European Journal of Information Systems*, **17** (3), 290–304.

Galloway, A.R. (2004), *Protocol: How Control Exists after Decentralization*, Cambridge, MA: MIT Press.

Garfinkel, H. and A.W. Rawls (2002), *Ethnomethodology's Program: Working out Durkeim's Aphorism*, Lanham, MD: Rowman & Littlefield.

Garland, D. (1997), '"Governmentality" and the problem of crime: Foucault, criminology, sociology', *Theoretical Criminology*, **1** (2), 173–214.

Garsten, C. and K. Jacobsson (forthcoming), 'Post-political regulation: partnership, voluntarism and illusory consensus', *Critical Sociology*.

GDDI (2002), 'Better, faster, cheaper: developing and leveraging world class ICT Networks for social and economic advancement', Geneva, Global Digital Divide Initiative, WEF.

GeSCI (2005), '300 meet in Dublin for Global Forum on Harnessing the Potential of ICTs for Education', GeSCI, Dublin, press release, GeSCI available at: http://www.gesci.org (accessed 1 March 2011).

Goldsmith, J.L. and T. Wu (2006), *Who Controls the Internet? Illusions of a Borderless World*, New York: Oxford University Press.

Gordon, C. (1991), 'Governmental rationality: an introduction', in G. Burchell, C. Gordon and P. Miller (eds), *The Foucault Effect: Studies in Governmentality*, Chicago: Chicago University Press.

Gottweis, H. (2003), 'Theoretical strategies of poststructuralist policy analysis: towards an analytics of government', in M.A. Hajer and H. Wagenaar (eds), *Deliberative Policy Analysis: Understanding Governance in the Network Society*, Cambridge: Cambridge University Press.

Goven, J. (2006), 'Dialogue, governance, and biotechnology: acknowledging the context of the conversation', *Integrated Assessment Journal*, **6** (2), 99–116.

Graz, J.-C. and A. Nölke (eds) (2007), *Transnational Private Governance and its Limits*, London: Routledge.

Gross, D. (2005), 'Read My Lips; No New Internet Governance at U.N., Gross Says', *Washington Internet Daily*, 13 September, **6** (177) (available through Factiva).

Gössling, T., L.A.G. Oerlemans et al. (2007), *Inside Networks: A Process View on Multi-Organisational Partnerships, Alliances and Networks*, Cheltenham, UK and Northampton, MA, USA: Edward Elgar.

Haas, P.M. (1992), 'Introduction: epistemic communities and global policy coordination', *International Organization*, **46** (1), 1–35.

Hackett, E.J., O. Amsterdamska et al. (2008), *The Handbook of Science and Technology Studies*, Cambridge, MA: MIT Press; published in cooperation with the Society for the Social Studies of Science.

Hajer, M.A. and H. Wagenaar (eds) (2003), *Deliberative Policy Analysis: Understanding Governance in the Network Society*, Theories of Institutional Design, Cambridge: Cambridge University Press.

Hall, R.B. and T.J. Biersteker (eds) (2002), *The Emergence of Private Authority in Global Governance*, Cambridge Studies in International Relations, Cambridge: Cambridge University Press.

Hallström, K.T. and M. Boström (2010), *Transnational Multi-Stakeholder Standardization: Organizing Fragile Non-State Authority*, Cheltenham, UK and Northampton, MA, USA: Edward Elgar.

Hansen, H.K. (2009), 'Bribery risk governance: the politics of measurement in international anti-corruption', 50th ISA Annual Convention, New York.

Hansen, H.K. and D. Salskov-Iversen (2005), 'Remodelling the transnational political realm: partnerships, benchmarking schemes and the digitalization of governance', *Alternatives*, **30** (2), 141–64.

Hansen, H.K. and D. Salskov-Iversen (eds) (2008), *Critical Perspectives on Private Authority in Global Politics*, Basingstoke: Palgrave Macmillan.

Hassard, J., M. Kelemen et al. (eds) (2008), *Disorganization Theory – Alternative Explorations in Organizational Analysis*, New York: Routledge.

Heeks, R. (2008), 'ICT4D 2.0: the next phase of applying ICT for international development', *Computer*, **41** (6), approx. 26 pages.

Held, D. (1995), *Democracy and the Global Order: From the Modern State to Cosmopolitan Governance*, London: Polity.

Held, D. and A. McGrew (eds) (2002), *Governing Globalization: Power, Authority and Global Governance*, Cambridge: Polity Press.

Hernes, T. (2008), *Understanding Organization as Process: Theory for a Tangled World*, London and New York: Routledge.

Hoff, J. (2003), 'A constructivist bottom-up approach to governance: the need for increased theoretical and methodological awareness in research', in H.P. Bang (ed.), *Governance as Social and Political Communication*, Manchester: Manchester University Press.

Holohan, A. (2003), 'UNDP: the challenge of becoming a network organization', available at: http://mediaresearchhub.ssrc.org/undp-the-challenge-of-becoming-a-network-organization/attachment (accessed 2 March 2011).

Hunt, A. and G. Wickham (1994), *Foucault and Law: Towards a Sociology of Law as Governance*, London: Pluto Press.

Hutchby, I. (2001), *Conversation and Technology: From the Telephone to the Internet*, Cambridge: Polity Press.

Hylland Eriksen, Thomas (1999), 'Globalization and the politics of identity', *UN Chronicle*, autumn, available at: http://folk.uio.no/geirthe/UNChron.html (accessed 3 March 2011).
ICC (2004), 'ICC roadmap for Internet governance', Department of Policy and Business Practices, Paris.
ICC Statement (2010), 'ICC basis closing statement at the UN Commission on Science and Technology for Development', UN Commission on Science and Technology for Development, 13th session, 17–21 May, Geneva.
IG-Caucus (Internet Governance Caucus) (2004), notes from IG Caucus meeting.
IG-Caucus (2004–05), Mailing list contributions, available at: www.net-gov.org.
IGF (2008), 'IGF timeline', available at: www.intgovforum.org/cms/hyderabad.../IGF.Timetable.03.09.2008.doc (accessed 2 November 2010).
ITU (1998), 'Resolution 73 of the ITU Plenipotentiary Conference', ITU.
ITU (2008), 'Report on the WSIS stocktaking', available at: http://www.itu.int/wsis/stocktaking/docs/2008/WSIS-Stocktaking2008-e.pdf (accessed 28 February 2011).
Jackson, P.T. and D.H. Nexon (1999), 'Relations before states: substance, process and the study of world politics', *European Journal of International Relations*, **5** (3), 291–332.
Jacobsen, J.K. (1995), 'Much ado about ideas: the cognitive factor in economic policy', *World Politics*, **47**, 283–310.
Jensen, W. (2005), 'Recommendations of the WGIG', public meeting on Internet governance, Ministry of Science and Technology, Copenhagen, 14 September.
Jones, C., W.S. Hesterly et al. (1997), 'A general theory of network governance: exchange conditions and social mechanisms', *Academy of Management Review*, **22** (4), 911–45.
Juris, J.S. (2008), *Networking Futures: The Movements against Corporate Globalization*, Durham, NC: Duke University Press.
Kamalipour, Y.R. (ed.) (2002), *Global Communication*, Belmont: Wadsworth/Thomson Learning.
Karlsen, M.P. and K. Villadsen (2008), 'Who should do the talking? The proliferation of dialogue as governmental technology', *Culture & Organization*, **14** (4), 345–63.
Keck, M.E. and K. Sikkink (1998), *Activists beyond Borders: Advocacy Networks in International Politics*, Ithaca and London: Cornell University Press.
Kendall, G. (2004), 'Global networks, international networks, actor

networks', in W. Larner and W. Walters (eds), *Global Governmentality: Governing International Spaces*, London: Routledge.
Kendall, G. and G. Wickham (2001), *Understanding Culture – Cultural Studies, Order, Ordering*, London: Sage.
Keogh, D. and T. Wood (eds) (2005), *Village Phone Replication Manual*, UN ICT Task Force Series, New York: UNICTTF.
King, K. and S. McGrath (2004), *Knowledge for Development? Comparing British, Japanese, Swedish and World Bank Aid*, London: Zed Books.
Klein, H. (2006), 'Understanding the WSIS: an institutional analysis of the UN World Summit on the Information Society' in J. Dean, J.W. Anderson and G. Lovink (eds), *Reformatting Politics – Information Technology and Global Civil Society*, London: Routledge.
Kooiman, J. (2003), *Governing as Governance*, London: Sage.
Krasner, S.D. (ed.) (1983), *International Regimes*, Ithaca: Cornell University Press.
Laffey, M. and J. Weldes (2005), 'Policing and Global Governance', in M. Barnett and R. Duvall (eds), *Power in Global Governance*, Cambridge: Cambridge University Press, pp. 59–79.
Larner, W. and W. Walters (eds) (2004), *Global Governmentality: Governing International Spaces*, London: Routledge.
Latham, R. and S. Sassen (eds) (2005), *Digital Formations: IT and New Architectures in the Global Realm*, Princeton and Oxford: Princeton University Press.
Latour, B. (1986), 'The powers of association', in J. Law (ed.), *Power, Action and Belief: A New Sociology of Knowledge?* London: Routledge and Kegan Paul.
Latour, B. (1987), *Science in Action: How to Follow Scientists and Engineers through Society*, Cambridge, MA: Harvard University Press.
Latour, B. (1988), *The Pasteurization of France*, Cambridge, MA: Harvard University Press.
Latour, B. (1997), 'On actor network theory: a few clarifications plus more than a few complications', working paper, available at: http://www.cours.fse.ulaval.ca/edc-65804/latour-clarifications.pdf (accessed 2 March 2011).
Latour, B. (2000), 'When things strike back', *British Journal of Sociology*, **51** (1), 105–23.
Latour, B. (2004), 'Why has critique run out of steam? from matters of fact to matters of concern', *Critical Inquiry*, **30**, 225–48.
Latour, B. (2005a), *Reassembling the Social: An Introduction to Actor-Network Theory*, Oxford: Oxford University Press.
Latour, B. (2005b), 'What is the style of matters of concern?' Department of Philosophy, University of Amsterdam.

Latour, B. (2010), *The Making of Law: An Ethnography of the Conseil d'Etat*, Cambridge and Malden, MA: Polity.
Law, J. (1994), *Organizing Modernity*, Oxford and Cambridge, MA: Blackwell.
Law, J. (2000), 'On the subject of the object: narrative, technology, and interpellation', *Configurations*, **8** (1), 1–29.
Law, J. and J. Hassard (1999), *Actor Network Theory and After*, Oxford and Malden, MA: Blackwell/Sociological Review.
Law, J. and A. Mol (2008), 'Globalisation in practice: on the politics of boiling pigswill,' *Geoforum*, **39** (1), 133–43.
Law, J. and V. Singleton (2005), 'Object lessons', *Organization*, **12** (3), 331–55.
Law, J. and J. Urry (2004), 'Enacting the social', *Economy and Society*, **33** (3), 390–410.
Lessig, L. (1999), *Code and Other Laws of Cyberspace*, New York: Basic Books.
Liikanen, E. (2001), 'European Commission response to report of high-level group of advisers on ICT', letter to UNICTTF Director, private UNICTTF Archives.
Lipschutz, R. (2005), 'Global civil society and global governmentality', in M. Barnett and R. Duvall (eds), *Power in Global Governance*, Cambridge: Cambridge University Press.
Lipschutz, R.D. and W.J.K. Rowe (2005), *Globalization, Governmentality, and Global Politics: Regulation for the Rest of us?* London and New York: Routledge.
Mandaville, P. (2002), 'Reading the state from elsewhere: towards an anthropology of the postnational', *Review of International Studies*, **28** (1), 199–207.
Mansell, R. and U. Wehn (eds) (1998), *Knowledge Societies: Information Technology for Sustainable Development*, UN Commission on Science and Technology for Development, Oxford: Oxford University Press.
March, J.G. and H. A. Simon (1958), *Organizations*, New York: Wiley.
Marcus, G.E. and E. Saka (2006), 'Assemblage', *Theory, Culture & Society*, **23** (2–3), 101–9.
May, C. (2002), *The Information Society: A Sceptical View*, London: Polity Press.
Mayer-Schonberger, V. and M. Ziewitz (2007), 'Jefferson rebuffed: the United States and the future of Internet governance', *Columbia Science and Technology Law Review*, **188**, 188–228.
Miller, P. and N. Rose (1990), 'Governing economic life', *Economy and Society*, **19** (1), 1–31.

Mol, A. (2002), *The Body Multiple: Ontology in Medical Practice*, Durham: Duke University Press.

Mosco, V. (2004), *The Digital Sublime: Myth, Power, and Cyberspace*, Cambridge, MA: MIT Press.

Mueller, M. (2002), *Ruling the Root: Internet Governance and the Taming of Cyberspace*, Cambridge, MA: MIT Press.

Mueller, M. (2010), *Networks and States: The Global Politics of Internet Governance*, Cambridge, MA: MIT Press.

Mumby, D.K. (2005), 'Theorizing resistance in organization studies: a dialectical approach', *Management Communication Quarterly*, **19**, 19–44.

Napoli, P. (2001), *Foundations of Communications Policy: Principles and Process in the Regulation of Electronic Media*, New York: Hampton Press.

Napoli, P. (2008), 'Diversity as an emerging principle of Internet governance', McGannon Center Working Paper Series, no. 16.

Neumann, I.B. and O.J. Sending (2007), ' "The international" as governmentality', *Millennium: Journal of International Studies*, **35** (3), 677–701.

Nicolini, D. (2009), 'Zooming in and out: studying practices by switching theoretical lenses and trailing connections', *Organization Studies*, **30** (12), 1391–418.

O'Mahony, S. and B.A. Bechky (2008), 'Boundary organizations: enabling collaboration among unexpected allies', *Administrative Science Quarterly*, **53** (3), 422–59.

O'Rourke, D. (2006), 'Multi-stakeholder regulation: privatizing or socializing global labor standards?' *World Development*, **34** (5), 899–918.

Ong, A. and S.J. Collier (2004), *Global Assemblages: Technology, Politics and Ethics as Anthropological Problems*, Malden, MA and Oxford: Blackwell.

Orr, J.E. (1998), 'Images of work', *Science Technology & Human Values*, **23** (4), 439–55.

Panel, ICT (2000), 'Report of the High-level Panel on Information and Communication Technology', New York, United Nations, ECOSOC: 32.

Porter, T. (2008), 'Disaggregating public and private authority in global governance', in H.K. Hansen and D. Salskov-Iversen (eds), *Critical Perspectives on Private Authority in Global Politics*, Basingstoke: Palgrave Macmillan.

Porter, T.M. (1995), *Trust in Numbers: The Pursuit of Objectivity in Science and Public Life*, Princeton, NJ: Princeton University Press.

Power, M. (2007), *Organized Uncertainty: Designing a World of Risk Management*, Oxford and New York: Oxford University Press.

Prahalad, C.K. (2010), *The Fortune at the Bottom of the Pyramid:*

Eradicating Poverty through Profits, Upper Saddle River, NJ: FT Press, Pearson Education.

Pugh, D.S. (1997), *Organization Theory: Selected Readings*, Hardmondsworth and New York: Penguin.

Rabinow, P. (2005), 'Midst anthropology's problems', in A. Ong and S. J. Collier (eds), *Global Assemblages: Technology, Politics and Ethics as Anthropological Problems*, Malden, MA and Oxford: Blackwell Publishing.

Ragin, C.C. and H.S. Becker (eds) (1992), *What is a Case? Exploring the Foundations of Social Inquiry*, Cambridge: Cambridge University Press.

Rasche, A. and G. Kell (eds) (2010), *The United Nations Global Compact: Achievements, Trends and Challenges*, Cambridge: Cambridge University Press.

Risse, T. (2000), '"Let's argue!": communicative action in world politics', *International Organization*, **54** (1), 1–39.

Rose, N. (1999), *Powers of Freedom: Reframing Political Thought*, Cambridge: Cambridge University Press.

Rose, N. and P. Miller (1992), 'Political power beyond the state: problematics of government', *British Journal of Sociology*, **43** (2), 173–205.

Rosenau, J.N. (1999), 'Toward an ontology for global governance', in M.Hewson and T.J. Sinclair (eds), *Approaches to Global Governance Theory*, New York: State University of New York Press.

Rosenau, J.N. and E.-O. Czempiel (eds) (1992), *Governance without Government: Order and Change in World Politics*, Cambridge: Cambridge University Press.

Ruggie, J.G. (2001), 'global_governance.net: the global compact as a learning network', *Global Governance*, **7**, 371–8.

Ruggie, J.G. (2002), 'The theory and practice of learning networks: corporate social responsibility and the global compact', *Journal of Corporate Citizenship*, **5** (Special Issue on International Perspectives of Corporate Citizenship), 27–36.

Santos, F.A. and K.A. Eisenhardt (2005), 'Organizational boundaries and theories of organization', *Organization Science*, **16** (5), 491–508.

Schech, S. (2002), 'Wired for change: the links between ICTs and development discourses', *Journal of International Development*, **14**, 13–23.

Schechter, M.G. (ed.) (2001), *United Nations-Sponsored World Conferences: Focus on Impact and Follow-up*, Tokyo: UNU Press.

Schram, S.F. and B. Caterino (eds) (2006), *Making Political Science Matter: Debating Knowledge, Research and Method*, New York and London: New York University Press.

Scott, W.R. (2004), 'Reflections on a half-century of organizational sociology', *Annual Review of Sociology*, **30**, 1–21.

Sending, O.J. and I.B. Neumann (2006), 'Governance to governmentality: analyzing NGOs, states, and power', *International Studies Quarterly*, **50** (3), 651–72.

Sennett, R. (1980), *Authority*, New York: Knopf.

Shore, C. and S. Wright (1997), 'Policy: a new field of anthropology', in C. Shore and S. Wright (eds), *Anthropology of Policy: Critical Perspectives on Governance and Power*, London: Routledge.

Singleton, V. (1998), 'Stabilizing instabilities: the role of the laboratory in the United Kingdiom cervical screening programme', in M. Berg and A. Mol (eds), *Differences in Medicine: Unravelling Practices, Techniques and Bodies*, Durham, NC: Duke University Press.

Siochrú, S.Ó. and B. Girard (2002), *Global Media Governance: A Beginner's Guide*, New York: Rowman and Littlefield.

Slaughter, A.-M. (2004), *A New World Order*, Princeton, NJ: Princeton University Press.

Smircich, L. and G. Morgan (1982), 'Leadership: the management of meaning', *Journal of Applied Behavioural Studies*, **18**, 257–73.

Star, S.L. and J.R. Griesemer (1989), 'Institutional ecology, "translations" and boundary objects: amateurs and professionals in Berkeley's Museum of Vertebrate Zoology, 1907–39', *Social Studies of Science*, **19** (3), 387–420.

Stark, D. (2009), *The Sense of Dissonance: Accounts of Worth in Economic Life*, Princeton, NJ: Princeton University Press.

Stauffacher, D., W. Drake et al. (eds) (2005), *Information and Communication Technology for Peace – the Role of ICT in Preventing, Responding to and Recovering from Conflict*, UN ICT Task Force Series, New York: UNICTTF.

Stauffacher, D. and W. Kleinwächter (eds) (2005), *The World Summit on the Information Society: Moving from the Past into the Future*, UN ICT Task Force Series, New York: UNICTTF.

Tamm Hallström, K. and M. Boström (2010), *Transnational Multi-Stakeholder Standardization: Organizing Fragile Non-State Authority*, Cheltenham, UK and Northampton, MA, USA: Edward Elgar.

Therien, J.-P. (2004, 'The Global Compact: UN's bid for a world social contract', ISA, Montreal.

Thussu, D.K. (2000), *International Communication: Continuity and Change*, London: Arnold.

Trompette, P. and D. Vinck (2009), 'Revisiting the notion of boundary object', *S.A.C. Revue d'anthropologie des connaissances*, **3** (1), 3–25.

UN (2000), 'UN Millennium Development Goals', available at: http://www.un.org/millenniumgoals (accessed 7 March 2011).

UNDP (2001), 'UNDP Thematic Trust Fund: information and communication technology (ICT) for development', New York.
UNDP employee, UNICTTF (2000a), aide memoire, UNICTTF Archive, New York.
UNDP employee, UNICTTF (2000b), 'Plan for consultations', fourth draft, UNICTTF Archive, New York.
UNDP employee, UNICTTF (2000c), letter, UN ICTTF Archive, New York.
UN-GAID (2009), 'Summary of discussion and recommendations', Fourth Meeting of the Strategy Council, Global Alliance for ICT and Development, New York, United Nations Department of Economic and Social Affairs.
UN-GAID (2010), available at: http://www.un-gaid.org/About/tabid/861/ItemID/554/Default.aspx (accessed 28 February 2011).
UN General-Assembly (1999), 'Resolution 54/231: Role of the UN in promoting development in the context of globalization and interdependence', 87th plenary meeting, UN, New York.
UN General Assembly (2010), 'Continuation of the Internet Governance Forum – note by the Secretary-General', UN General Assembly, New York, document no A/65/78–E/2010/68, available at: http://ods-dds-ny.un.org/doc/UNDOC/GEN/N10/354/73/PDF/N1035473.pdf?OpenElement (accessed 1 March 2011).
UN General Assembly (2011), 'Resolution adopted by the General Assembly: information and communications technologies for development', UN General Assembly, New York, document no A/RES/65/141, available online at http://daccess-dds-ny.un.org/doc/UNDOC/GEN/N10/521/00/PDF/N1052100.pdf?OpenElement (accessed 1 March 2011).
UNICTTF (2000a), A framework for consultations on the ICT Task Force: Aide-memoire, UN ICT Task Force Archives, New York.
UNICTTF (2000b), ICT Task Force consultations, 14–23 November, UN ICT Task Force Archives, New York.
UNICTTF (2000c), ICT TF and Trust Fund – charter documents, UN ICT Task Force Archives, New York.
UNICTTF (2000d), Summaries of consultations, UN ICT Task Force Archives, New York.
UNICTTF (2001a), 'Mission statement and plan of action', draft, UN ICT Task Force Archives, New York.
UNICTTF (2001b), 'Plan of action', draft, United Nations Information and Communication Technologies Task Force, UN ICT Task Force Archives, New York.
UNICTTF (2002), 'Plan of action of the ICT Task Force', UN ICT Task Force Archives, New York.

UNICTTF (2004a), Business plan for the UN ICT Task Force for 2004 available at: www.unicttaskforce.org (accessed 7 March 2011).

UNICTTF (2004b), 'Second annual report of the Information and Communication Technologies Task Force', ECOSOC: 1–20, UN ICT Task Force Archives, New York.

UNICTTF (2005), 'Draft: principles/elements for the establishment of a Global Alliance for ICT and Development', UN ICT Task Force Archives, New York.

UNICTTF, Nordic Baltic Regional Seminar (2000), Summary of meeting/ minutes, 21 December, UN ICT Task Force Archives, New York.

Unwin, T. (ed.) (2009), *ICT4D – Information and Communication Technology for Development*, Cambridge: Cambridge University Press.

USA (2000–01), US government comments on consultation documents.

Utting, P. (2001), 'Regulating business via multistakeholder initiatives: a preliminary assessment', UNRISD.

Utting, P. (2002), 'Regulating business via multistakeholder initiatives: a preliminary assessment', in *Voluntary Approaches to Corporate Responsibility: Readings and a Resource Guide*, Geneva, NGLS.

Wade, R.H. (2002), 'Bridging the digital divide: new route to development or new form of dependency?' *Global Governance*, **8,** 433–66.

Wasserman, S. and K. Faust (1994), *Social Network Analysis: Methods and Applications*, Cambridge: Cambridge University Press.

Weber, M. (2002), *The Protestant Ethic and the Spirit of Capitalism*, Harmondsworth: Penguin.

Weiss, T.G. and R. Thakur (2010), *Global Governance and the UN: An Unfinished Journey*, Indianapolis: Indiana University Press.

WGIG (2004–05), 'Lists of participants, Open Consultations', available at: www.wgig.org (accessed 15 May 2006).

WGIG (2005), 'Report of the Working Group on Internet Governance', Geneva, available at: http://www.wgig.org/docs/WGIGREPORT.pdf (accessed 27 February 2011).

Williams, C., S.P. Wainwright, K. Ehrich and M. Michael (2008), 'Human embryos as boundary objects? Some reflections on the biomedical worlds of embryonic stem cells and pre-implantation genetic diagnosis', *New Genetics and Society*, **27**, 7–18.

WSIS (2003a), 'Declaration of principles', World Summit on the Information Society, Geneva.

WSIS (2003b), 'Plan of action', World Summit on the Information Society, Geneva.

WSIS (2005a), Tunis Commitment, published by ITU, 18 November, document no WSIS-05/TUNIS/DOC/7-E, available at: http://www.itu.int/wsis/docs2/tunis/off/7.html (accessed 1 March 2011).

WSIS (2005b), Tunis Agenda for the Information Society, published by ITU, 18 November, document no WSIS-05/TUNIS/DOC/6(Rev. 1)-E: available at http://www.itu.int/wsis/docs2/tunis/off/6rev1.html (accessed 1 March 2011).

WSIS Caucuses (2004–05), contributions to Plenary Mailing List: available at http://mailman-new.greennet.org.uk/pipermail/plenary (accessed 1 April 2011).

Wunsch-Vincent, S. and J. McIntosh (eds) (2005), *WTO, E-commerce and Information Technologies: From the Uruguay Round through the Doha Development Agenda*, UN ICT Task Force Series, New York: UNICTTF.

Zittrain, J.L. (2009), *The Future of the Internet – and How to Stop it*, New Haven, CT: Yale University Press.

Index